Caribbean Labor and Politics

Dedicated to the memory of Alma Harrington Young

Caribbean Labor and Politics

*Legacies of Cheddi Jagan
and Michael Manley*

EDITED BY

Perry Mars

AND

Alma H. Young

Wayne State University Press Detroit

African American Life Series

For a complete listing of the books in this series please visit our website at http://wsupress.wayne.edu

Series Editors:

Melba Joyce Boyd
Department of Africana Studies, Wayne State University

Ron Brown
Department of Political Science, Wayne State University

Copyright © 2004 by Wayne State University Press,
Detroit, Michigan 48201. All rights are reserved.
No part of this book may be reproduced without formal permission.
Manufactured in the United States of America.
08 07 06 05 04   5 4 3 2 1

Library of Congress Cataloging-in-Publication Data

Caribbean labor and politics : legacies of Cheddi Jagan and
Michael Manley / edited by Perry Mars and Alma H. Young.
  p. cm.

"This edited volume grows out of a conference held at Wayne
State University in April 1998 that analyzed the lives and
politics of two great leaders of the Caribbean, Cheddi Jagan
of Guyana and Michael Manley of Jamaica"—Acknowledgements.
Includes bibliographical references and index.

ISBN 0–8143–3211–0 (pbk. : alk. paper)
1. Labor movement—Caribbean Area—Congresses. 2. Caribbean
Area—Politics and government—1945—Congresses. 3. Labor
unions—Guyana—History—Congresses. 4. Labor unions—
Jamaica—History—Congresses. 5. Jagan, Cheddi—Congresses.
6. Manley, Michael, 1924—Congresses. 7. Guyana—Politics
and government—1966—Congresses. 8. Jamaica—Politics and
government—1962—Congresses. I. Mars, Perry. II. Young,
Alma H.

HD8193.5.C36 2004

331.88'09729—dc22   2003028063

∞ The paper used in this publication meets the minimum requirements of the
American National Standard for Information Sciences—Permanence of Paper for
Printed Library Materials, ANSI Z39.48-1984.

Contents

Acknowledgments · vii

Introduction · ix
PERRY MARS AND ALMA H. YOUNG

PART I
Life and Times of the Men

1 Michael Manley: A Personal Perspective · 3
   NORMAN GIRVAN

2 Legacies of Cheddi Jagan · 10
   BRINDLEY H. BENN

3 Dr. Cheddi Jagan: The Making of a Movement Intellectual · 18
   MAURICE ST. PIERRE

4 Michael Manley, Trade Unionism, and the Politics of Equality · 40
   ANTHONY BOGUES

5 Colonialism, Political Policing, and the Jagan Years · 64
   JOAN MARS

PART II
Labor-Politics Nexus

6 Guyana, Jamaica, and the Cold War Project: The Transformation of Caribbean Labor · 89
   HILBOURNE WATSON

7 Globalization, Economic Fallout, and the Crisis of Organized Labor in the Caribbean · 126
   CLIVE THOMAS

8 Ethno-Politics and the Caribbean Working-Class Project: Contributions of Cheddi Jagan and Michael Manley   143
PERRY MARS

9 Women Trade Union Leaders in the Anglophone Caribbean   166
A. LYNN BOLLES

PART III
Critical Current Challenges

10 Global Economic Crisis and Caribbean Women's Survival Strategies   183
ALMA H. YOUNG AND KRISTINE B. MIRANNE

11 The Caribbean and Drugs: Challenges in Local-Global Context   200
IVELAW L. GRIFFITH

12 The Role of Emigration in the Caribbean Development Process   225
MONICA H. GORDON

Selected Bibliography   243
ELLA DAVIS

Contributors   251

Index   255

Acknowledgments

This edited volume grows out of a conference held at Wayne State University in April 1998 that analyzed the lives and politics of two great leaders of the Caribbean, Cheddi Jagan of Guyana and Michael Manley of Jamaica. We are grateful to those who made presentations at the conference, many of whom are contributors to this volume. The conference would not have been possible without the able assistance of Sabrina Williams, at that time a doctoral student at Wayne State, and Debbie Hardie-Simpson of the Africana Studies Department.

We would like to thank Monita Hollis Mungo for her professionalism in preparing the final draft of the manuscript. I [Alma Young] also appreciate her efforts in managing my schedule so that there was time to complete this project. Thanks also go to Treena Dundas for her research and bibliographical assistance, and to Doug Towns, cartographer in the Wayne State Center for Urban Studies, for the map that appears at the beginning of the volume.

We appreciate the permission to publish the photographs that appear in this volume. Photographs of Cheddi Jagan are from the *Guyana Chronicle*, and those of Michael Manley are from the *Daily Gleaner* and the Jamaica Information Service. We also thank Dudley Kishore of the Cheddi Jagan Research Institute in Georgetown and Opal Mars of Arawak Publications in Kingston for their kind assistance.

Again, the cooperation and patience of the contributors to this volume have been invaluable, as have been the suggestions of the anonymous readers of the manuscript. We appreciate the excellent working relationship with members of the Wayne State University Press, and the support of the editors of the African American Life Series, Melba Boyd and Ronald Brown. We are honored by the support of the Coleman A. Young endowment in Wayne State's College of Urban, Labor and Metropolitan Affairs, an endowment named in recognition of another great political and labor leader.

Our inspiration comes of course from the lives of the two great men we honor with this volume, Cheddi Jagan and Michael Manley. Their contributions to the Caribbean and beyond remind us that much can be accomplished when individuals decide that the time has come for change.

Many thanks to Dennis Young and Alden Young, and to Joan Mars and Jason Mars, for their encouragement and support.

Alma H. Young
Perry Mars
August 2003

Alma Young passed away in March 2004 as this book was going to press.

INTRODUCTION

PERRY MARS AND ALMA H. YOUNG

When Cheddi Jagan of Guyana and Michael Manley of Jamaica died on the same day, March 6, 1997, the Caribbean lost two giants who had helped to redefine the region and, more generally, the Third World. The two heads of state were bold and creative in their ability to connect labor and politics, and in so doing, left a powerful legacy with important ramifications for political and economic struggles throughout the Caribbean region and beyond. Their mission was to create the kind of change that would improve the lives of the disadvantaged and the dispossessed. This volume provides a critical analysis of the life, work, and contributions of these two dynamic political leaders.

The Caribbean region, which provided the context for their struggles, is indeed a volatile terrain for the realization of the bold and challenging political and economic changes they sought. Historically, the region as we have come to know it was artificially created for the deliberate exploitation and plunder by foreign powers and adventurous fortune seekers. Slavery, indenture, colonialism, and the most predatory forms of imperial capitalism, manifested principally in the ubiquitous plantation system, were the problematic legacies of this peculiar history. The mostly darker-skinned Caribbean peoples were forced into subordination to white European rule, which further created a legacy of entrenched racism and ethnic conflicts. Within this context, also, the labor of the subordinate or subject peoples was destined to play largely an oppositional role in the political and economic future of the region. The major problematic, therefore, emerging from this context in which Jagan and Manley were to make their greatest contributions, revolved around the value of labor in the political economy as a whole, the meaning of democracy under foreign and elite control, and the necessity of political and economic transformation in the region.

Cheddi Jagan and Michael Manley, Caribbean men coming from different social and cultural backgrounds, were linked in the pursuit of a common agenda: the forging of a labor-political nexus in their struggles toward social, economic and political change in their respective countries and, indeed, the Caribbean region as a whole. In doing so, they succeeded in catapulting the region into unprecedented levels of international significance. Their influence, in both domestic and international arenas, was often inspiring, although quite as often unsettling. Their vision of change appeared at times radical, at other times revolutionary, but moved consistently in a progressive and humanitarian direction until, unfortunately, the squeeze of economic globalization helped to eclipse, or derail, their efforts.

Cheddi Jagan (1918–1997)

As Cheddi Jagan remarked in one of his many books, *The West on Trial*, "Mine was the role of 'politics of protest,' with the weapons of exposure and struggle. If the legislature was my forum, the waterfront, the factories, plantations, mines and quarries were my battleground" (Jagan 1972, 43). Jagan's parents had come to what was then British Guiana as indentured laborers from India to work on the sugar plantations. The eldest of eleven children, Jagan was born on March 22, 1918, just a year after labor migration from India to British Guiana had ended. After emancipation and the abolition of slavery in the English-speaking Caribbean in 1834, sugar plantation companies, which dominated the political, social, and economic life of the colony, had drawn their labor force mainly from British India. Jagan was born on a sugar plantation, but his parents worked hard to make sure that he would receive an education. In 1942 he finished training as a dentist at Northwestern University in Chicago. His six years in the United States, including undergraduate training at Howard University, broadened his understanding of social and economic injustice and turned him into a Marxist. In 1943 he married Janet Rosenberg, who shared his political and social views.

He returned to Guyana in October 1943 and began to work for political change. In 1946, he, Janet Jagan, Jocelyn Hubbard, and Ashton Chase, among others, formed the Political Affairs Committee (PAC). In 1947, running as an independent, he won a seat on the Legislative Council. In 1950 he and his political associates in the PAC formed the first modern mass political party in Guyana, the People's Progressive Party (PPP). One of the goals of the party was to foster unity among the two groups most negatively impacted by the colonial system, people of African and East Indian descent. Thus Forbes Burnham, an Afro-Guyanese lawyer recently returned from England, was asked to join Jagan as a leader in the party. In the first elections under adult suffrage in 1953, the PPP, led by Cheddi Jagan, won overwhelmingly.

However, the PPP's first term in office lasted only 133 days (see Chase 1954). Heavily influenced by Cold War politics, the British government labeled the PPP's nationalist-reformist program Communist (see Watson, this volume). On October 9, 1953, the British government sent in troops, suspended the constitution, and removed the PPP government from power. Restrictions were placed on leaders of the PPP, many of whom, including Jagan, were imprisoned. During this period, Burnham challenged Jagan for the PPP leadership, and in effect succeeded in splitting the party. In 1957 Burnham and his followers founded a new party, the People's National Congress (PNC). In the process, Burnham was helped by the British and the American governments who supported what they believed were his more moderate politics in Guyana.

Still, Jagan won the general elections in 1957 and again in 1961, and embarked upon welfare programs in health, education, and housing. During this time the PPP also stepped up its campaign for Guyana's political independence. But in 1963, at a constitutional conference in London, the British gave open support to the opposition, changed the electoral system (from first-past-the-post to proportional representation), and ordered new elections in 1964, before independence would be granted. After these elections, the PNC formed the government in coalition with the more conservative United Force (UF), even though the PPP received the highest proportion of votes. When independence came in 1966, Jagan was leader of the opposition, a position he held for the next twenty-eight years. From 1964, Burnham would remain leader of the government for the next twenty years. His regime became extremely controversial in that he often resorted to violence, election irregularities, and patronage in governing.

After the death of Forbes Burnham in 1985, the more pragmatic Desmond Hoyte became president. By the late 1980s, the PPP had toned down its political and economic agenda and was emphasizing its belief in a mixed economy and democratic politics. Thus by the early 1990s, with the end of the Cold War and the subsequent changing geopolitical landscape, the United States was prepared to accept Jagan's return to office. However, an

Map of the Caribbean

intense struggle had to be waged by the PPP and other opposition groups to force Hoyte to agree to electoral reforms that would result in free elections. Jagan lobbied very actively in the international arena to get the world's support for a return to greater democracy in Guyana. Despite his long years in the opposition, Jagan maintained his stature as an international figure. In the first free and fair elections since 1964, Jagan was elected president of Guyana on October 5, 1992. He returned to office in a country demoralized by years of mismanagement. Less radical perhaps than he was in his younger years, he set about reforming the government and instituting social and economic policies. He suffered a heart attack on February 14, 1997, and died at the Walter Reed Army Medical Center in Washington, D.C. on March 6, 1997. His wife and political associate, Janet Rosenberg Jagan, was elected president in the December 1997 elections. Amid political turmoil, she resigned the presidency in 2000.

Michael N. Manley (1924–1997)

Michael Norman Manley led Jamaica as prime minster from 1972 to 1980, and again between 1989 and 1992. While he is most known for his political leadership, Manley's career included being a prominent trade unionist, a journalist, and author. In his book, *Jamaica: Struggle in the Periphery* (1982), Manley suggests that the history of the hemisphere and the history of Jamaica, is the story of the interaction between the forces that work for change and the forces that defend the status quo. Through it all, he saw the United States as the deciding factor.

His father, Norman Manley, a barrister and founder of the People's National Party (PNP), led the independence movement in Jamaica during the 1950s. However, Norman Manley lost the 1962 election that would have made him the first prime minister of an independent Jamaica. Anthony Bogues suggests that Norman Manley's political and social ideas framed the Jamaican Creole nationalist movement, a legacy that separated politics from economic advancement (2002). It was this legacy that his son tried to address by bringing economics and the needs of the working class into the political agenda. Michael's mother, Edna Manley, was an artist of some renown. Thus Michael Manley was born into a privileged middle-class Creole family. After graduating from Jamaica College in Kingston, Michael Manley studied at the London School of Economics. While in England, he worked as a journalist and served in the Royal Canadian air force. He returned to Jamaica in 1952 and became active in the National Workers Union (NWU) (see Bogues, this volume). During his twenty years as an active trade unionist, he strongly believed that the progress of the nation was tied to the progress of the working classes. His political career included being appointed to the Senate (1962–67), being elected to the House of Representatives (1970), and becoming leader of the People's National Party in 1969, following the death of his father. In 1972 he became prime minister. He was reelected in 1976, defeated in 1980 and 1983, and returned to power in 1989. He stepped aside in 1992 because of illness and was succeeded by P. J. Patterson.

Running on the slogan, "Better must come," Manley's PNP came to power in 1972 with thirty-seven of fifty-three parliamentary seats. Declaring that Jamaica was to be "a land of social justice," Manley embarked on an agenda of democratic socialism. He remained committed to the democratic process, but believed that there was a major role for the state in the economic development of the country. During his term in office, he was an outspoken advocate for Jamaica's poor and instituted many important social programs, including housing, education, and agricultural reforms. In order to finance social programs and to save foreign exchange, his government instituted price freezes and limited imports, especially on some luxury goods. He renegotiated his government's contracts with the six North American bauxite companies operating in the country, making it possible for Jamaica to receive increased taxes and acquire majority interest in the country's important bauxite mines. In international affairs, he became very active in the nonaligned movement. The close ties he developed with Cuba caused immediate tensions with the United States, but many of his policies of economic nationalism and social progress were viewed critically by the U.S. government. Manley was reelected in 1976, but soon faced a severe economic decline and sharp political divisions within the country.

In 1977 his government was forced to accept very harsh terms from the International Monetary Fund to address the deteriorating balance-of-payments situation. Efforts to destabilize his government after some of the social and economic changes were instituted led to his party's defeat in the 1980 elections, after a campaign marred by violent clashes. He was reelected prime minister in 1989 on a platform that advocated more free market principles. Unfortunately, due to ill health, he had to resign in 1992. Throughout his political career, Manley was also a leader in the international arena, being elected vice-president of Socialist International in 1979 and chairing the organization's economic commission in 1983. In 1993, the Caribbean Community (CARICOM) named him its ambassador at large. Out of political office, but still very much an actor on the national and international political scene, he died on March 6, 1997.

Promoting Working-Class Democracy

As we have seen, both Jagan and Manley were educated abroad, and thus exposed to different cultures, crises, and ideas (see Gordon, this volume). While studying in the United States, Jagan became acutely aware of the indignities that African Americans suffered in their daily lives. Through his future wife and others, he was exposed to the teachings of socialism. In London, Manley studied political philosophy with the socialist Harold Laski. Tim Hector argues that while abroad, Manley was "incorporating into himself the whole previous history of western civilization, in order to change it . . . in order to change the world" (Hector 1997).

Both men combined political leadership with leadership of trade unions. Jagan had been head of the Sawmill and Forest Workers Union (SFWU) during the 1950s and the Guyana Agricultural and Workers Union (GAWU) in the 1960s and 1970s, both of which were closely affiliated with the party he led, the People's Progressive Party (PPP). What cemented the historical and practical nexus between labor and politics in Jagan's experience was the 1948 massacre of striking workers by colonial police at Plantation Enmore, when Jagan vowed by the blood of the slain Enmore martyrs that he would commit the rest of his life to political struggle on behalf of the causes of the working classes (Jagan 1972). Michael Manley became involved with the union movement upon his return to Jamaica in the 1950s (see Bogues, this volume) through the National Workers Union (NWU), which was affiliated with the People's National Party that he would go on to lead from the 1970s until shortly before his death in 1997. In 1959 Manley led one of the biggest sugar strikes in Jamaica, which resulted in the setting up of a commission to investigate malpractices by the economically and politically powerful white planters. He argued that "class relations [in Jamaica] were stark in their intolerance. There was no subtlety, and little mobility because a man's class was stamped upon his skin as much as upon his clothes" (as quoted in Hector 1997).

For these reasons among others, Cheddi Jagan and Michael Manley were poised to play significant roles in Caribbean intellectual and political history. Their specific contributions relate to the catalytic role they played, particularly in the 1960s and 1970s, in emancipatory struggles toward elevating the political and class consciousness of the working classes in particular, and realizing political and economic transformations within their countries in general, and possibly at regional and international levels as well. Their recognition of the working classes (broadly defined) as pivotal to this wider emancipatory project reflected strong commitments on their part to a fundamentally democratic basis of national development. Their democratic commitment was demonstrated not simply by their adherence to the Westminster liberal-democratic tradition with its emphasis on free and fair elections and parliamentary representation, but more fundamentally by their striving toward an essentially inclusive, participatory politics that elevated the status of marginalized or repressed groups within Caribbean society (see Manley 1974, Jagan 1972).

The struggle for democratic justice on all fronts was characteristic of their political leadership. Michael Manley, for example, demonstrated this inclusive sense of democratic justice at the domestic level in the 1970s with his political embrace and elevation of the Rastafarian movement which had, since its inception in the 1940s, been socially and culturally ostracized by the Europeanized middle classes of Jamaican society. Manley's acceptance of Jamaican Marxists on his political platform in the 1970s similarly reflected the democratic inclusion of the traditionally maligned and ostracized left within Jamaican society (see Munroe 1990). In Guyana, Jagan's indefatigable struggle for the political empowerment of the Guyanese people against colonial control in the 1950s and 1960s, his attempts from the 1960s to democratize the problematic Guyana labor movement (see Reno 1964, St. Pierre 1999), and fight against the dictatorial powers of Forbes Burnham in the 1970s and 1980s, reflect these aspirations for democratic justice.

But it was at the international level that some of the most impressive contributions of both Jagan and Manley manifested themselves. Manley's pioneering fight for what was then termed a New International Economic Order (NIEO) represented a courageous call for international efforts to reduce significantly the economic gap between rich and poor nations. This was seen as a precondition for reducing inequities within Caribbean and other Third World societies (Manley 1974, 1991). Although the quest for the NIEO was effectively torpedoed by efforts of the more economically advantaged nations (the United States in particular), Manley's stature as an international statesman rose to unprecedented heights. Manley also pioneered closer interstate relationships between the Jamaican and Cuban governments at a time when most Caribbean and Latin American states were afraid to do so because of the intensity of U.S. animosities toward Castro's Cuba. In doing so, Manley demonstrated the intellectual and political fortitude that earned him the reputation of being an independent international statesman.

Jagan also saw his international stature elevated as a result of his diplomacy in the 1980s, which would seem to have upturned history both at home and abroad. His efforts to gain international support for returning his country to more democratic rule led to an amazing result when Arthur Schleisenger, adviser in the 1960s to U.S. President Kennedy, apologized to Jagan for helping initiate the violent destabilization of his government during the 1960s. Second, Jagan's magnanimity during his struggles at home to undo the U.S. and British sponsored dictatorial regime led by Burnham, earned him strong support from international quarters, including the U. S. Congressional Black Caucus and Senator Edward Kennedy, as well as from formerly implacable ideological foes within the U.S government. The result was a more humanitarian intervention from the United States and others in 1992 to restore free and fair electoral democracy in Guyana. Jagan's winning of the restored democratic elections that year seemed therefore well earned and richly deserved. Shortly before his death, Jagan issued a call for what he termed a "New International Human Order," which he hoped would blunt the rough impact of increasing capitalist globalization on the Third World, including Caribbean countries (see Benn, this volume; also Jagan 1999).

International and Political Impact

To fully understand the ramifications of the international diplomacy of Jagan and Manley in the course of their political careers, one has to understand the nature and significance of the Cold War (1947–89), and the interventionist proclivities of powerful states, particularly the United States, Britain, and the Soviet Union, in the domestic affairs of weaker states. In the Cold War context, the Caribbean, long considered "the American backyard," had often been viewed as—and used as—a pawn in the deadly international ideological conflicts between the powerful capitalist states, the United States and Britain, on the one hand, and the Soviet Union and satellite "communist" or "socialist" states, including Cuba, on the other (see Watson, this volume). The objective of the United States and Britain was to check or eliminate the apparently growing influence of Cuba, the Soviet Union and other international socialist states or movements, throughout the Caribbean and around the world. In this process, the strategy of inducing "low intensity warfare" (see Watson, this volume) aimed at destabilizing or destroying all leftist influences in a region became an intrinsic aspect of U.S. foreign policy employed particularly throughout the Caribbean region.

During this period, several interrelated strategies were used to destabilize what were regarded as communist ideological influences throughout the hemisphere. These destabilization efforts, covering military, political, economic, and cultural elements, involved both overt intervention and covert or subversive strategies by foreign forces, often in league with supportive elements among the domestic elite. Hemispheric history is replete with incidents involving U.S. efforts to destabilize governments, including the overthrow of democratically elected leftist governments such as the Jagan PPP government in 1953 and again in 1963–64, the Arbenz government in Guatemala in 1954, the Bosch government in the Dominican Republic in 1965, the Allende government in Chile in 1973, and the Manley government in Jamaica in 1980. The Central Intelligence Agency (CIA) was also involved in intrigues in several British Caribbean territories, including Guyana (1963–64), Jamaica (1976–80), and Grenada (1980–83), which left a legacy in these territories of bitter political divisiveness, ethnic polarization, violent conflict, and economic destitution (see Pearce 1981, Searle 1983, Mars 1998, and Watson, this volume).

The experiences of visionary, committed and progressive leaders in causes that support disadvantaged peoples throughout the Third World have often been marked by misfortune or tragedy. Jagan and Manley's experiences both followed this pattern, as evident in a series of destabilizing pressures meted out against them. The high point of the experiences of these two leaders coincided with the height of the Cold War. The British dismissal of the popularly elected Jagan government in 1953, and the violent CIA interventionism against what was considered to be a communist government in the 1960s represent the most significant examples in the Guyana case. The period 1953 to 1964 was perhaps the most volatile and traumatic in Guyana's political history. The 1953 Waddington Constitution, which gave Guyana its first democratic elections based on universal suffrage, saw the PPP under Cheddi Jagan sweeping the polls by a landslide. The British, embarrassed that a supposedly Marxist party could govern a territory within the British empire, swiftly contrived to suspend the constitution, dismiss the new government from office, and then proceeded to repress the movement by first incarcerating the leaders, including Cheddi Jagan, and subsequently engineering a split within the leadership of the PPP. The 1955 split in the party pitted the British cultivated "moderate," Forbes Burnham, who was then chairman of the party, against the so-called extremist Cheddi Jagan, who was then leader of the party.

Subsequent elections, however, in 1957 and again in 1961, saw the Jaganite faction of the PPP still victorious at the polls. By this time both the Burnhamists, who by 1958 had changed the name of their party to the "People's National Congress" (PNC), and the British colonial authorities had become desperate to see Jagan out of power. So the British, the PNC, and another opposition political party in Guyana, the United Force (UF), contrived to dramatically change the Guyana electoral system from the traditional "first past the post" multiconstituency system to the proportional representation system. Since it had been observed that Jagan's party never commanded more than 42 percent of the total national polls, which nevertheless secured most of the seats under the former system, the proportional representation system would ensure his proportionate loss at the next election scheduled for 1964. As anticipated, therefore, both the PNC and the UF combined to form the majority coalition government after the 1964 elections (see St Pierre, this volume).

In Jamaica, Manley's relatively mild efforts toward structural change did not avoid the unfortunate fate experienced by his counterpart, Cheddi Jagan. Foreign (including CIA) financing of opposition violence and the instigation of mutiny in the Jamaican army, as well as the fitting out of a private mercenary invasion against the Manley government during the 1970s, are the main examples in the Jamaican case (see Mars 1998). These actions led to Manley's electoral defeat in 1980 by the more socially and fiscally conservative Edward Seaga, leader of the Jamaica Labor Party (JLP). Seaga was preferred by the Americans in this case. It was typical of the times that foreign political destabilization would combine with pressures from global economic actors to stem the bold working-class projects of both Jagan and Manley.

External pressures precipitated destructive middle-class conflicts over political power, fostering in their wake ethno-political mobilization, ethnic divisiveness and violence, which continue to threaten the very fabric of Guyanese and Jamaican societies today (see P. Mars, this volume). Such pressures appear to have overwhelmed the leadership capabilities of both Jagan and Manley. Eventually, like most political leaders throughout the Third World, Jagan and Manley abandoned their structural transformation programs and policies of the 1970s in favor of the draconian structural adjustment measures demanded by the World Bank and the International Monetary Fund (IMF). The economic and social hardships suffered by Caribbean and other Third World countries as a consequence of structural adjustment policies are already well documented (see MacEwan 1990, McAffee 1991, and Young and Miranne, this volume).

Two specific aspects of these global pressures served to undermine and overturn the programs of Jagan and Manley that were oriented specifically to what is here called their "working-class project" (see P. Mars, this volume). The first relates to the erosion of the sovereign independence of nation-states due to the subjugation of their economies to international (basically World Bank and IMF) monitoring and other conditionalities, and thus the reduction of state leaders to mere puppets of foreign interests. The second pertains particularly to the labor movement. The usual IMF demands to cap wages and reduce labor costs, in order to attract more foreign investments, tend to weaken labor's economic base and hence its mobilizing capabilities, as well as to impoverish the working classes as a whole. Undoubtedly, these two dimensions of structural adjustment account for the major proportion of the destructive forces operating against the working classes. Thus, the "working-class project," with its emphases on fulfillment of labor demands and elevating the masses and working classes to a more prominent and influential position in the political process, which Jagan and Manley championed at the height of their political careers, was sidetracked by foreign and domestic pressures. While toward the end of his career, Manley more stoically accepted the terms of the IMF for addressing the economic and fiscal crises in Jamaica (see *Sunday Gleaner* 1992, Hart 1997), Jagan appeared to be more skeptical of the neoliberalist IMF requirements, which he saw as an inevitable but temporary evil (see *NACLA* 1997, 32–34).

Given the relentless onslaught of economic globalization on weak or disadvantaged states and peoples in the international system, several questions need to be raised about the relevance of the "working-class project," which both Jagan and Manley consistently pursued for the greater part of their political careers. The working-class project is here conceived in terms of the efforts of both leaders to elevate workers and the subordinate classes to positions whereby they can earn a greater share of the political and economic resources within their respective societies. Jagan's and Manley's emancipatory vision in the working-class project, enshrined in their continuing legacies, embraced (1) expansions in the democratization of the Guyanese and Jamaican societies to fully embrace the masses, including the political involvement of labor and the working classes; (2) struggles toward the realization of a more egalitarian political and economic universe, in which the labor movement itself was enabled to become a more self-confident player in the domestic and international political economy; and (3) support for the sovereign independence of Third World states and the egalitarian restructuring of the international economic and political order. As a result, the working classes in Guyana and Jamaica increasingly gained greater voice in, and access to, the processes of economic and political decision making. Similar gains in political and economic participation were achieved by workers throughout the rest of the English-speaking Caribbean.

But within the context of structural adjustment, how relevant to Caribbean conditions today are the legacies of the politicization of labor, the prioritization of the working classes as the principal agents of necessary political change, and challenges to economic inequality? Did Jagan and Manley's commitment to liberal democratic principles help or hinder the prospects of realizing their emancipatory and transformative projects? Was the fact of their middle-class socioeconomic status a self-defeating contradiction to their leadership of a working-class project? To what extent, therefore, was the eventual collapse of these transformative projects inevitable, or associated with the defeat of socialism on a world scale? Or are these projects part of a longer process of change, which is still ongoing?

The politicization of labor in the Caribbean enabled it to take part in a more constructive engagement in the process of needed social, political, and economic changes. Indeed, the labor movement in both Guyana and Jamaica historically produced many of the Caribbean's most able social and political reformers, including H. N. Critchlow, Ashton Chase, Jane Phillips-Gay, Ken Hill, and Richard Hart, along with Cheddi Jagan and Michael Manley. At the same time, the labor orientation of Jagan and Manley helped ground Caribbean politics in the experiences and struggle of the working classes who had long been regarded as the productive social forces. This approach, therefore, earned for the forces of radical and revolutionary struggle some semblance of political legitimacy, at least as far as the underprivileged Third World peoples were concerned. In 1996, shortly before his death, Jagan summed up his contribution to these labor-political groundings as follows:

> I have always associated myself with the ideology of the working class, and I have led a strong working-class party for the past 47 years. Different people see and call working-class ideology by different names, but what was important were the concrete historical conditions in Guyana and the creation of a programmatic platform that caters to the needs of the working class.... For me, Marxism was not nor is a dogma, but a scientific guide to action. It gave me strong ethical beliefs in social justice, particularly in helping the poor, the underprivileged and the exploited. (*NACLA* 1997, 32)

Theoretical Considerations

To fully understand the significant role of Jagan and Manley in elevating the working-class project, it is necessary first to come to grips with the theoretical and practical underpinnings of the relationship between capital and labor in developing societies such as in the Caribbean. That relationship in the Caribbean context is fundamentally historical, in that it is imbedded in slavery and the plantation system based on the availability of cheap labor and raw materials that was responsible for the development of capitalism in Europe, and consequently worldwide. It was a system characterized by the subordination of dark-skinned laborers and attendant class exploitation and racism. Labor resistance, originally associated with black and indentured resistance, was consequently the order of the day and intrinsic to this characteristically exploitative system (see Rodney 1981). Challenges to the system were to reach a peak in the 1930s when spontaneous labor resistance erupted everywhere throughout the English-speaking Caribbean. During this time were first created what were then termed "Working Men's Associations," the embryo of the modern trade union movements throughout the region.

Although these early movements were led by typically middle-class men, labor militancy was nevertheless always apparent among the working classes themselves (see Bogues 2002), and quickly became associated with leftist politics and ideology throughout the region. This labor-political nexus on the left was the space within which both Jagan and Manley quickly carved out their niche. Their interpretation of this linkage was to bring the labor movement in line with, and under the tutelage at least, if not the firm control of, the political party. But this militant or progressive labor-political trend soon became eclipsed by the reaction of capital with the aid of British colonialism and U.S. imperialism, particularly during the Cold War era (1947–89) when labor militancy itself was consistently identified with communism and Marxism. Colonial capitalism and imperialism responded with a variety of coercive and violent measures, including divide-and-rule tactics, incarceration of labor and political leaders of the left, violent repression of mass protest and movements associated with leftist politics, and cultivation of middle-class leadership to contain labor and political militancy, thus creating what is today recognized as a Caribbean labor aristocracy.

Today, global capitalism, primarily through IMF structural adjustment policies aimed at Third World and Caribbean countries, significantly furthers the weakening and impoverishment of labor and protest movements through imposed conditionalities including restriction on wage increases, massive unemployment through downsizing of industries, curtailment of labor agitation and strikes, and compulsory privatization of public enterprises with negative implications for workers' benefits. For these reasons of violent destabilization and containment of labor on a world scale, the Caribbean labor movement is seemingly caught in the critical dilemma of having to choose between depoliticization and apathy, on the one hand, and risking its own destruction at the hands of the powerful forces of global capital, on the other. It is this dilemma imposed by the hegemony of global capital that is of pivotal interest in this volume and that is brought out forcefully in the discussions of several of the chapters, particularly those in part 2. It is important, therefore, to address at this stage some of the more crucial issues involved in the dilemma facing the Caribbean working classes arising from this hegemony of global capital, and how Jagan and Manley might have responded to them.

The argument, fashionable today, that the global economy mandates a separation between labor and politics in the interest of capital growth and the encouragement of needed foreign investments has often been applied to discredit the efforts of political reformers like Jagan and Manley. However, in the intellectual tradition from which these men came, it was argued that the resolution of underdevelopment, material deprivation, and immiseration of people in the Caribbean (and the Third World generally) required the committed and energetic intervention of human effort, and not just the action of market forces in the abstract. In practical terms, the more salient aspects of these human efforts take the form of the state or collective (mainly party) activism. Notwithstanding the pervasiveness of the globalization arguments that generally elevate the significance of blind market forces, Jagan and Manley were energized by their view of the necessity of human agency, and they in turn energized others on that basis. They were indignant that the Caribbean, like most of the Third World, still experiences what could be termed incomplete or arrested modernization (see Chilcote and Johnson 1983), compared to the more developed capitalist world. Herein lies the necessity of their struggles for social, political, and economic change. For there continues to exist severe tensions between the incomplete modernization seen in terms of truncated or stifled industrialization in the South, and the global dynamics that largely enabled the North to complete its modernization phase and begin to display postindustrial characteristics.

But again, it could be argued that even if human agency is significant for some types of social and political change, there is no necessary association of such agency solely with labor and the working classes. In today's complex world, there are a number of social movements and organizations that compete for influence and power. Indeed the argument is often advanced that civil society as a whole, particularly through the work of nongovernmental organizations (NGOs), holds the key to the important processes of change in the modern world (see Giddens, 1994). Within this perspective, therefore, it is usually argued that politics and the state should play a minimal role in the national economy. But the relevance of the Jagan/Manley working-class project within the Caribbean context is that civil society in this region is either too minimal or nonexistent; that is, "civil society"—defined in terms of a supposedly neutral, nonpoliticized middle ground capable of playing a politically independent role in bringing about the changes acceptable to all sides in the Caribbean political process—is too weak for the task at hand. Caribbean civil society, particularly in Guyana and Jamaica, is strongly polarized around fundamentalist and ethnically divisive political forces, and within it labor plays a most significant role as being the more self-consciously organized for, or committed to, the type of economic and social changes necessary for reducing the ever increasing gap between the rich and the poor in the region.

The labor movement indeed is part of civil society. But the call for strengthening civil society appears to be contradicted by a major thrust of the economic globalization process toward the weakening of the labor movement. This is one of the basic contradictions of neoliberalist ideology that Jagan and Manley in their heyday fought so vigorously to contain or overturn. However, foreign intervention and the asymmetrical impact of capitalist globalization, both advancing the neoliberalist cause, proved overwhelming for both Jagan and Manley, particularly in their efforts toward sovereign and self-sufficient development. It was precisely at the juncture of forging the labor-political nexus that their efforts were hardest hit. Foreign intervention and economic globalization were primarily instrumental in dwarfing and dividing the labor movement, and in changing the very character of the Caribbean working class. Increasing structural unemployment, insecurity of the workforces through privatization policies without guarantees of welfare benefits, and transition from a relatively stable to a mainly casual and part-time labor force are some of the indicators of the changed character of Caribbean labor (see Young and Miranne, this volume). The combination of these circumstances is being felt in the increasing domination of foreign capital throughout the region.

Yet the changed and weakened character of Caribbean labor does not negate the fact that the workers' contribution to the national economy is still significant (probably pivotal), compared to most other elements within Caribbean civil society. For this reason, the elevation of labor by both Jagan and Manley in the Caribbean political and economic processes and structures appears to a large extent justifiable, particularly in a context where the economy relies largely on production of raw material rather than large-scale capital exchanges. If on a world scale labor is not necessarily, in a Marxist sense, historically ordained to play the vanguard role in the inevitable social revolution, its role, nevertheless, cannot be ignored or slighted in the Caribbean context. For in the Caribbean capital is scarce, and even in the favorable structural adjustment (neoliberalist) climate, it is still not being invested in the region in significant proportions as anticipated. Thus the massive pressures toward privatization of former public enterprises and concomitant appeals since the 1980s for large-scale influx of capital have largely fallen on deaf ears among foreign investors.

The wider issue of the struggle by Jagan and Manley to reduce economic or class inequalities within their countries would be, under the neoliberalist globalization perspectives today, considered not only idle and idealistic, but even antiprogressive or retrograde. The globalization argument holds that economic inequalities are not only inevitable, given the competitive nature of the historically given capitalist system, but also creative in the sense that the skillful entrepreneurial elite it produces is necessary to stimulate further economic growth and, indeed, the continual regeneration of the economic system as a whole (*Stabroek News* 2000). But within recent years it has become more evident, as if to revive the egalitarian perspectives of Jagan and Manley, that these arguments do not hold in reality. After several decades of structural adjustment programs, the actual gap between the few rich and the vast majority of poor has been increasing considerably both between and within states in the international system (Thomas 2000, Brecher 2000). The surprising immensity of the inequality gaps throughout the world has today generated serious concern and rethinking even from among the strongest advocates of structural adjustment and global capitalism, including the IMF and the World Bank. And the events in Seattle in 1999 and in Davos, Switzerland in 2000, involving massive popular and violent protests against the World Trade Organization that is seen in effect to be promoting increasing poverty, immiseration, massive unemployment, and environmental devastation around the world, would seem to provide endorsement for the foresight of earlier "idealists" like Manley and Jagan who argued for a more egalitarian and just world.

The economic globalization argument champions the pluralistic liberal democratic framework as being compatible with competitive market approaches. But the demonstrable commitment of Jagan and Manley to Westminster pluralistic and electoral democracy did not prevent the destabilization of their political projects by the very champions (especially Britain and the United States) of democratic politics in the first place. Contrary to their overt claims, these developed capitalist countries have always put the control of Third World resources above maintaining democratic processes and institutions throughout the world (see Robinson 1996). Moreover, the democracy promoted by these foreign powers in the Third World, including the Caribbean, has always been limited to elite (middle-class) political control. The elite are generally interested in preserving the interests of foreign capital and gaining what they can for themselves. This kind of democracy is not what Jagan and Manley envisioned, which is the popular political involvement of the masses in struggle for a greater share of the economic pie.

Was defeat of the working-class project inevitable? It appears that like their radical and revolutionary counterparts among the Third World political leadership, both Jagan and Manley underestimated the strength and determination of Western hegemonic powers in their efforts to impose or maintain capitalist enterprises abroad, and to thwart attempts to challenge or upset the established capitalist world system. Second, there was hardly an alternative world system, despite the earlier assumptions about the Soviet socialist system, that was capable or willing to defend the fledgling efforts toward political change among Caribbean and Third World peoples. To this extent, therefore, the quest of Jagan and Manley for political alternatives at both the national and international levels appears to have been either illusory or premature. But to say that the defeat of the working-class project of Jagan and Manley was predictable, given the reactionary nature of the global capitalist system, is not to say that such an outcome is necessarily permanent or irreversible. Current waves of popular protests around the globe against the impoverishment and devastation wrought by the IMF and the World Bank, the recent anticapitalist protests in Europe, North American challenges to the global asymmetries and inequities produced by world trade, and the apparent return of the left to significant power positions in many of the leading European states are only some of the indicators pointing to the possibility that issues of human emancipation and equality are once again on the agenda of national and global politics alike.

Finally, what were the consequences of the contradictions between the essentially middle-class status of Caribbean political leadership, which included Jagan and Manley, and the ostensibly working-class struggles they were supposed to lead? While on the one hand, middle-class leaders were vulnerable to external influences and thus might be, wittingly or not, tools of the destabilizing forces, on the other hand, they often had the necessary education, skills, and resources to guide the movement. They provided the organizational experience to lead the movement at a particular moment in the historical development of the Caribbean. The contradiction is not likely to be completely overcome, but it can be minimized by the leaders' willingness to seek greater understanding of the needs of working people, to seek participation of and collaboration with the working class, and to create organizations that practice democracy and articulate social, political, and economic justice. Jagan and Manley seemed to have been conscious of this contradiction and to have worked to create organizations and agendas that reflected the contributions of these perennially disadvantaged classes. Thus they spoke not only on behalf of the working classes, but *with* the working classes (see St. Pierre, this volume; Bogues, this volume). In the case of Jagan and Manley, the two classes worked together in complementary ways.

What seemed to be central to the theoretical underpinning of the working-class project as conceived by Jagan and Manley is the issue of the extent to which trade unionism must become politicized in the interest of advancing fundamental change in the social system as a whole. For both Jagan and Manley, a political unionism is necessary and crucial for such a task, as well as for building the social and class consciousness of working peoples. However, such a labor politicization was narrowly conceptualized in terms of the labor movement subordinating itself to leadership by a particular party. This conceptualization is today largely criticized in academic circles that are conscious of the totalizing and destabilizing impact of capitalist globalization. For some, labor itself remains ideologically dependent on the globalizing system, with little wiggle room to challenge the system. In this perspective, labor is seen as an intrinsic extension of such global capitalist destabilization as witnessed, say, in the role of many Caribbean labor unions in conjunction with the AFL-CIO in destabilizing progressive Caribbean regimes and leftist political movements in the region, particularly during the Cold War period (see Watson, this volume). The implication here is that without some aggressive political militancy on the part of trade unionism, or what Moody

(2001) termed "social movement unionism," whether in the Caribbean or elsewhere, the prospects for the working-class project are bleak.

For others, labor is seen as too overly political, too closely allied to and dependent on the political party, with negative impact on the economy and society as a whole. A more independent trade unionism is, therefore, the recommendation for this diagnosis (see Thomas, this volume). However, one does not have to eliminate politics from unionism to make it less partisan or dependent on the political party. An independent trade union movement is not necessarily incompatible with a politically or ideologically conscious unionism (see P. Mars, this volume). The moment a trade union movement supports widely national issues beyond the particular constituency of the trade union itself, such as the national minimum wage, solidarity strikes, or opposition to IMF and WPO policies and strategies, then a certain level of political advocacy or ideological commitment becomes as obvious as it is necessary for the advancement of the working-class project.

Beyond the working-class project and the strengthening of the labor-political nexus, Manley and Jagan explored other aspects of society that kept inequalities in place. As Manley (1982, 48) noted, "The . . . majority of the Jamaican people, held to be equal in the constitution, were not equal in law, in opportunity nor, most profoundly, in the unspoken and unwritten assumptions which underlay the social order." One of these inequalities was the role of women, especially in relation to employment opportunities. Another was the welfare of children, especially those born outside of marriage. Attempts were made to provide greater access to education, as well as to make the curriculum more relevant to the needs of Caribbean societies.

However, these issues remained relatively subdued in relation to the more prominent working-class and economic concerns of Jagan and Manley. The rights of women, for example, although conceptualized within the context of the inegalitarian structural tendencies of capitalism, were left largely unexplored as an issue in its own right. Women within the labor movement and within politics were accorded a secondary role to that of men (see Bolles, this volume), and thus women continue to be hampered by economic and political inequities (see Young and Miranne, this volume). Yet the gendered aspects of labor are very much a part of economic globalization today and need careful conceptualization. Growing numbers of women have entered the labor force over the past twenty years, and now women are often the major breadwinner in the family. In fact, in some industries, such as manufacturing and business services, women have become preferred employees, "playing central, critical roles in the process of structuring the global economy" (Christopherson 1995, 191). At a time when structural adjustment policies result in growing male unemployment due to the closure of many firms in traditional sectors, the recasting of jobs as casual labor, and the dismantling of government programs, women are encouraged to enter the labor force because they can be mobilized as low-wage workers (see Sassen 2000). Under these conditions, they are likely to work for lower wages, fewer benefits, and less than full-time status due to their domestic responsibilities. Women then can be used to break any notion of a "labor aristocracy."

Thus, women entering the labor force often find that their salaries are low and their families still poor, and they must struggle to make ends meet. The impacts of the changing global and national economies are felt most keenly in the domestic household, where a deterioration of living standards is apparent. Given these situations, women seek any number of alternative means for making a living, and are encouraged to do so by governments, who then can (and do) take less responsibility for providing for the social welfare of women and their families (see Young and Miranne, this volume). Thus an emphasis is put on privatizing solutions for immiseration, rather than developing public responses and policies, which is what Jagan and Manley considered so important in their working-class project.

When labor is viewed from a gendered perspective, it is also possible to see how global and national economies benefit in other ways. For instance, the work that women do in the informal sector is often central to the work that is being done in the formal sector, for example, piecework done more cheaply in the home that becomes part of a finished manufactured product. The national government benefits from hard currencies that have been generated from the work that women do, work that is often invisible and poorly remunerated (see Sassen 2000, Fernandez Kelly and Sassen 1995). Women's work may be essential to the household economy, the national economy, and even the global economy, but for the most part it is being done privately, without benefit of collective or organized effort (but see Trotz and Peake 2001, Reddock 1998). Thus the logic of globalization keeps the working class at a distinct disadvantage. Much work remains to be done on the gendered aspects of economic globalization.

There were other issues that were not included in the working-class project as orginally conceived, but that have gained prominence in more recent years. One of these is the narco-trafficking problem, which is also conceptualized as the hidden and undeclared hand of modern aggressive capitalism, and one which still overwhelms the capacity of the Caribbean to contain or eliminate (see Griffith, this volume). Another issue that appears to take a minor place in the perspectives of Jagan and Manley is that of the level of criminality and its relationship to ethno-political violence that recently escalated in both Guyana and Jamaica. Here we refer to the continual incidents of neighborhood political gangsterism in Jamaica and violent and politicized criminal gangs in Guyana. These incidents have occasionally merged with political protest, making them difficult to contain or control. Although both Manley and Jagan in their published works touched on rebellion and destabilization, both overt and covert, they tended to slight specific discussions on conflict resolution, short of the need to call out the security forces and appeal to the opposition political forces to help stop the violence. The fact that the security forces have often been unreliable in such a task, particularly in the case of Guyana under Jagan (see J. Mars, this volume), must be seriously considered in efforts toward successful ethno-political conflict resolution in the region. What is needed is a more systematic approach to conflict resolution, inclusive of mediation, economic incentives, political and economic participation, and a more critical assessment of the zero-sum implications of Westminster "democratic" politics that both Jagan and Manley unflinchingly championed.

Structure and Scope

This volume grows out of a conference organized to commemorate the lives and contributions of Cheddi Jagan and Michael Manley, and to critically evaluate their impact on the Caribbean. The conference, "Caribbean Perspectives on Labor and Politics: Legacies of Cheddi Jagan and Michael Manley," was held at Wayne State University in April 1998, hosted by the Department of Africana Studies and the College of Urban, Labor and Metropolitan Affairs. The majority of the chapters in this volume were first presented at this conference, but all have been substantially revised. Five of the chapters were commissioned expressly for this volume. Held a year after Jagan and Manley's deaths (both died on March 6, 1997), the conference presented an opportunity for remembering the impact that these men had on the Caribbean as they struggled to free their countries from colonialism, imperialism, and dependency, and to provide their peoples with more democratic and just societies.

Much has been written about Cheddi Jagan and about Michael Manley, and each man was prodigious in his own writings. However, this volume is the first comparative analysis of the contributions of the two men. While Jagan and Manley were clearly different in a number of respects, they both struggled to transform their societies in very fundamental ways. This volume examines their legacies by placing them within the context of what is here called the "working-class project." The possibilities embedded in this project, as well as the external and internal challenges that confronted it, are analyzed. However, the chapters in this volume do not reflect a uniformity of views with respect to Jagan and Manley or the concept of the working-class project. In fact, the differences that might be detected from chapter to chapter are encouraged in the interest of furthering the debate and addressing the contentions that have surrounded these men and the issue of the working-class project from the inception. Contention and debate can only further scholarship in the field and help develop insights into more creative policy interventions in the issues that were focal to the lives and contributions of these two capable Caribbean political and labor leaders.

This volume is divided into three interrelated parts. The first is "The Men and Their Times," in which is discussed the life, contribution and impact of these two leaders in both their domestic and international environments. The second part, "Labor-Politics Nexus," discusses the close interrelationship between labor and politics throughout the region, and the specific contributions of Jagan and Manly to the origins and development of that interconnection, particularly within their own countries, Guyana and Jamaica. The third part, "Critical Current Challenges," considers several issues that were not adequately addressed by the leaders but that continue to affect the possibility of transformation in the region. At the end of the volume is a listing of the major writings and speeches of Jagan and Manley.

The first part includes five chapters, two tributes from the men's contemporaries (Girvan and Benn), and three (St. Pierre, Bogues, and J. Mars) that critically examine the forces that influenced their personal and political growth and the impact these leaders had on the development of their countries and the Caribbean region as a whole. In Girvan's insightful tribute, he represents Manley's contributions as highly relevant not only during the 1970s, when struggles toward social, political, and economic transformations were fashionable in the region, but even today, despite the claims of globalization to have superseded the transformative potentialities of the state through free-market strategies that are little more than thinly disguised forms of yesterday's strategies of imperialism.

The Honorable Brindley H. Benn, Guyana high commissioner to Canada at the time of the conference, presents a chronology of Cheddi Jagan's contributions to the political and economic development of Guyana and his influence in the international field. Benn himself had been closely associated with Jagan, especially in the early years of the struggle and the creation in 1950 of the People's Progressive Party. Both Benn and Jagan were incarcerated by the British in the 1950s and 60s for their defiance of British oppressive control, as they were ardent campaigners against colonialism and imperialism alike. Benn brings a lot of memories of their anticolonial and anti-imperialist struggles to the discussion, and in his chapter Jagan's contributions are cast principally in this light.

Maurice St. Pierre discusses Jagan's role as an activist-intellectual who became a principal architect of the movement for political independence in Guyana. St. Pierre is particularly interested in how Jagan's ideas and intellectual framing of the situation of struggle against British colonialism and American interventionism help contribute to the overall knowledge base of the country, and indeed contribute to similar struggles in the Caribbean as a whole. Anthony Bogues follows with an in-depth analysis of the origins of Michael Manley's politics in the Jamaican labor movement and the ramifications of this experience for Manley's political practice within Jamaican society as a whole. According to Bogues, while Manley's contribution to the development of political unionism in Jamaica helped sharpen his oratorical skills and his remarkable ability to communicate with the Jamaican popular masses, it was the narrower partisan and conflictual aspects of political unionism that facilitated the defeat of his quest for social equality within the context of his vision of democratic socialism.

Next, Joan Mars gives a forthright analysis of the role of Jagan in attempting to gain the support of the Guyana police while it was still under the control of British colonial authority during the heyday of the Cold War period in the 1960s, and how the colonial politicization of the force then has continued to contribute significantly to the overall pattern of political and ethnic instability in Guyana. After delineating a clear connection between the colonial police practices and the continued political policing today in Guyana, she concludes with pertinent recommendations for reforming the force to make it more civic and community oriented, and as such more capable of mitigating rather than exacerbating conflicts in ethnic plural societies such as Guyana.

Part 2 of this volume, "The Labor-Politics Nexus," addresses specifically the ramifications of the interrelationships between labor and politics, and the extent to which this interrelationship was influenced by, as well as impacted by, the political careers of both Jagan and Manley. Hilbourne Watson begins the part by locating Jagan and Manley's political contributions within both the domestic "labor" and international "global capital" dimensions while at the same time demonstrating the linkages between these two interrelated spheres of activities. A significant thrust of Watson's analysis is that the very rootedness of Jagan and Manley's domestic politics in labor relations ran up against the contradictions of the international capitalist system in which foreign labor was used to undermine and ultimately derail the labor-political projects of both men at the domestic level and their quest for fundamental structural change at the international level. Watson helps us understand how the Cold War affected the domestic and international agenda of these two men. For Watson, the Cold War project was the crowning principle of postwar American hegemony, even though it was masked as the moral idea of freedom. The experiences of Jagan and Manley, Watson contends, pose important lessons for the Caribbean left in general, even in the post–Cold War world of increasing capitalist globalization.

Clive Thomas analyzes the condition of the Caribbean labor movement within a crisis-ridden political context. Thomas concludes with some pertinent advice to labor and political leaders about the way forward for a more viable trade union movement. Most prominent among his recommendations are the initiation of legislation to help Caribbean labor maintain the international standards set by the International Labor Organization (ILO), and the development of strategic alliances with other significant groups and organizations within the particular Caribbean society.

Perry Mars considers the perils of divisive ethno-politics on what he termed the "working-class project" sponsored by both Jagan and Manley. Mars suggests that this project was undermined by basic contradictions inherent in the leaders' strategy of dependence on communal, ethnic, or what Manley himself called "tribalistic" loyalties mobilized toward the attainment and maintenance of political power.

Lynn Bolles concludes this part with an insightful analysis of the role played by women in the Caribbean labor movement. She argues cogently that although the activism of Caribbean women in building trade unionism was essential, recognition of their work was not forthcoming. Their work here, as in other aspects of society, was "invisible," based on the assumption that it would be males who speak for the labor movement. Women's roles would be in the background. This thinking has resulted in few women in leadership positions within either labor or political movements in the Caribbean.

Part 3 of this volume, "Critical Current Challenges," deals with some of the wider issues surrounding the main quest of Jagan and Manley for liberation, equality, and democracy both politically and economically, and at both domestic and international levels. These are issues not systematically addressed by either man during his lifetime but which clearly impact the ability to carry out the agendas that they left us. First, Alma Young and Kristine Miranne examine the role of women within the context of the Caribbean welfare state that is shrinking due to the privatizing impact of structural adjustment conditionalities and increasing capitalist globalization. In such a context, women and their families are clearly at a disadvantage in having their needs met by government or capital, and so must find ways to ensure their own survival. Young and Miranne also discuss ways in which women are organizing to address issues of their empowerment while working to enhance transformational development opportunities in Caribbean societies.

Ivelaw Griffith follows with a wake-up call to regional governments and to the population as a whole to face the deadly problem of increased drug trafficking throughout the region. He addressed the issue of combating drugs both comprehensively and in terms of drug trafficking's impact on the policies of Jagan and Manley in Guyana and Jamaica. Since Griffith wrote this analysis in early 2000, the nexus among drugs, crime, and ethnic politics has become more apparent in Guyana as crime has escalated due to disputes among those involved in drug activity. Unfortunately, much of this criminal activity is being cast in ethnically polarizing terms, making it all the more difficult to deal with the drug problem. Griffith contends that the drug problem is one in which, to use Martin Carter's poetic phrase, "all are involved," and if neglected, all might eventually become "consumed" by it.

Finally, Monica Gordon scrutinizes the phenomenon of Caribbean migration in terms of both its outward and homeward trends. She refers to the "going away" and "coming home" phenomenon as part of a singular process of the circulation of Caribbean populations both during colonial and postcolonial times. She examines the influence of this migratory phenomenon on the life and politics of both Jagan and Manley, and on the political and economic development of the Caribbean region as a whole. She reminds us once again that globalization is not only about the movement of capital and goods, but also about people.

Concluding Remarks

To a large extent, the experiences of Jagan and Manley demonstrate the limitations of the ostensibly sovereign state in the Third World in the wake of increasing economic and cultural globalization. Their political and ideological projects were potentially far-reaching and catalytic in bringing about fundamental changes within an extremely inegalitarian world. But beyond their borders, in the global and international environment, the Achilles' heel of their radical projects became immediately revealed, and so inevitably met serious setbacks and defeats.

But it appears also that they operated within a peculiar historical time—a time of cold wars, foreign destabilization, and enforced structural adjustments—which leaves the story of the future pregnant with the possibility of eventual vindication of much of what they fought for in the interest of labor, the working classes, and those whom Fanon termed "the wretched of the earth." A new groundswell involving international alliances across classes, borders, and ethnicities in attempts to reform or reverse the perils of the global economy—what Brecher et al. call "globalization from below" (2000)—might be the beginning of a new historical phase that is more in keeping with the interest of the disadvantaged peoples of the globe whom both Jagan and Manley championed so loudly and with such deep commitment. Only time will tell.

References

Bogues, Anthony. 2002. "Politics, Nation and Postcolony: Caribbean Inflections." *Small Axe* (March): 1–30.

Brecher, Jeremy, Tim Costello, and Brendan Smith. 2000. *Globalization from Below: The Power of Solidarity*. Cambridge, Mass: South End Press.

Chase, Ashton. 1954. *133 Days Toward Freedom in Guyana*. Georgetown: People's Progressive Party.

Chilcote, Ronald H., and Dale L. Johnson. 1983. *Theories of Development: Mode of Production or Dependency.* Beverly Hills: Sage Publications.

Christopherson, Susan. 1995. "Changing Women's Status in a Global Economy." In *Geographies of Global Change: Remapping the World in the Late Twentieth Century,* ed. R. J. Johnston, Peter Taylor, and Michael Watts. London: Blackwell.

Fernandez Kelly, M. P., and S. Sassen. 1995. "Recasting Women in the Global Economy." In *Women in the Latin American Development Process,* ed. Christine Bose and Edna Acosta-Belen. Philadelphia: Temple University Press.

Giddens, Anthony. 1994. *Beyond Left and Right: The Future of Radical Politics.* Stanford: Stanford University Press.

Hart, Richard. 1997. *Michael Manley: An Assessment and Tribute.* London: Caribbean Labor Solidarity.

Hector, Tim. 1997. "Michael Manley—Prince of the People's Struggle (Part I)," *Fan the Flame,* http://www.candw.ag/~jardinea//ffhtm/ff970314.htm.

Jagan, Cheddi. 1999. *A New Global Human Order.* Milton, Ont.: Harpy.

———. 1972. *The West on Trial.* Berlin: Seven Seas Books.

MacEwan, Arthur. 1990. *Debt and Disorder: International Economic Instability and U.S. Imperial Decline.* New York: Monthly Review Press.

McAffee, Cathy. 1991. *Storm Signals: Structural Adjustment and Development Alternatives in the Caribbean.* Cambridge, Mass.: South End Press.

Manley, Michael. 1991. *The Poverty of Nations: Reflections on Underdevelopment and the World Economy.* London: Pluto Press.

———. 1982. *Jamaica: Struggle in the Periphery.* London: Writers and Readers.

———. 1974. Budget Speech Debate. *Hansard,* 29 (May).

Mars, Perry. 1998. *Ideology and Change: The Transformation of the Caribbean Left.* Detroit: Wayne State University Press; Mona: University Press of the West Indies.

Moody, Kim. 2001. *Workers in a Lean World: Unions in the International Economy.* London: Verso.

Munroe, Trevor. 1990. *Jamaican Politics: A Marxist Perspective in Transition.* Kingston: Heinemann/Lynn Reinner.

North American Congress on Latin America (NACLA). 1997. 31, no. 1.

Pearce, Jenny. 1981. *Under the Eagle: U.S. Intervention in Central America and the Caribbean.* Cambridge, Mass.: South End Press.

Reddock, Rhoda. 1998. "Women's Organizations and Movements in the Commonwealth Caribbean: The Response to Global Economic Crisis in the 1980s." *Feminist Review* 59: 57–73.

Reno, Phillip. 1964. *The Ordeal of British Guyana.* New York: Monthly Review Press.

Robinson, William I. 1996. *Promoting Polyarchy: Globalization, U.S. Intervention, and Hegemony.* Cambridge: Cambridge University Press.

Rodney, Walter A. 1981. *A History of the Guyanese Working People.* Baltimore: Johns Hopkins University Press.

Sassen, Saskia. 2000. "Women's Burden: Countergeographies of Globalization and the Feminization of Survival." *Journal of International Affairs* 53, no. 2: 503–24.

Searle, Chris. 1983. *Grenada: The Struggle Against Destabilization.* London: Writers and Readers.

Stabroek News. 2000. February 24.

St. Pierre, Maurice. 1999. *Anatomy of Resistance: Anticolonialism in Guyana 1823–1966.* London: Macmillan.

The Sunday Gleaner. 1992. May 17.

Thomas, Caroline. 2000. *Global Governance, Development and Human Security.* Kingston: Arawak Publications and Pluto Press.

Trotz, D. Alissa, and Linda Peake. 2001. "Work, Family and Organizing: An Overview of the Contemporary Economic, Social and Political Roles of Women in Guyana." *Social and Economic Studies* 50, no. 2: 67–101.

Waters, Malcolm. 1995. *Globalization.* London: Routledge.

PART I

Life and Times of the Men

1

Michael Manley: A Personal Perspective

NORMAN GIRVAN

This is about Michael Manley. It is a personal perspective.

Michael Manley was born to privilege, but he spent most of his life fighting against the entrenched structures of privilege in his native Jamaica and in the wider world. His father, Norman Manley, had been in his youth an outstanding athlete, and a veteran of World War I, who went on to become Jamaica's most outstanding barrister of his day and then to become, in effect, the father of the Jamaican nation. If Marcus Garvey's mission was black pride and panAfricanism, and Alexander Bustamante's was to launch a national labor movement, Norman Manley's was to launch the national movement for self-determination and to forge a national identity where none existed before.

In the closing speech of his political career, the elder Manley declared that the mission of his generation was to secure political independence; winning economic independence was the mission of the generation to follow. The younger Manley was to take up the challenge. The goal proved elusive. Today, some would say economic independence is irrelevant in the era of globalization. I beg to differ. Its substantive significance, I will argue, remains as relevant at the close of the 1990s as it was at the beginning of the 1970s.

Michael's mother, Edna Manley, was a brilliant and talented artist whose forte was sculpture. She is widely credited with inspiring and nurturing the Jamaican art movement that paralleled the emergence of the nationalist movement of the 1930s and 40s—and hence with being the "mother" of Jamaican art. Michael Manley grew up in a household in which political ideas and events were the fodder of daily conversation, artistic expression was a passion, and sport a subject of continuing interest, in a family that had embraced service to the nation as a lifelong vocation. When Michael won the leadership of the People's National Party in 1969, in an election in which everyone agrees his father maintained strict neutrality, an intergenerational heritage of political leadership was confirmed. But it was a tradition, not a dynasty.

Throughout Michael's own life, he seemed to wrestle with the manifold drives of his two unusual parents: of political struggle, of love of sport, and of artistic expression—the mind, the body, and the spirit. The tension, if never fully resolved, became the wellspring of his own unique brand of creativity. There are still those who argue that of his books, which included *A Voice at the Workplace, The Politics of Change,* and *Struggle in the Periphery,* the best is the last—his monumental *History of West Indies Cricket.* His parents were indeed a hard act to follow. But for Michael, theirs were the only act he *could* follow.

As a youth, Michael signaled his instinctive intolerance of injustice when he chose to leave, prematurely, the elite high school Jamaica College rather than to accept a caning—widely regarded as a symbol of Jamaica's colonial educational culture—from a headmaster. As his father was, by that time, already campaigning against Jamaica's colonial political order, it is a safe bet that Michael was applying at school the political principles he was learning at home. After a stint with the Royal Canadian Air Force, he went to the London School of Economics, where he majored in government and was strongly influenced by the great socialist political philosopher Harold Laski.

His involvement with the cause of labor began almost immediately after his return to Jamaica in 1951. It was his mission to organize the National Workers Union as the trade union base of the PNP, which had recently lost its base in the labor movement as a result of the expulsion of the Marxist left from the party, which controlled the Trade Union Congress. Michael soon established a reputation as a skilled negotiator who combined an excellent grasp of the tactics of bargaining with a remarkable capacity to communicate complex issues with great simplicity and, in doing so, to find common ground between management and labor.

The experience of a remarkable string of successfully resolved labor disputes in which he was able, in effect, to persuade management to make concessions in their own long-term self-interests was to be put to use in the 1970s. Michael tried to reform Jamaica's entrenched structure of class and

Michael Manley. Courtesy of the Jamaican Information Service.

economic power through a combination of mobilization of the masses and persuasion of the classes. On the international front he campaigned for a new international economic order by a combination of strategic alliances with radical governments in the south and progressive leaders in the north, supported by careful reasoning and brilliant rhetoric. But, as we now know, the structures of power, both domestic and international, proved stubbornly impervious to the formula that had worked so well in labor-management negotiations. Perhaps the confidence in his own capacities that Michael had developed in his trade union years made him unduly optimistic about the possibilities for negotiated change.

One cannot fail to note that Michael's vision for labor developed beyond immediate concerns of wages and working conditions to embrace broader questions of worker power. The fraternal relations that Michael developed with Hugh Shearer of the BITU (Barbados Industrial Trade Union), and their joint bargaining with the sugar and bauxite industries, spoke of an approach in which trade union rivalry was subordinated to the broader interests of the workers. Further, in *A Voice at the Workplace,* Michael Manley outlined his proposals for worker participation in management—a program that was to be adopted as official policy in the 1970s and resurrected in the 1990s in the form of an Employee Share Ownership scheme.

My own father, Thom Girvan, worked with Norman Manley in the Jamaica welfare movement that the latter founded in 1937. I myself first met Michael Manley in the early 1960s. At that time I could have been described as a leftist nationalist, and Michael was, if anything, suspicious of a left that tended to view his father, and by extension himself, as an irredeemable "middle-of-the-roader." After his election to the party leadership in 1969, however, Michael Manley welded together a remarkable coalition of PNP old guard, young black nationalists, socialist populists, and disenchanted capitalists to sweep the polls in 1972. The Manley administration set about implementing the most sweeping program of social and economic reform that Jamaica has ever seen in so short a time. The aim was to drastically reduce unemployment, poverty, and inequality; to distribute land to landless small farmers; to guarantee the rights of workers, women, and those born out of wedlock; to provide training and educational opportunities for the disadvantaged and excluded; and to wrest the levers of economic control from the multinational corporations and the local elite. Internationally, he joined the campaign led by OPEC (Organization of Petroleum Exporting Countries) nations for a New International Economic Order, fought for an end to the isolation of Cuba, campaigned militantly against South African apartheid, and generally became a thorn in the side of Uncle Sam.

Helped by the revenues from the bauxite levy, the democratic socialist project prospered at first and Manley's PNP won an overwhelming election victory in 1976. But the consequences of capital flight, retaliation by the bauxite companies, a U.S.-sponsored campaign of economic and political destabilization, and excessive public spending brought the economy to the brink of bankruptcy and into the jaws of the International Monetary Fund (IMF). I joined the administration in early 1977 as part of a group charged with finding an alternative production program to the package of devaluation and spending cuts advocated by the IMF. In the end, Manley did go to the IMF, largely because there was at the time a sympathetic administration in Washington and neither the Soviets nor the oil-rich states could come up with the money that the IMF could offer.

The rest, as they say, is history. The private sector never put their confidence back in the PNP. In spite of the IMF programs, investment continued to falter and the economy continued to deteriorate. The 1980 election was to be fought in a setting marked by acute shortages of basic goods, growing unemployment, and extreme violence. The people, whom Michael loved, and who loved him, voted him out of office. They had their reasons. Two remarks, in my view, summed it up. In the words of one man: "I love Michael, but I voted for Mr.[Edward] Seaga because he knows how to get the money. Next time I'll vote for Michael because he knows how to spend it." And in the words of one woman: "I love Michael, and that's why I voted for the Labor Party. If the PNP had won, the Police and the Army would have taken over, and they would have killed him." Such is the wisdom of the working people.

But for Michael Manley it was perhaps the bitterest disappointment of his life. It is impossible, in my view, to understand Manley's later ideological turnaround without a sense of the trauma that the 1980 defeat inflicted on him. To add to this, there was the dramatic shift in the global balance of power in the 1980s, a decade that began with the ascendance to power of Margaret Thatcher in Britain and Ronald Reagan in the United States, that continued with the Latin American debt crisis and the entrenchment of neoliberalism and structural adjustment, and that ended with the collapse of state socialism and of the Soviet Union. If Manley had embraced the theology of globalization and the market by 1989 when he was reelected to office, it stemmed from his own personal disillusionment with the negative aspects of the 1970s experience, together with a pragmatic reading of the global constellation of forces. He was in effect doing penance for the harm that the polarized politics of the 1970s had done to the people and to his beloved

Jamaica. There was, in my humble opinion, a genuine conviction that the market could succeed where the state had failed in bringing improved conditions of life to the population. And for Michael, it was results that mattered.

What can one say now of these policies, after the structural adjustment of the 1980s and the currency and financial liberalization of the 1990s, and as the juggernaut of market and financial globalization tries to sweep aside everything in its path? Sadly, the Jamaican economy has continued to falter, with little or negative growth in the 1980s and 1990s, steep devaluation—after Guyana, Jamaica's currency is the lowest in the English-speaking Caribbean—and recurrent bouts of high inflation and high interest rates. The experience of currency and financial liberalization has been disastrous, with a bill for financial assistance to troubled financial institutions that now approaches U.S.$1.6 billion, equivalent to about one-quarter of Jamaica's annual GDP.

As for globalization, it should be clear to everyone after the Asian financial crisis of the 1990s that this is nothing but a facade for the untrammeled power of global players on global financial markets, and of the transnational corporations, to garner profits whenever and wherever they wish throughout the globe, no matter what the social and political costs, and that far from meaning the end of the nation state, it weakens some and strengthens others, particularly the United States. In other words, the neoliberal experience shows that there is no substitute for a socially managed economy, both nationally and internationally, an economy in which the market is guided and regulated by an active and democratically governed state, in partnership with business and with an active civil society, including organized labor and a wide spectrum of citizen organizations. And this principle holds true for the global economy, if global poverty and inequality are to be effectively addressed and if the planet's life-support systems are to be sustained in the interests of present and future generations. *In short, the market, whether national or global, must be subordinated to the common good.*

Michael Manley's death elicited a collective outpouring of love amongst Jamaicans, the likes of which I have never seen before. The closest thing, in my experience, was the love poured out to Nelson Mandela on his triumphal visit in 1991. Though I have to say, I was not in Jamaica at the time of the funeral of Bob Marley in 1981 or of Norman Manley in 1969. The newspapers' banner headlines, for coverage occupying the entire front page in several editions, tell the story: "NATION MOURNS MANLEY," "THEY CALLED HIM JOSHUA," "FAREWELL, MICHAEL," "HERO'S FAREWELL," "MANLEY BURIED."

As I read the papers one year later in preparing this tribute, I could feel the chills running up and down my spine, and I began to choke up, as I did when I filed with thousands of others past his lifeless body, and I thought about the Michael Manley of the 1970s, this beacon of hope, this David who took on Goliath, who stirred the minds of men and the hearts of women with his eloquence, his passion, his vision, and his love. The tributes from every quarter are revealing of the esteem with which Michael Manley was held.

But the last word is from the Jamaican cartoonist Clovis. He shows Michael Manley and Cheddi Jagan, both having just passed through the pearly gates of Heaven, looking mischievously angelic, and Michael is saying "Cheddi, are you thinking what I'm thinking? Let's REFORM this place!" One Love Michael. One Love Cheddi.

2

Legacies of Cheddi Jagan

BRINDLEY H. BENN

Persistent poverty has been the condition of the people in the British West Indies, now CARICOM (the Caribbean Community), since the days of slavery and indenture. Every few years, some have been allowed to escape from this pit of despair. But there has been no dramatic long-term progress. Every now and again, as the masses despaired of deliverance, they used the strike weapon or they rioted. Invariably, many were imprisoned, many were shot. That was the situation throughout the British West Indies in the 1930s, and fears that there would be more unrest impelled the British colonial government to appoint a commission to investigate the conditions that caused the disturbances. The West Indian Royal Commission, led by Lord Moyne, was appointed in 1938.

Because of the onset of World War II, the commission's findings were filed away to prevent their contents from being known by the German enemy, who could have used them to attack British imperialism. Yet the war produced a great deal of opportunities for enlightening the masses. The radio had become popular. Thousands of Caribbean youths enlisted in the British armed forces. U.S. forces were stationed in several territories under arrangements between the United States and Britain. It was out of these conditions that many progressive leaders developed. Among them were Cheddi Jagan and Michael Manley, both of whom passed away in 1997, within hours of each other.

Cheddi Jagan, the son of indentured Indian sugar workers whose parents could not afford to purchase him shoes until he was nearly twelve years old, studied hard, passed through the educational system, and earned a place in Guyana's most prestigious secondary school—Queens College. Later, he studied dentistry in the United States and came face to face with the problems of the working people there. He also studied political science and became adept at explaining the U.S. Constitution, and the New Deal implemented by President Franklin D. Roosevelt. When he returned home to Guyana, having married Janet Rosenberg, he spent a few years observing the political situation and setting up a practice. Thereafter he decided to enter politics, and took as his principal task the education of the working people.

His success at this task was beyond compare. This he did by regular public meetings, and by distributing pamphlets that he and his principal supporters produced. In Guyana this was quite new. He joined the trade union movement, organizing especially in the sugar industry as well as the sawmill and forest industry. He captured the leadership of the Rice Producers Association through his consistent good representation of the rice farmers. He was a socialist, and his immediate aim was to lead working people to fight for better wages, and improve living and working conditions. He also saw that it was effective to engage in the struggle for national independence.

By 1946 he had formed the Political Affairs Committee with Ashton Chase, H. J. M. Hubbard, and his wife, Janet. The group published the PAC Bulletin, which appeared everywhere—on the waterfront, on the sugar estates and wood grants, in offices, even on the desks of the bosses. Among the pamphlets that appeared were "Fight for Freedom," "Who Owns the Press," "Is Imperialism Dead" and "Bitter Sugar." The pamphlet "Who Owns the Press" showed the working people why their daily problems and other events differed from what was published in the newspapers. They learned that the newspapers were owned by their oppressors: the sugar industry, big business, and the chamber of commerce. The pamphlet "Is Imperialism Dead" used quotations from the American Declaration of Independence to demonstrate the people's right to independence. But it also included statements by King George V, Winston Churchill, Lord Trefgarne (first chairman of the Colonial Development Corporation), even John Strachey (a labor minister), all asserting bluntly the need for Britain to exploit her colonies. Indeed, John Strachey declared, "By one means or another, by hook or by crook . . . the primary production of all colonial territories is a life and death matter for the economy of Britain."

When studied together, the pamphlets were a manifesto of the movement. They dealt with the need for drainage and irrigation, for diversification of agriculture; they spoke against higher rice prices, devaluation, high profits, and low wages. In 1947, Dr. Jagan won a seat in parliament, the first

Cheddi Jagan. © Nadira Jagan-Broncier.

parliamentary election since 1935. In 1950 the People's Progressive Party (PPP) was formed. Prominent among the leadership were several trade unionists, including PAC members Ashton Chase, H. J. M. Hubbard, and Janet Jagan; L. F. S. Burnham as chairman, Sydney King, Jainarine Singh, Pandit S. Misir (an indefatigable distributor of party literature), Frank

VanSertima, Ivan Cendrecourt, Ivan Edwards, Dr. J. P. Latchmansingh (another trade union leader), and Jane Phillips Gay. The party also attracted a large number of public servants and teachers—who had to join surreptitiously if they were to keep their jobs—as well as the youth.

Dr. Jagan used his seat in parliament as a platform to fight for the rights of the workers to vote for the union of their choice, under a law modeled on the U.S. National Labor Relations Act. This was necessary because the sugar workers, particularly, were being represented by a union that owed allegiance to the sugar bosses. He demanded that Guyanese civil servants be permitted rights equal to those of expatriate British civil servants. He analyzed the nature of the bauxite companies operating in Guyana. He criticized their apartheid-like housing settlements, exposed their extraordinary profits, and demanded that they pay higher taxes within the country. He advocated the implementation of drainage and irrigation schemes to make agriculture safe and profitable to farmers, and to make local foods cheaper. He called for implementation of hydroelectric power, distribution of state lands to landless farmers, the provision of workers' houses in town and country, and the purchase of ranches in the Rupununi for conversion into cooperative ranches for the Amerindians.

Under Cheddi's leadership the party was opposed to the West Indies Federation that was being foisted on the Caribbean by Britain, but that was supported by Grantley Adams (Barbados), Dr. Eric Williams (Trinidad), and Norman Manley and Alexander Bustamante (Jamaica). It was a colonial-style institution that eventually collapsed. Of course he had made, early in his political career, contacts with other Caribbean labor leaders. These included John Rogers of the Oil Field Workers Union, the Trade Union Congress (TUC) president, and the head of the Sugar Workers Union in Trinidad and Tobago. He traveled widely in the Caribbean and tried to sell his ideas. Internationally, the party developed ties with the Progressive Working Class Movement, the World Federation of Trade Unions, the World Federation of Democratic Youth, and the Women's International Democratic Federation. The PPP supported the anticolonial struggles in Keyna, led by Jomo Kenyatta; in Ghana, led by Kwame Nkrumah; and in Malaysia and Cyprus as well as the struggle against apartheid in South Africa. Contacts were established with the British Communist Party, the Labour Party and several other groups in Britain that supported independence for the colonies.

Jagan had so many friends and supporters worldwide that he was able to get technical help for a wide range of programs. In some cases the assistance was afforded by friendly countries—India, the People's Republic of China, Ghana, the Soviet bloc—in others by universities, political groups, and by private individuals. The establishment of the University of Guyana in 1963 was one of his monumental achievements. Dr. Jagan kept straining at the colonial chains, and he was a pioneer in certain positive changes that took place. He was the first petitioner to appear before the U.N. Committee of Twenty-Four—the Committee on Decolonization. He evaded as much as possible peddling the United Kingdom line, even though as a nongoverning member at international conferences, Guyana had to be part of the U.K. delegation. While attending a Food and Agricultural Organization (F.A.O.) conference in Rome, at a time when their slogan was *"Freedom from Hunger,"* he broke ranks to explain Guyana's problems and demand independence over the objections of the leader of the U.K. delegation.

He harbored no illusions that independence in itself would solve Guyana's problems, or indeed the problems of any Third World country. He joined the campaign for socialism, imported Marxist literature, and established the Accabre Ideological College. The program of the PPP government during the 1960s was for a mixed economy—mixed in the sense that the major industries, sugar and bauxite, as well as banking, remained in foreign hands. The state controlled railways, harbor service, telephone, and drainage and irrigation. Only the Canadian-owned electricity company and a small internal air service were nationalized. Goaded by the United States, which feared that Jagan would take an independent Guyana along the Communist path, the British government used every device to ensure that the People's Progressive Party would be sidelined. The PPP, which won the majority of the vote and held ministerial posts in 1953, was dismissed from office when British troops landed. Dr. Jagan and many of his supporters were imprisoned, their movements restricted, and socialist literature banned, seized, and burned.

The party was split under the encouragement of the British government, yet, when the electoral system was restored, the party bounced back to the head of the polls in 1957. By 1961 crooked electoral arrangements had failed to dislodge the party, so strikes and violence were used to disrupt the PPP administration. With the PPP in power, the government was also starved of financial aid from all sources. This type of subversion continued throughout the early 1960s. However, by dint of struggle and intense work, the party ensured the people understood these tactics. In 1964, the British changed the electoral system to proportional representation, yet still the PPP won the majority of votes. However, it was unable to form the government due to an alliance between two opposition parties, the People's National Congress (PNC) and the United Force (UF). For nearly twenty-eight years afterward, every election was rigged, keeping the PPP from heading the government. Even so, the PPP continued its educational work and its struggle on behalf of working people, including public servants. The party maintained its international contacts, drawing and giving support in struggles for independence, for socialism, and for peace. Cheddi was an analyst of international economic trends, noting the extreme poverty of the majority in Asia, Africa, and Latin America; he also noted problems in the developed world. In a paper delivered in 1994, at the Twelfth Meeting of the Caribbean Group for Cooperation in Economic Development, he surveyed the general economic trends in this way:

> In this era of globalization and modernized, capital-intensive and high technology methods of production, recession and stagnation will be more prolonged than in the past and will occur with greater frequency. This is due to the fact that we are now faced with a cyclical, as well as structural, crisis. Cybernation and automation—computers and robots—are the hallmarks of the modern production process in the global market. This leads to intense trade competition, trade barriers and protectionism, as a result of deepening contradictions between the means of production and the relations of production, the growing social inequality and the widening gap between the rich and the poor.

It is out of such considerations that his government invited economists, diplomats, labor representatives, and others to a conference in Georgetown where a program for a *New Global Human Order* was enunciated. The Georgetown Declaration proposes:

1. To find a solution to the debt crisis, which involves the cancellation of the debt of the least developed countries (LDCs); significant reduction of multilateral debt; a reduction in the remaining debt stock to sustainable levels for other developing countries, with debt service payments limited to 10 percent of exports, provided that 50 percent of the saving is used for social sector development;
2. To significantly increase transfers of long-term development finance to developing countries, by attaining the existing Official Development

Assistance (ODA) target of 0.7 percent of GNP through mobilizing new and additional sources of finance, creating a new Global Development Fund, and introducing measures to stabilize the international monetary system and financial markets.
3. To establish a fair and equitable trading system, including the provision of reliable access to the markets of the North. Such a system should take account of the special needs of small developing states, ensure fair and stable commodity prices, and secure a renegotiation of the provisions of the World Trade Organization, especially with respect to the trade in investment, intellectual property rights and services;
4. To reduce and relax conditions attached to future financial transfers.
5. To give new emphasis to the expansion of production and growth for sustainable development and safe physical environment in the South.
6. To develop the social sector as focus of any New Program with emphasis on education, human resources, health and the development needs of women, children and indigenous peoples.
7. To democratize and strengthen the United Nations and restructure other multilateral and financial institutions to respond more effectively to the challenge of people-centered development.

This program was introduced by Dr. Jagan, his ministers, and diplomatic representatives at several international conferences, including the Commonwealth Conference in New Zealand, the UNCTAD IX in South Africa, the various CARICOM heads of government meetings, and the U.N. General Assembly in 1996, where Grenada joined with Guyana in calling for its implementation. So far, plans call for a Regional Integration Fund to be implemented, and the IMF/World Bank have agreed to modify their rules on debt forgiveness to assist the most highly indebted nations.

The New Global Human Order proposals embody to a large extent a summary of Cheddi Jagan's struggles and achievements. He can truly be considered the Guyanese who has made the greatest contribution to the hopes expressed in the program of the Guyana Labor Union, founded by Hubert N. Critchlow, "to do much to stamp out poverty and to usher in the glorious time when all children, all women and all men shall have an abundance of life's essentials, when all shall do their share of work and become thereby entitled to the results thereof."

Indeed Cheddi Jagan and Michael Manley have left us a rich legacy of dedicated and restless struggle for the liberation of their people, indeed of the wretched of the earth. It is up to us to ensure, by hard work and perseverance, that their efforts will not have been in vain.

References

Jagan, Cheddi. 1999. *A New Global Human Order.* Milton, Ont.: Harpy.

3

Dr. Cheddi Jagan: The Making of a Movement Intellectual

MAURICE ST. PIERRE

Dr. Cheddi Jagan, one of Guyana's foremost political leaders, emerged as a major force in the political landscape of that country during the period from the 1940s to the 1960s, when the political independence movement was on the upsurge. Dr. Jagan used the political independence movement to make space for himself and his ideas, and in that way contributed to the knowledge base of the country. Thus he can be classified as an intellectual whose stature was derived from his participation in the struggle for independence. The theoretical perspective of social movements guides this analysis. The data for this study are gathered from interviews with some of the movement's leaders, a perusal of colonial office (in Britain) and state department (in the United States) records, as well as other archival materials, including newspapers and political party documents that were gathered from the National Archives of Washington, D.C., and the National Archives of Guyana, in particular.[1]

Theoretical Guidelines

Over the years, social movements as a form of collective action have been viewed less as a manifestation of irrational behavior and more as representative of rational action on the part of participants who have made and hierarchized choices based on an assessment of the benefits and costs of such action.[2] This approach was influenced in no small measure by the Civil

Rights movement and other movements in the United States that were affected by it, as well as an assessment of various social movements that took place largely in Europe. From the premise of rationality associated with collective action emerged what, arguably, has become the dominant paradigm in social movement theory, namely, resource mobilization theory or RMT (Jenkins 1983, Cohen 1985, McCarthy and Zald 1977, and Morris 2000). This approach maintains that in an effort to deal with grievances that cannot be successfully addressed on an individual basis, collective action is undertaken by social movement leaders (to whom we shall refer as movement intellectuals) who educate, raise the consciousness of, and mobilize their followers by recourse to a number of resources that may be nonmaterial (such as time, trust, friendship, knowledge, values, and so on) or material (such as jobs, money, previously organized entities, and so on). Since, in keeping with the rationality argument, individuals are unlikely to incur the costs of participation (expenditure of time, loss of jobs, and even of life) if they can derive the benefits that will accrue to *all* members of the aggrieved group (for example, blacks and the Civil Rights movement or women and the feminist movement) without participation, they will tend to "free ride" (Cohen 1985, Olson 1971). As a consequence, movement leaders will seek to ensure participation by offering selective incentives, depending on the nature of the movement, such as the promise of jobs in a future administration or in the political party.[3]

Though of obvious usefulness, RMT is not as helpful for the purposes of this essay as the cognitive praxis approach to the study of social movements (Eyerman and Jamison 1991, Eyerman 1994). This perspective maintains that social movements are very often producers of new knowledge in the sense that, for example, leaders mobilize followers by providing their own analysis, novel interpretation, and solution to the grievance at hand. Thus knowledge production is an outcome of relationships between leaders, in the role of movement intellectuals, and both their followers and those that are being challenged. However, in order to achieve the status of movement intellectual, leaders have to make space within the political landscape for themselves and their beliefs, ideas, tactics, and strategies. This perspective is of greater contextual relevance in that it better demonstrates why leaders like Cheddi Jagan are described as movement intellectuals. Beyond that, the cognitive praxis approach better explains the role social movements play in transmitting scientific ideas into social and political beliefs, and the historical function of social movements as social laboratories for the testing of social theories and providing critiques for existing paradigms and structures (Eyerman and Jamison 1991, 92–93).[4] In other words, this approach helps show how social movements generate knowledge. However, as others have maintained with respect to the activities of intellectuals, as such, one needs to take into account a number of other factors. First, the production of new knowledge, generally typical of intellectual activity, is a function not only of a tradition of critical discourse (Gouldner 1979, St. Pierre 2000) but also the presence of various factors that present the intellectual with something to "rail" against—often this allows him or her to move a perceived grievance from the periphery to the center (Habermas 1989)—and perhaps, most importantly, the opportunity to communicate ideas (knowledge) to a chosen audience either verbally or through the written word.

To sum up, social movements allow for the mobilization of others by leaders who use various socially and culturally relevant resources; social movements also lead to the production of knowledge. However, this process is related to the extent to which the movement intellectual is able to institutionalize his or her presence in the society; the existence of systemic factors about which the movement intellectual is dissatisfied with and rails against; a culture of critical discourse that facilitates dialogue; as well as structures that permit the communication of information to selected audiences, notably by way of the printed word. All of these variables are crucial to an understanding of Jagan's role as a movement intellectual.

Jagan as Political Independence Movement Intellectual

Since the sociological imagination is in a large measure fueled by the intersection of biography and history, we begin with a statement about Jagan's background.[5] In Jagan's autobiographical work (Jagan 1975), we are told about life on the plantation, historically and contemporaneously, for East Indian indentured laborers and their families. Jagan states, for example, that the dwellings of the indentured laborers could be entered any time. The indentured workers were forced to work even though ill, and they were punished physically for all kinds of reasons: penalized for failure to answer a daily muster roll, or for failure to complete a prescribed number of tasks, or for absence from work for seven consecutive days, which was tantamount to desertion in the eyes of the planters (Jagan 1975).

As we consider further Jagan's role as a movement intellectual we need to look also at how he made space for himself in the political fabric. He returned to the colony in 1943 with his American-born wife after spending seven years in the United States preparing himself for economic independence by training to be a dentist. This meant that he could criticize the colonial system and the establishment with impunity because he was not beholden to them for a job. His recollections of racism in America and his experiences as a student selling worthless medicine door to door to unsuspecting, poor African Americans—as he put it, he was selling hope not a cure—undoubtedly impacted upon his eventual concern with alleviating the condition of the economically dispossessed and the politically disenfranchised. In this task, he would be ably assisted by Janet Jagan who, as a Jew, had herself experienced racism in America (St. Pierre 1999, 62–63). She played the roles of wife, mother, dental assistant, political advisor, party activist, and movement intellectual in her own right.

Then in November of 1946, the Political Affairs Committee (PAC) was founded by the Jagans and Jocelyn Hubbard, a light-complexioned Water Street clerk and trade unionist, and Ashton Chase, a black trade unionist. The PAC evolved out of various discussion groups that actually started after the Jagans invited a number of leading intellectuals to their residence in Kitty (a suburb of the capital, Georgetown, where they lived from the late 1940s to 1950, and that was likely to be beyond the gaze of colonial officials) to deliberate on the workings of the society and how best it could be improved for the masses. The committee aimed, as Chase put it, to "enlighten and mould or form public opinion" and to mobilize and educate the masses for political action oriented toward achieving political independence. The PAC surfaced in response to the undemocratic colonial controls of the 1940s and the fact that, as Jagan felt, existing political organizations were "opportunistic and not interested in the masses." The group's discussions were characterized by a predisposition for polemic that was not pervasive in Guyanaese society, and allowed for the airing of views that would not have normally been discussed. This was an important precursor to the culture of critical discourse that was to follow when the PAC moved its activities into the open.

Martin Carter, another movement intellectual and foremost Guyanese poet at the time, recalls that the PAC, which was originally called the Kitty Adult Education Association, was definitely a "communist front." The notion of communism as an ideology, and as an alternative form of government to democracy—which at the time did not exist in Guyana—was not something of which most Guyanese were aware and, as we shall see, was an important facet of the new knowledge that emanated from the relationship between Jagan and his followers. Again, the PAC's aims suggested an effort to create a new strategy for the dissemination of information, especially with political independence in mind. Lastly, the original name of the group and the somewhat clandestine manner of its early operation are all indicative of a strategy designed to reduce the likelihood of a negative reaction on the part of colonial officials, and to keep its communist ideology private.

Another dimension of intellectual activity concerns the various techniques used by Jagan and his cohorts to connect with other members of the colonized stratum through a printed medium, which of course speaks to the ongoing efforts by Jagan to make space for himself along the political spectrum. As Chase puts it, "We met as a committee on any situation, decided on a line and then published a broadsheet." Apart from the fact that this meant that resources such as time, technical knowledge about the ramifications of colonialism and its negative effect on the colonized, a printing machine, and paper were being used to mobilize Guyanese, we notice a further accretion to strategies of mobilization that emanated from the activities of movement intellectuals.

But as the PAC moved from a latent organization to a more overt one, its mobilization efforts, as well as those designed to raise the consciousness of the masses, took other more direct forms that added to political knowledge both in the form of information and in the development of tactics and strategies. Thus, Jagan and other PAC leaders held political meetings at marketplaces and unused open spaces (such as the parade ground and Bourda pasture) as the movement gained momentum. And as the significance of the information dispensed became more public, private yards and sugar estates were pressed into service in order to carry their message to the people. The choice of each one of these settings was of major historical import. For example, marketplaces always assured an audience as people shopped or passed by. Yards in the city contained an "ecological concentration" (St. Pierre 1999, 80) of lower class and poor urban dwellers who had a subculture of their own. For instance, the only means to obtain water was from a pipe set in a concrete base in the yard where inhabitants gathered to wash things, discuss matters of interest, even quarrel with other residents, all of whom experienced considerable economic deprivation. Finally, the choice of rural sugar estates as sites for political campaigns had deep historical significance, since these locations were portrayed by the PAC as the physical embodiment of plantation exploitation of the Guyanese working classes.

In addition, visits to these locations were meant to assure even the most dispossessed that they had a role to play in the movement. The personal appearances enabled Jagan and his colleagues to engage in a back-and-forth dialogue with their listeners. Also, face-to-face contact enabled the PAC's executive to become known to the people in terms of both ideas and physiognomy. In the absence of television, this was an extremely important strategy that further institutionalized the presence of Jagan. Beyond that, whenever a sugar estate manager prevented Jagan from visiting workers living on estates in his constituency on the grounds of "trespassing," this was used to denigrate the system and to increase the value of Jagan's political currency in the society.

This kind of mass politicization, which capitalized on the contributions of other organized entities, involved a dialogue with the masses that produced an unprecedented wealth of new knowledge in Guyana. However, it was also an effort at consciousness raising, using everyday language, and powered by a practical and ideological mode of action that provided interpretations for various experiences, like poverty, estate life, and the inability to vote. Furthermore, since ideology conceivably separates adherents from nonbelievers, the PAC's message allowed the former to cooperate with one another for the achievement of a collective good (see Gouldner 1976)—like the ending of exploitation in the sugar industry and colonial domination. This was another important facet of the PAC's political strategy, whereby efforts were made to particularize and locate a set of experiences within a specific ideological context. This produced a consciousness of kind among listeners that made them all the more receptive to the messages of Jagan and his colleagues.

The 1947 Legislative Experience

Jagan's portrayal of what I would call the existential dimensions of life on the sugar estates and the plantation critically shaped his subsequent political ideas and action in another manner, as he never lost sight of the important exploitative role of the plantocracy and relevant multinational corporations like Bookers' Brothers, or of the pivotal importance of sugar to the economy of the country. During his first term in the legislature, after his victory in the

1947 elections, the twenty-nine-year-old Dr. Jagan continued to make space for himself in the political fabric but using a different posture. In the first place, he regarded his electoral victory in 1947 as "the people's victory" and a beginning of the struggle against the "sugar gods" and the bauxite companies. He was clearly bent on using the legislature as a stage upon which to find out and expose the exploitative practices of big business. As he put it:

> Politics, it is said, is the science of "who gets what, when and how." Mine was the role of the "politics of protest," with the weapons of exposure and struggle. If the legislature was my forum, the waterfront, the factories, plantations, mines and quarries were my battleground. I brought a new dimension to the politics of protest, continuity between the legislature and the street corner; the legislature was brought to the "streets" and the "streets" to the legislature. The Legislative Council was no longer the hallowed Chamber where "gentlemen" debated and had their words recorded in *Hansard* for posterity. The legislature at last became part and parcel of the struggle of the people. (Jagan 1975, 70)

The above statement is contextually significant. It is evident, for example, that Jagan was using his election to the legislature to continue to make space within the political landscape for himself and his ideas, especially regarding politics, protest, and the prescriptively symbiotic relationship between the people and the government. Again, making it plain that he was keenly aware of what needed to be fixed, as intellectuals are wont to do, he was using the legislature as a stage to rail against what he felt was problematic, fully cognizant of the fact that his words and actions would be recorded for posterity in the printed, and official, version of the proceedings of that body—the *Hansard*. Finally, in breaking with the past, he made it clear that he regarded the legislature as the chamber of the people and not that of a few privileged gentlemen.

Turning his attention to the sugar industry once again, Jagan observed that when a sugar estate employee left the job—which meant having to leave his dwelling—he was forced to seek other employment or become a peasant farmer. And because, as often happened, neither option was attractive, he had to return to the plantation, which meant the sugar planters were able to keep wages low. This led him to introduce, in 1950, a minimum wage bill in the Legislative Council, which, however, was supported by only four of his colleagues.

Industrial Action

In Guyana, as elsewhere in the West Indies, professional politicians at the helm of the political independence movement, as Jagan admitted during an interview, deliberately exploited the possibilities of becoming involved with trade unions, thereby acting as spokespeople for labor within the Legislative Council. This meant that trade unionism in Guyana, as in other West Indian territories, developed with an emphasis upon the political rather than the industrial role of labor organization.[6] It was thus not surprising that Jagan himself would use trade unionism to further establish himself in the society. For example, during 1946–47, he was treasurer of the Man Power Citizens Association (MPCA), which he left to become president of the Sawmill Workers Union, after which he was associated with the Guyana Agricultural Workers Union (GAWU).

Jagan's relationship with the trade union movement also enabled him to act as a spokesperson for the workers and the betterment of their condition. This effort to make space for himself was facilitated by various industrial disputes and strikes that took place at this time that were portrayed as struggles between labor/the working class represented by the unions, and capital/big business represented by the two largest capitalist enterprises in the country—the Demerara Bauxite Company (Demba) and King Sugar. The Demba strike, which lasted from April 13 to June 16, 1947, and whose causes were rooted in the unequal relationship between capital and labor, was at the time characterized by geographical separation of the two groups, the right of the company to enter a worker's place of abode "without any notice," and, in the event that he fails to leave the plantation when ordered, "the right to take possession and evict [him] without recourse to law."[7] There were marked similarities between the condition of the bauxite worker and that of his sugar estate compatriot, which in the case of the former was further exacerbated by the contempt on the part of company officials for the efforts of African Guyanese workers to unionize themselves (St. Pierre 1972, 1975). The strike, therefore, presented Jagan with another opportunity to make his presence known by performing important directional and propaganda tasks for the workers.

In addition, Jagan got involved in the aftermath of the Enmore estate strike, which started on April 22, 1948, and, it might be argued, was in reality a confrontation between the Guiana Industrial Workers Union (supported by the Jagans and future minister of government, Dr. J. P. Lachmansingh) and the Sugar Producers' Association (SPA), which favored the MPCA. The ensuing clash between the police and the strikers on June 16, 1948, which resulted in the deaths of five East Indian sugar workers and serious injury to fourteen others, enabled the Jagans, along with Lachmansingh and activist Jane Phillips-Gay, to become more involved in the workers' struggle. Jagan used the strike as an occasion to dramatize his presence by leading the funeral procession of the five slain workers to the capital city of Georgetown, thereby identifying himself with the masses while underscoring what he conceived to be the evils of capitalism and colonialism.

The PAC eventually gave way to Guyana's first mass-based political party, the People's Progressive Party (PPP), which came into existence in January 1950 with the specific aim of obtaining political independence for Guyana. For our purposes, two factors are paramount. The first is that the PPP provided Jagan with another stage on which to continue both his delegitimation of the colonial system and the legitimating of the political independence movement. Thus, he (and the PPP) used the publication of the Waddington Commission Report to demand full self-government and an end to the governor's authority. For example, in a press statement in early November 1951, to which the public obviously had access, Jagan castigated the governor's right to have a deciding vote in the Legislative Council and to nominate individuals of his own choosing to fill ministerial portfolios, which he contended would make the six elected ministers "mere puppets." He therefore declared that although the Guyanese people anxiously sought to cooperate with the British for their mutual advantage, they wished to do so "not as *subjects* [my emphasis] but as real partners," and that the PPP was preparing to "carry out a vigorous countrywide campaign for immediate independence and self-government" (Jagan 1951).

The second factor is that the party's deliberations allowed for the promulgation of its ideology and the delineation of various tactics and strategies, which fall within the realm of the production of knowledge by a social movement. The party's ideology, for instance, conceptualized political independence as not merely involving an end to the metropole-colony relationship, which had countenanced the "exploitation of the human and natural resources for the benefit of the few," but the end of gubernatorial hegemony. It is evident that Jagan's comments were designed to get to the heart of democracy, in that participants in this form of government typically are *elected* by the people (demos) and not *selected* by some higher authority who himself is not elected. Jagan concluded that the checks written into the

Waddington Constitution were primarily intended to protect the imperialist interests of the British government—with its need for primary products—as well as those of the colony's capitalists (Jagan 1954, 45). His opposition to the checks and balances in the report, it might be added, showed a clear understanding of the role of the colonies in British mercantilism and perhaps, not surprisingly, elicited an assurance from British minister of state Alan Lennox-Boyd that Britain's constitution also had checks and balances that were, indeed, a "very desirable feature of all democratic constitutions."[8]

Furthermore Jagan's actions were conceivably part of his ongoing effort to institutionalize the culture of critical discourse, which treats the relationship between those who speak it and those *about whom* it is spoken as a relationship between those who judge and those who are judged. Participation in this critical discourse means to be "emancipated *at once* from lowness in the conventional social hierarchy, and . . . a subversion of that hierarchy" (Gouldner 1979, 59). Thus Jagan's actions in this context, and with the PAC, were political acts and, as part of the culture of critical discourse, a crucial precursor to the eventual attainment of universal adult suffrage and democracy, particularly as stated by the British. Not surprisingly, he voted against the Waddington proposals and, as it turned out, was the only member of the legislature to do so.

Meanwhile, Jagan's views and those of the PPP, especially with regard to big business and the role of capital in the colony, had begun to occasion some concern both locally and in Britain and especially in the United States. Locally, for instance, Lionel A. Luckhoo, a well-known East Indian lawyer, and then president of the MPCA, introduced into the Legislative Council in March 1952 a bill "to prohibit the entry into this country of literature, publications, propaganda or films which are subversive or contrary to public interest." The legislative debate on the bill, and the interest it generated by way of press statements and letters to the editor, was a continuing exemplification of the culture of critical discourse. As part of the political independence movement, this discourse produced more knowledge about communism and its allegedly undesirable implications. This is illustrated by the comment of one individual that freedom to read was the lifeblood of democracy and that he knew nothing about communism until the bill seeking the banning of "communist" and other "subversive literature" was discussed.[9]

The bill, which contained a clause (clause 4) that made such an offense punishable by a fine not exceeding G$500.00, or not more than twelve months in prison, or both, was passed into law on February 27, 1953. Luckhoo, who had previously expressed alarm at PPP efforts "to create trouble," had also tried to obtain "definite proof" as to whether the Jagans were connected with the communist movement.[10] Opponents of the bill were joined, eventually, by Cheddi Jagan and his wife who, along with other party members, used the opportunity to register their own opposition to the bill with such slogans as "Ban illiteracy not books," "We want to read, think, and understand; don't ban books," and "Who must decide what is undesirable?" For his part, Jagan subsequently, but unsuccessfully, requested that the officer administering the government be advised to withhold his assent to the bill.[11] Clearly, Dr. Jagan was actualizing his philosophy of protest and the idea regarding the people's parliament, in this case, by using the placard as a medium for educating and raising the consciousness of the masses.

The 1953 PPP Government

Though space does not permit a full discussion of the activities of the PPP's truncated tenure in office in 1953 (see St. Pierre 1999, chap. 5), it is instructive that in various instances efforts were made to use the House of Assembly (Parliament) as a stage to promulgate the party's vision of an independent Guyana and, as such, to produce new knowledge. In a major policy speech on August 9, 1953, for example, Jagan in his role as leader of the House of Assembly declared that he was "a confirmed socialist—perhaps too red and too outspoken for some people" and that just as capitalism had replaced feudalism, "socialism itself will evolve into a higher communist stage of society," and that he was a great admirer of the Soviet Union and the People's Republic of China. He also condemned the "propaganda about the Soviet Union and slave camps" and characterized the Russian revolution as having fought "not to bring about oppression, but to end it." Nevertheless, he maintained that local capitalists did "have a role to play," that they would be offered every protection, but that "they must regard themselves as partners in a joint programme of development" with the emphasis being "not on what can be taken out, but on what can be contributed." The U.S. consul general based in Trinidad noted that Jagan's assurance of protection to capitalists was hardly intended to inspire confidence on the part of foreign investors in view of the qualifications attached to his assurances.[12]

In an effort to reduce the effect of religious instruction in schools, then PPP minister of education Forbes Burnham introduced a white paper (as a precursor to what was later known as the Dual Control Bill) in early October 1953 ultimately designed to "revise the curriculum and textbooks of schools to give them the true Guyanese socialistic and realistic outlook," and to remove the control that the Church had over the management of primary education. This involvement had led to the coupling of admission to these schools with adherence to a particular faith. As a consequence, East Indians who refused to renounce Hinduism were denied a basic education, and Jagan's inability to get a job in the civil service, and the suggestion that he and his father become Christians in order to achieve this goal, were probably significant factors in the choice made by the PPP's leaders to abolish the system of dual (or church) control.

The government also introduced a labor relations bill designed to place the power of government behind the process of union recognition by giving the minister of labor the right to decide "who shall be classed as worker for the purpose of taking part in a ballot in any industry, trade or undertaking."[13] In addition, the bill sought to secure for workers the right to join a trade union of their choice, free of victimization, and to force the Sugar Producers Association (SPA) and "King Sugar" to recognize the Guiana Industrial Workers' Union instead of the MPCA, which was considered to be a company union, and which at the time was led by Lionel Luckhoo.[14] As such, it was clearly an attempt to strengthen the position of workers, which Jagan had stated was a paramount consideration.

Finally, the PPP government attempted to remove the ban on the entry of certain West Indians into Guyana, and introduced legislation to repeal the Luckhoo-sponsored Undesirable Publications Ordinance that had been passed in 1952.[15]

As is known, the British government was so disenchanted with the activities of the PPP government that it suspended the constitution on October 9, 1953, and dismissed the ministers. This action elicited a number of reactions from Jagan, which was part of his ongoing orientation toward protest. For example, after his arrest on April 3, 1954, for violating a restriction order, he asked to be exempted from the order on the grounds that his presence beyond the confines of the restricted area was due to his practicing dentistry rather than political activity. The authorities were not impressed with Jagan's explanation, as a result of which he was charged with breaking his restriction order, found guilty, and sentenced to six months in prison with hard labor.

While in prison, Jagan used his knowledge of politics and his leadership skills to start "a small study group on the theory and practice of socialism," and to use the "almost limitless time for reading and writing." His articles for the *Thunder*, the organ of the PPP that had replaced the PAC Bulletin, were smuggled out on toilet paper (Jagan 1975). The prison experience, as others have shown, can be used as a resource for the purpose of mobilizing others. It is also clear that Jagan continued to ensure that his thoughts and experiences would be committed to print and therefore accessible to his audience. In this case it was the relationship between Jagan and the challenged that produced knowledge.

Also of importance was the successful effort made by the British to delegitimate Jagan and the movement by blaming the "extremists" for the dismantling of the constitution, of whom Jagan was considered to be one of the leaders, and declining to condemn the "moderates," among whom Forbes Burnham was considered to be the leader.[16] This distinction led to a split in the movement and the subsequent formation of a new party, the People's National Congress, led by Burnham. However, despite the communist label attached to them, Jagan and the PPP won the next three elections, held in 1957, 1961, and 1964. The United States, which by this time had been told by the British of their expectation that they should play an important part in the future of Guyana, harbored grave doubts about Jagan and his policies. These doubts by the United States were intensified especially because they felt that they had been deceived by Cuban leader Fidel Castro, who had presented himself as a reformer but who subsequently had established ties with the Soviet Union and refused to hold elections.

However, in order to have a good look at Jagan, the Americans invited him to visit the United States in October 1961 to present his case, which included a request for aid, before President John Kennedy and his top advisors. During the visit the Guyanese premier delivered an address before the National Press Club. In this address, which was of extreme importance to Jagan's political future, he began by saying that he was told that since he is "a controversial figure" it was his first duty to put his personal position briefly and clearly. After stating that he was generally dismissed as a communist, and after giving various definitions of communist, he went on to state that he was, first of all, "a passionate anticolonialist" who like the forefathers of the Americans believed that "colonialism is wicked." After pointing out that two of the major industries—sugar and bauxite—in Guyana were foreign owned, he went on to outline his socialist policy for economic advancement, which he said was second only to his passion for independence of his people.[17]

Further, he reminded his audience that he had won his place in the political life of the country in three successive general elections, that he had not come to power by revolution or coup d'état, and that he believed in parliamentary democracy. Also, Jagan stated that in order to carry out the program of social and economic reform he had in mind, he needed both trade and aid. But, as he put it, because "of the immensity of our problems I am forced like India and some other underdeveloped countries to seek aid from all possible sources." He then ended by saying, "it is not our concept of democracy which is now on trial, but yours."[18] He would also, during an audience with U.S. officials, accuse "certain US forces" of subsidizing his political rivals during the 1961 elections and reiterate the view that aid was urgently needed to carry out his domestic program.

Jagan's statements were another example of the extent to which, by way of his role as movement intellectual interacting with the challenged, knowledge was produced. We note, for example, his distinction between communism and socialism and his perception of democratic socialism, which involved (1) the right to nationalize key industries in the interest of the nation so as to ensure a fairer distribution of the country's wealth and (2) the preservation of basic rights and freedoms as well as regular and honest elections, an impartial judiciary, and an independent civil service, all of which were clearly consistent with Western notions of democracy.

As it turned out, the Americans felt that his visit left more questions than answers. Consequently, aid was not forthcoming and efforts were made to destabilize the Jagan government, especially by fomenting internal social disorganization and bringing pressure to bear on the British government to get rid of Jagan. For example, after the disturbances that took place in early 1962, a few months after Jagan's 1961 electoral victory, U.S. secretary of state Dean Rusk communicated to British foreign secretary Lord Home that, based on reports of Jagan's communist connections, Rusk had determined that it was "not possible for us to put up with an independent British Guiana under Jagan [and] it seems to me that new elections should now be scheduled, and I hope we can agree that Jagan should not accede the power again."[19] This was followed by a number of actions that culminated with Britain, with strong U.S. support, replacing the first-past-the-post electoral system with proportional representation (PR): in order for a party to form the government (at independence) it would have to get more than 50 percent of the votes cast. Since Jagan and the PPP had again failed to do so, especially during the 1964 elections, which were the last ones before independence was gained, Burnham in a coalition with the United Force party was in office when political independence was achieved. An obviously disappointed Jagan promised "hurricanes of protest," called on Guyanese to rail against this "brazen injustice and join the mass protest," and alluded to the possibility of violence when he stated that Guyanese may well question the efficacy of the "electoral and parliamentary road" to independence.[20] He boycotted the last preindependence constitutional conference in November 1965.

The Race Question

Before concluding, some attention should be paid to the question of race as far as Jagan was concerned. It should be noted that the race question is something that confronted other movement intellectuals in Guyana, notably Forbes Burnham and Eusi Kwayana. We have already noted Jagan's adherence to socialism and possibly communism, which made any connection with racial politics incompatible. Indeed, in his book *Forbidden Freedom,* Jagan seemed to champion the cause of the working class and mentioned that the PPP had succeeded in uniting all the racial groups. As political scientist Perry Mars later put it: "That the class issue was consistently made to supersede the racial issue is reflected, for example, in the contention of Janet Jagan . . . that while race cannot be ignored in Guyanese politics, the 'decisive factor . . . was not race but economics.' It was also this typical Marxist 'base-superstructure' argument that led Cheddi Jagan to conclude during the early part of his political career that 'race is only skin deep'" (1998, 73). Jagan was apparently more concerned with class than with race.

However, the British reaction in suspending the constitution and its previous policy of racial balancing, which had occurred since the middle of the nineteenth century with the introduction of East Indian laborers to work on the sugar plantations, along with the fact that Jagan drew his support primarily from the East Indian population, made it very difficult for him to disavow totally any connection with racial politics. For example, in an address soon after the split in the PPP, which he attributed in part to Burnham's "right wing opportunist deviationism," Jagan contended that "feeling as they do a sense of oppression the Indians are 100 percent against Federation."[21]

Eusi Kwayana, Martin Carter, and Rory Westmaas, the most important black members of the PPP who remained with Jagan after the split in 1955, felt this constituted a reversal of the party's position on Guyana's inclusion in the proposed West Indian Federation, which would have comprised a large majority of blacks in the other West Indian territories.

Again, as others have noted, PPP policies between 1957 and 1961 seem to have privileged East Indians as opposed to blacks (Despres 1967, Greene 1968, Milne 1981, Spinner 1984, and King [Kwayana] 1999). Denis Benn suggests that Jagan's posture was merely a pragmatic gesture as "the logic of political survival forced the party to consolidate its electoral base by seeking the support of the large number of East Indian rice farmers and sections of the urban-based East Indian merchant/capitalist class." But Benn concedes that the result was an intensification of ethnic divisions and racial conflict (1987, 124). Finally, the comment by a top-ranking black member of the party, that by 1961 Jagan had become "an election animal" (that is, that the PPP leader saw elections as a way to continue being in office), indicates that Jagan knew that East Indians were likely to vote for his party as opposed to others. Various statements by a governor, colonial officials, and U.S. state department officials suggest that, in order to drive home protest against the proportional representation (PR) election system, the PPP tried to fill all vacancies in the civil service with East Indians.[22] Most of all, Eusi Kwayana's revelations and trenchant criticisms suggest that the PPP leader was not altogether indifferent to the question of racial politics.[23]

Concluding Remarks

In closing, two points must be addressed. The first is why was Dr. Jagan, as movement intellectual, unsuccessful in leading Guyana to political independence. After all, he was at the epicenter of the movement and was, possibly, the most active of the movement intellectuals. In the context of the political independence movement, Jagan was able to draw attention to what he considered to be the ills of colonialism, which he expressed in the form of a grand narrative. The narrative spoke to the historical domination of the colony's economy by the sugar and bauxite industries and their exploitative role that disadvantaged workers, to the pivotal position of the governor, to the gradualist philosophy of the colonial power that manifested itself in an incremental baring of the colonial framework, and to the policy of divide and rule that had such detrimental consequences for the political independence movement, particularly in the form of interracial strife in the early 1960s.

A major issue was Jagan's Marxist approach to the colonial problem, involving nationalization of the commanding heights of the economy while simultaneously espousing a democratic ethos that involved critical discussion, safeguards of citizen rights, and independence of the judiciary and the civil service. These democratic ideals notwithstanding, Jagan's beliefs and actions posed serious problems for British and U.S. foreign policy in that, although he consistently won elections in a democratic manner, his posture appeared to have embraced communism and involved ties to the Soviet Union, both of which were considered unacceptable to the United States, at the time in the midst of a cold war crisis with the Soviet Union. This forced the United States in particular to devote many resources (time, money, manpower, technical expertise, and so forth) in order to deal with what they perceived as Guyana's political enfant terrible. The result was that the United States was placed in the uncomfortable position of having to explain to the British why on the one hand it was championing the doctrine of independence for colonies in the United Nations while on the other hand it was urging Britain to get rid of Jagan by nondemocratic means, which eventually conduced to strains in the Anglo-American alliance.

Apart from Anglo-American intervention, an important answer to the question concerning Jagan's eventual failure to lead the colony to independence is to be found in a dimension of Caribbean movement intellectuals that has seldom been explored (but see Deosaran 1981), and to the best of my knowledge never been dealt with concerning Jagan. It concerns the social psychological dimension, in this case Jagan's inflexibility, to which some of his former colleagues in the PPP have adverted. For example, one noted that Jagan had his head in a book and very often against the wishes of others sought to apply Marxist principles to Guyana's problems without regard to the peculiarities of the situation. The commission on the 1962 disturbances opined that Dr. Jagan did not possess the "nimbleness of intellect" that would have made him realize that his policies after the 1961 elections, especially the 1962 austerity budget, could only have lamentable consequences. Indeed, although the budget was variously described as "courageous and economically sound," there were some elements, such as its compulsory savings component, that elicited deep misgivings from black industrial and civil service workers in Georgetown because "It was easy for the government to deduct such savings from wages at source [from the black industrial and civil service workers], but much more difficult to apply the same law to the Indian individual rice growers [and] Jagan's past speeches and actions gave no reason to believe that he would not favor his Indian supporters at the expense of his Negro opponents."[24] Furthermore, Jagan had refused to rule out seeking aid from communist countries as well as to limit visits to these countries. He was of course well within his rights to have adopted these measures. The real political issue was the timing and the likely costs to his political future given the realities of the situation, and Britain's signal that the United States would be playing a major role in the proceedings.

The second point regards the theoretical perspective. Jagan used a number of culturally relevant resources to mobilize and educate his followers with respect to political independence as a collective good while at the same time making space for himself in the political fabric. In showing this process, we were able to get some sense of his beliefs, ideas (especially with respect to the efficacy of protest), tactics and strategies, and in general, his vision of an independent Guyana. We also noted the extent to which political independence as a social movement permitted Jagan to apply various ideas associated with Marxist theory and very importantly with respect to democratic socialism. Political independence as a social movement enabled Jagan and others to delegitimate the grand narrative of colonialism, *both in Guyana and the United Kingdom and the United States,* by pointing to its shortcomings. Jagan highlighted the notion of emancipatory as well as other forms of new knowledge that would become part of the Guyanese lexicon. This included concepts such as communism, nationalization, universal adult suffrage, dual control, proportional representation, and so forth, as well as his own brand of oxymoronic aphorisms, such as "bitter sugar." Last but by no means least, we noted how Dr. Jagan used organizations, like the trade unions, the PAC, and the PPP, to make space for himself and his vision of an independent Guyana.

In light of the foregoing, therefore, we can argue that the construction of a movement intellectual (and possibly that of intellectuals in general) is a process that is characterized primarily by making space and railing against perceived systemic concerns in a manner that produces new knowledge, as intellectuals interact both with fellow challengers and the challenged. Specifically in the case of the movement intellectual, however, it is the movement that provides the stage for intellectual activity as use is made of an organizational framework (unions, political parties, and so on), as well as of the spoken and especially the printed word, to institutionalize and internationalize his or her position. Since the movement intellectual is at the forefront of displacement politics (the termination of the colonial order and the removal of its supporters), knowledge directed to this end tends to be bifurcated in terms of *theory* and *praxis*.

Finally, the most lasting facet of Jagans legacy is that he helped to create an atmosphere whereby protest became a critical feature of the everyday lives of Guyanese, and political office something to which anyone regardless of his or her station in life could aspire. The Jagan family is perpetuating this legacy as efforts are made to assure access to his papers, which will enhance the careers of political activists and scholars alike. In this manner, Guyana's political independence movement becomes what was earlier referred to as a social movement industry.

Notes

1. Colonial office documents from the Public Records Office in London begin with the letters CO, those from the National Archives, Washington, D.C., have the prefix NAR, and those from the National Archives in Guyana have the prefix NAG. Except where otherwise noted, information from movement intellectuals comes from interviews.

2. Proponents of this perspective include Neil Smelser (1965, 1969) who viewed the belief systems of collective behavior participants as akin to "magical beliefs."

3. McCarthy and Zald refer to these as social movement organizations (SMOs) that become so entrenched that they provide careers for collective action activists, in which case they become a social movement industry (SMI). Ultimately they become integrated in the business and political sectors, in which case they become a social movement sector (SMS). For a discussion of how the family of Martin Luther King has turned the Southern Christian Conference into a SMI and a SMS, see Dyson (2000).

4. For a discussion of the extent to which social movements enable the testing of social theories and the translation of ideas into social action, see Bottomore (1969, chapter 6).

5. The usefulness of the intersection of biography and history generally is discussed by Mills (1961), and in terms of the Caribbean in Oxaal (1968) and St. Pierre (1999).

6. Development of Trade Unionism in British Guiana, CO 111/97. In fact, the Venn Commission, which investigated the 1948 Enmore labor riots in 1949, was so concerned about the use of labor organizations for political action that it recom-

mended, in an effort to exclude the professional politician, that only regular workers in an industry be permitted to hold paid office in a trade union.

7. See Labor Ordinance No. 2 of 1942. Report of a Committee of Inquiry appointed to inquire into the causes of dispute between the Demerara Bauxite Company and its employees and generally upon conditions of employment under the company, July 5, 1947, p. 14.

8. Mayle to Governor Woolley, November 10, 1951, CO 1031/776.

9. Letter to the editor, *Daily Chronicle,* March 7, 1953, p. 2.

10. Luckhoo to Burke, No. 109, Enclosure No. 2, March 8, 1951, confidential, 741D.00/3-851.

11. Jagan to the secretary of state for the colonies, March 7, 1953, CO 1031/776.

12. Maddox to Department of State, No. 55, August 20, 1953, 741D.00/8-2053.

13. Proceedings and Debates of the First House of Assembly, September 29, 1953, Cols. 613–31, NAG.

14. Ibid., Col. 621.

15. Proceedings and Debates of the First House of Assembly, July 24, 1953, Col. 288, NAG.

16. For a list of charges against the PPP after the suspension of the constitution in 1953, see "Report of the British Guiana Constitutional Commission," Cmnd. No. 9274, London: HMSO, 1954, known as the Robertson Report.

17. See "Toward Understanding, the Text of an Address to the National Press Club," by Cheddi Jagan, premier of British Guiana, Washington, D.C., October 1961.

18. Ibid.

19. Rusk to Home, No. 264, February 19, 1962, top secret, priority, eyes only, NAR, FRUS XII.

20. Text of a letter from the premier of British Guiana to the prime minister of the U.K. government on the decision of the secretary of state for the colonies at the British Guiana Independence Conference, dated November 7, 1963.

21. See "Address to 1956 Congress of the People's Progressive Party," reprinted in the *Daily Chronicle,* December 22, 1956.

22. Incoming telegram to Department of State, Action Department 168, November 13, 1963, NAR, POL 25-3BRGU.

23. See in particular Sydney King (Eusi Kwayana) ([1962] 1999). This is a powerful document all the more relevant in view of the current political situation in Guyana. The new editions introduction is written by King, a movement intellectual, now considered a public intellectual, with an intimate knowledge of Guyana's political history.

24. Analysis of Premier Jagan's letter to the president, April 16, 1963, enclosure to memorandum for Mr. McGeorge Bundy, the White House, from William H. Brubeck, confidential, NAR, POL BR-GU.

References

Ben, Denis. 1987. *The Growth and Development of Political Ideas in the Caribbean, 1774–1983.* Mona: Institute of Social and Economic Research (ISER), University of the West Indies.

Bottomore, T. B. 1969. *Critics of Society: Radical Thought in North America.* New York: Vintage Books.

Cohen, Jean. 1985. "Strategy or Identity: New Theoretical Paradigms and Contemporary Social Movements." *Social Research* 52, no. 4: 663–716.

Deosaran, Ramesh. 1981. *Eric Williams: The Man, His Ideas, and His Politics: A Study of Political Power.* Port of Spain, Trinidad: Signum Publishing.

Despres, Leo. 1967. *Cultural Pluralism and Nationalist Politics.* Chicago: Rand McNally.

Dyson, Michael. 2000. "Reaping Riches." *Emerge* 11, no. 4: 48–55.

Eyerman, Ron. 1994. *Between Culture and Politics: Intellectuals in Modern Society.* Cambridge, Mass.: Polity Press.

Eyerman, Ron, and A. Jamison. 1991. *Social Movements: A Cognitive Approach.* University Park: Pennsylvania State University Press.

Gouldner, Alvin W. 1976. *The Dialectic of Ideology and Technology: The Origins, Grammar, and Future of Ideology.* New York: Seabury Press.

———. 1979. *The Future of Intellectuals and the Rise of the New Class.* New York: Seabury Press.

Greene, J. E. 1974. *Race Versus Politics in Guyana: Political Cleavages and Political Mobilisation in the 1968 General Election.* Mona: ISER, University of the West Indies.

Habermas, Jurgen. 1989. *The Structural Transformation of the Public Sphere: An Inquiry into a Category of Bourgeois Society.* Trans. Thomas Burger with Frederick Lawrence. Cambridge, Mass.: Polity Press.

Jagan, Cheddi. 1951. Press statement, November 1, 1951, CO 1031–76.

———. 1954. *Forbidden Freedom: The Story of British Guiana.* London: Lawrence and Wishart.

———. 1975. *The West on Trial: The Fight for Guyana's Freedom.* Berlin: Seven Seas Books.

Jenkins, J. Craig. 1983. "Resource Mobilization Theory and the Study of Social Movements." *Annual Review of Sociolgy* 9: 527–53.

King, Sydney (Eusi Kwayana). [1962] 1999. *Next Witness: An Appeal to World Opinion, Commentary on the Commission of Inquiry into Disturbances in British Guiana in February 1962.* Georgetown: Free Press.

Mars, Perry. 1998. *Ideology and Change: The Transformation of the Caribbean Left.* Detroit: Wayne State University Press; Mona: University of the West Indies Press.

McCarthy, John D., and Mayer N. Zald. 1977. "Resource, Mobilization and Social Movements." *American Journal of Sociology* 82, no. 6: 1212–41.

Mills, C. Wright. 1961. *The Sociological Imagination*. New York: Grove Press.

Milne, R. S. 1981. *Politics in Ethnically Bipolar States: Guyana, Malaysia, Fiji*. Vancouver: University of British Columbia Press.

Morris, Aldon. 2000. "Reflections on Social Movement Theory: Criticisms and Proposals." *Contemporary Sociology* 29, no. 3: 445–54.

Olson, Mancur. 1971. *The Logic of Collective Action: Public Goods and the Theory of Groups*. Cambridge: Harvard University Press.

Oxaal, Ivar. 1968. *Black Intellectuals Come to Power: The Rise of Creole Nationalism in Trinidad and Tobago*. Cambridge, Mass.: Schenkman.

Smelser, Neil. 1965. *Theory of Collective Behavior*. New York: Free Press.

———. 1969. "Theoretical Issues of Scope and Problems." In *Readings in Collective Behavior*, ed. Robert Evans. Chicago: Rand McNally.

Spinner, Thomas J., Jr. 1984. *A Political and Social History of Guyana, 1945–1983*. Boulder, Colo.: Westview Press.

St. Pierre, Maurice. 1972. "The Sociology of Decolonization: The Case of Guyana Bauxite." *New World Quarterly* 5, no. 4: 50–62.

———. 1975. "Race, the Political Factor, and the Nationalization of the Demerara Bauxite Company, Guyana." *Social and Economic Studies* 24, no. 4: 481–503.

———. 1999. *Anatomy of Resistance: Anticolonialism in Guyana, 1823–1966*. London: Macmillan.

———. 2000. "The Inception of Critical Discourse and Democracy in Guyana." Paper read at the Twenty-Fifth Annual Conference of the Caribbean Studies Association, St. Lucia, June.

4

Michael Manley, Trade Unionism, and the Politics of Equality

ANTHONY BOGUES

Despite an inauspicious start in 1952 when he was made a member of the National Workers Union's (NWU) negotiating team for the Ariguanbo Mill workers, Michael Manley remained deeply attached to the Jamaican labor movement throughout his career. His political thought and practices were profoundly influenced by twenty years of active trade unionism. Manley's trade union experiences also shaped his political communication skills, his style of political rhetoric, and the political relationship between himself and ordinary Jamaicans. In the last few months of his life he was involved with two labor-oriented projects. First, he attempted to reduce the rivalry between the two major unions in the bauxite industry, the National Workers Union (NWU) and the University and Allied Workers Union (UAWU). Second, his last major public appearance was to chair a conference with the island's leading trade unionists and sections of the island's management elite group in an effort to develop employee share ownership programs (ESOPs) in Jamaican enterprises. Both projects marked continuities in his labor and political practices.

Early Period

The labor movement, which Manley joined in 1952, was divided and plagued by "political unionism." The history of formal trade unionism in Jamaica began with the organization of the Jamaica Union of the Teachers and the

Artisans Union in the nineteenth century.[1] In the early twentieth century Marcus Garvey also formed a trade union. Prior to the 1938 rebellion, the major trade union activity was led by Allan George Coombs and the man reputed to be Jamaica's first Marxist, Hugh Buchanan, an important figure in 1930s Jamaican working-class politics. In the aftermath of the 1938 rebellion, the Bustamante Industrial Trade Union (BITU), led by Alexander Bustamante, became the base of the Jamaica Labor Party (JLP), with union branches and the party organization being one and the same.[2] In the early days after 1938, the People's National Party, which was formed in September of that year as an anticolonial nationalist movement, saw itself as the political movement with the BITU as the labor wing. Both would cooperate in the anticolonial struggles. However, after the 1943 split between the leadership of the PNP and the BITU, the PNP's left wing organized the Trade Union Congress (TUC) as that party's union base to compete with the BITU. From thence onward unionism and party politics were intertwined in Jamaica, creating what has been commonly referred to as "political unionism."

In 1952, the year Manley officially became an official of the NWU, the PNP leadership, influenced by cold war politics, expelled its left wing. This action required that the party leadership build an alternative mass/union base. The birth of the National Workers Union (NWU) occurred, then, not only as a response to the mass political needs of the PNP but was also shaped by cold war influences. Munroe details how the U.S. state department was at this time very concerned with "the Jamaican communists [who were] being welded into a single striking force by aggressive and competent leadership" (Munroe 1992, 72). U.S. foreign policy at the time was organized around cold war conflict, and all foreign relations were seen through this prism. As part of U.S. foreign policy, the state department encouraged the formation of unions whose leadership was anticommunist. Given the split in the PNP and the party's need to form a trade union, important sections of the U.S. labor movement became financial and political allies in the early days of the NWU. So deep was this alliance that one member of the NWU, Kenneth Sterling, was for many years on the payroll of the United Steelworkers of America (Munroe 1992, 94).

Michael Manley's intervention into Jamaican party politics and trade unionism was against the Marxist-Leninist left. When, at the behest of the PNP leadership, he conducted a mass speaking program amongst party members, it was to conduct a political education program on the differences between democratic socialism and communism. It is ironic that twenty-eight years later, both the U.S. political elite and local conservative opposition would ferociously attack his regime as being communist. Manley's democratic socialism at the beginning of his career was rooted in mainstream social democracy. Writing on March 8, 1953, in his regular column in the nationalist paper *Public Opinion*, Manley stated that "democratic socialism . . . means the . . . preservation of free political institutions, pledged to the preservation of the freedom of the individual . . . and was for planned economic progress of Jamaica." The article also gestured to the politics of the cold war and suggested that the core difference between democratic socialism and communism was the former's attachment to liberal democratic political practices and norms. In later interviews, Manley claims that the single most important intellectual influence on his political thought was the British political theorist Harold Laski (Bogues 1996b). However, while Laski's lectures in the 1940s at the London School of Economics were inspirational to Manley, they could not adequately prepare him for the vigorous life of rival political unionism in Jamaica.

What factors accounted for Manley's entrance into trade unionism? Manley was drawn to public life; his family, including his mother, Edna Manley, and father, Norman W. Manley, were both prominent public figures.[3] In making a decision about public life, the question Manley faced was the sphere of his contribution. Political journalism was attractive but, while intellectually stimulating, was not enough for a young person with an activist temperament. Intense involvement with party politics would inevitably lead to comparisons between Manley the father and Manley the son, and accusations of political dynasty. Therefore trade unionism seemed to be the other option (Bogues 1996b). Manley entered the Jamaican labor movement with the following commitments: to pursue policies that would ameliorate the conditions of the Jamaican working class, policies with a political and social conception of human equality. He also came with the perspective of a positive view of regionalism, something he had learned from the West Indian student movement in London in the 1940s (Bogues 1996b).

The Jamaican labor movement offered Manley an opportunity to be active around issues of human equality in Jamaica's rigid class-color colonial plantation system. In his book, *A Voice at the Workplace*, which details his own understanding of the Jamaican labor movement, Manley makes the point, "It is no exaggeration to say that until quite recently in our history, the working class did not exist as human beings for the privileged" (Manley 1975, 54). The racial/color/class attitudes of the Jamaican upper class were an effrontery to Manley's conception of human equality. These attitudes were rooted in the historic white planter bias of Jamaica and were deeply embedded within the workplace. In the 1950s it meant that workers on the sugar plantations were treated in many instances like their African slave ancestors had been. In such circumstances, notions of labor rights were anathema to employers since the dominant white and brown mulatto economic elite perceived the black Jamaican worker as a beast of burden.

Manley's entrance into this domain of Jamaican life allowed him an opportunity to break with the traditional mold of the brown privileged middle class. His involvement with trade unionism profoundly shaped his political ideas for his entire public life. It meant that he was a consistent advocate for the rights of the working class and for forms of workplace democracy. Manley's family background, his conceptions of public duty, and his politics of democratic socialism would eventually draw him into vigorous attempts to negotiate and reconcile the sharp class differences of Jamaican society. These attempts were conducted on the basis of actions and policies that he thought were more humane for the ordinary Jamaican worker. These attempts by Manley to negotiate the labyrinth of Jamaican postcolonial class and color relations made him a complex political personality.

The central political value that organized Manley's political and labor practices was that of equality. For Manley, equality had a foundational aspect that was embedded in laws, a political dimension that was expressed in a democratic politics of participation, and an economic value elaborated in economic structures that would facilitate equal opportunity.

All colonial societies are built upon foundational human inequalities. The native or the colonized is declared nonhuman or an inferior species by the colonizer and excluded from the human polity with no legal, civil, or political rights. In the Caribbean this foundational inequality was compounded by a system of antiblack racial oppression. So black Caribbean people in the colonial system were not creatures of equal human worth because they were both of African descent and colonized. Human inequality then was inscribed in every pore of colonial society. The Creole nationalist movements of the late 1930s and 1940s in the Caribbean challenged only one dimension of this construction of inequality. The movements advocated only political equality, the right to vote. This was a crucial moment in Jamaica's anticolonial history, but, given the decisive weight of the western episteme in the political outlook of the Creole nationalists (see Bogues 2002), they did not challenge politically the overarching notions of human inequality based on race and class hierarchies. As a consequence, they did not practice a kind of politics that tapped into the deepest aspirations of the Jamaican popular classes. By the time Michael Manley entered the labor movement, the battle for political equality had been settled but the ones for equal opportunity and for justice had yet to be won.

Sugar Workers

In the labor movement, Manley claims that his aim was to overturn the legacy of the old white planter model of social relationships (Bogues 1996b). His first major assignment, given to him by Vernon Arnett, then the center-left general secretary of the PNP, took him to the heart of this model—the Jamaican sugar industry. The assignment was a complex one. It was partly motivated by the facts that there were no sugar workers in the NWU, that the BITU controlled the labor movement in the island, and that the PNP could not win a general election unless they penetrated and won a significant section of the sugar industry, at that time the single largest employer. The matter was further complicated because the TUC had won bargaining rights on two sugar estates and minority rights on others. So Manley faced a huge challenge—not only was he set the task of breaking the dominance of the BITU but he had to challenge the TUC as well. In an atmosphere of sharp union rivalry, the young Manley began to earn his spurs in the labor movement.

The conditions of the sugar workers were an eye-opener for Manley who, until this time, had never been on a sugar estate. He writes, "Very few estates bothered with simple expressions of concern like providing tents for shade and clean drinking water for thirsty field gangs still slogging it out under the merciless midday sun after a predawn start" (Manley 1975, 92). The campaign to win sugar workers to the NWU took Manley to many villages throughout the island. During this campaign he listened carefully to the concerns of the sugar workers and grappled with the form and language in which they were expressed. It was this experience and his subsequently long involvement with the sugar workers that profoundly shaped his practical knowledge of the everyday lives of ordinary workers. Manley claims that his democratic instincts were honed during this experience, and it was these instincts that facilitated his success. What is clear is that Manley's oratorical skills were crafted during this initial experience in the sugar industry, although he claims that his first attempts at public speaking were failures

(Bogues 1996b). However, his extensive time in the villages and the sugar estates gave him a feel for the concrete life of the sugar worker, and he quickly learned how to distill and represent this life in a series of speeches that culminate in a call for the worker to join the NWU. In these speeches he was careful not to attack Bustamante in any way nor did he bring the PNP leadership into the campaign until the last moment. The NWU won the polls in late 1953 and finally gained a foothold in the sugar industry. With this victory, Michael Manley's trade union career was successfully launched.

The sugar campaign sharpened Manley's organizational skills. He typically began his organizational work quietly with a few key persons building the base of the organization. From this base he moved to village and estate meetings with workers. Each stage of the organization was normally tested before he moved to the next. In this organizational mode, Manley developed a keen sense of tactics, which later become an essential part of his political skills. Importantly the sugar experience developed in Manley's armory of political gifts an exceptional antenna that allowed him to pick up on moods of a mass audience. It honed his skill at political communication in which he gave back to an audience their mood embellished with a tactical or strategic objective. This quality has been called by Isaiah Berlin "political judgment." Berlin argues that it is a quality by which one is able to "grasp the unique combination of characteristics that constitute [the] particular situation" (Berlin 1996, 147).

What were Manley's contributions to the struggle of sugar workers during this period? Manley found that winning the polls was a pyrrhic victory since the employers in the industry initially refused to budge on the NWU demands. Although none of the NWU demands were revolutionary, they sought to establish a modern collective bargaining system in the industry. Manley reflects, "[T]he years that followed were a mixture of accomplishment and frustration. It proved incredibly difficult to make any major breakthrough which would lead to the rationalization and modernization of workers condition in the industry" (Manley 1975, 99). Manley states that his major contributions to the sugar workers struggles were his participation in the Goldberg Commission in 1959 and his role in marshaling a joint trade union position (Bogues 1996b). What he brought to the negotiating table were his talents as a labor advocate and the forensic skills that dissected the accounts of the island's sugar companies. The former was achieved in spite of the NWU/BITU union rivalry and cemented a lifelong friendship with Hugh Shearer, who would become the island's third prime minister and president of the BITU. This personal fact became an important element in Manley's last years when he attempted to encourage the once hostile unions to develop a common platform of policy and action.[4]

It was in the sugar industry that Manley faced one of the biggest challenges to his trade union leadership. In the 1960s, Hugh Small, then a young radical leftist lawyer and a member of the left-wing group the Young Socialist League, had recently returned from England. In England, Small's politics had been shaped by the political and intellectual influence of Stuart Hall, a leading Caribbean intellectual, and by Marxist and Fanonist ideas (Bogues 1996a). Small wished to join the labor movement and his return passage to Jamaica was paid by the NWU. However, he quickly became critical of the NWU, arguing in worker and delegate forums that the union should have a strike fund. He also advocated strict accountability of workers' dues. Small combined this trade union work with political activity in the Young Socialist League (YSL). The YSL's ideological outlook was a mixture of Fanonist and Leninist ideas, and it was composed of individuals who had been encouraged by Vernon Arnett and Allan Issacs to join the PNP (see Gray 1991). However by 1964, the relationship between the league and the PNP leadership had soured, and the leadership of the YSL was ousted from the party. Before this occurred, however, Small and the NWU had parted company.

In 1965, sugar workers began a massive series of unauthorized wildcat strikes. In the town of Frome in the parish of Westmoreland, the site of the spark of the 1938 rebellion, some workers approached Small to organize an alternative nonpolitical union to the BITU and NWU. He agreed and began a series of meetings to form the Workers Liberation Union. On May 9, 1965, in the village of Grange Hill in the parish of Westmoreland, Hugh Small made a public speech that severely criticized all of Jamaica's trade unions. He said, "Last week Wednesday . . . men and women who stand for the destruction of political unionism . . . held a meeting . . . they made it clear [they] wanted to form their own worker control trade union. Nobody comes here talking politics, because we have heard promises . . . and we know what politics tied with unionism have done."[5] Small continued to flay the practices of mainstream trade unionism by calling political unionism "cousin unionism," making reference to the familial relationships between the leaders of the two major unions. For his efforts Small was summoned before the party and expelled. The charges against him stated that he was "currently engaged in subversive activities against the People's National Party by renouncing the political affiliation between the National Workers Union and the Party."[6] It is clear that Small had committed a cardinal sin by wishing to break the stranglehold of politics on trade unionism.

If many structural features of Jamaica's political system drew their inspiration from the former colonial Westminster political system, then to the superficial observer the party-union link would seem to be another feature. However, this was not so. In the British Labour Party, the historic link between party and union was one whereby the unions had some influences over policy and candidate selection. This was not an unproblematic relationship. However, in the Jamaican case, the unions were often subordinated to the party and the party's recognition of the union primarily symbolic. This meant that "political unionism" was a structural feature of Jamaican politics that subordinated working-class politics.[7] Internally Jamaican unions may have operated in authoritarian ways but their larger relationship was to the political party. This relationship defined their policy directions, created the grounds for silent agreements, and facilitated the rise of a union bureaucracy integrally tied to the state whenever a particular political power held state power. So deep were these links that the history of political violence among Jamaican political parties was integrally linked with the competitive violence of political unionism.

It is clear that Manley's trade union activity did not break this established mold of trade union practice in Jamaica. He did not conduct any analysis about the need for an independent labor movement and took political unionism as a fixed and integral part of the field of Jamaican unionism and modern party developments. This was in opposition to the left, who in the immediate postindependence period sharply critiqued political unionism.[8] As part of the structure of political unionism, then, Manley is vulnerable to the criticism that he blunted the independent class aspirations of the island's working class. Small's effort to organize the sugar workers into an alternative independent union failed. However, in the postcolonial period there were other independent left attempts to organize the sugar workers, and the workers in "King Sugar" would once again be placed in the forefront of left political activity.

JBC and Civil Disobedience

According to Manley, his most significant trade union activity was the Jamaica Broadcasting Corporation (JBC) strike of 1964.[9] The catalyst for the strike was the unfair dismissal of newsroom workers in what was then the government-owned broadcasting station. The dismissal of the JBC workers created waves of sympathy among sections of the middle class. Negotiations between the JLP-led government and the NWU quickly arrived at a stalemate, however, and it seemed as if the strike would fizzle out. At this crucial juncture, Manley decided upon the tactic of public civil disobedience in Kingston, the island's capital city. This tactic called for blocking the major arterial routes from the island's airport into the city. One month into the strike, Manley began these series of roadblocks. With each roadblock the number of persons grew, with support cutting across class lines.

What is interesting about Manley's reflections on this strike was that he preferred to use the tactic of civil disobedience to gather public support rather than that of sympathy strikes. He writes, "I still had the weapon of sympathy strikes up my sleeve but this is a tricky card to play and I was determined to hold it as a last resort" (Manley 1975, 176). Why was it that Manley went the route of developing broad public support for the strikers rather than using the standard labor tactic of the sympathy strike? Apart from the fact that this would have created an unstable situation in the country and broken the silent codes of labor practices, which had by then developed in the island, there was another reason.

In the 1960s Manley believed that the labor movement had three historic phases. The first phase was the basic right to union organization and the traditional rights of collective bargaining. In the second phase, mutual rights based upon a notion of natural human rights were extended to the workplace. Central to this phase was the structure of authority and the grounds for dismissal. For Manley, the JBC strike was an expression of this second phase. Manley therefore saw the campaign around the JBC strike as one that should be centered on the violation of natural human rights; hence his broad-based tactical appeal. The third phase in Manley's schema of the development of the labor movement was one in which the nature of the workplace organization changed as democracy replaced hierarchical authority workplace structures (Bogues 1996b, Manley 1975).

The campaign around the JBC strike gave Manley additional credibility as a consistent defender of human rights. It broadened his base of support to sections of the middle class and made him a national figure. Manley was able to successfully combine the threat of sympathy strike action in bauxite and sugar along with the actions of civil disobedience to bring the government to the negotiating table. His own assessment of the strike is noteworthy. He writes that "the strike was a unique experience for all Jamaicans, provoking intense controversy, idealistic involvement and contributing to the self image of a young nation" (Manley 1975, 186). While this assessment is perhaps too sweeping, one certain result was that Manley was now firmly on the road from unionism to party politics. By 1967 he was a representative in the House of Parliament and two years later won the PNP leadership contest, becoming party president.

The other major area of Michael Manley's trade union involvement was the bauxite industry. In this domain two things were important. First, the demand of the NWU in November 1952 for 4 shillings an hour created a new bar for wage claims and set in motion a process where for many years bauxite workers became the vanguard for levels of wage compensation. Second, Manley's activities in the industry led him into establishing regional links with other mineworkers in the Caribbean that in time led to the organization of the Caribbean Bauxite Mine and Metal Workers Union. Aspects of Manley's trade union experiences in bauxite subsequently found their way into his policy actions in the early 1970s. In January 1974, when the PNP government began to negotiate over the bauxite levy, Manley did so from the standpoint of his experiences with the companies. These experiences as a labor leader in the bauxite industry also consolidated his position as an advocate of international commodity organizations, which would give newly developing countries economic bargaining power in the international economic system. In his efforts to forge alliances for a new international economic order (NIEO), Manley hoped that in the same way the Caribbean workers had developed a level of solidarity and cooperative action toward the mining companies, Third World countries endowed with similar resources would cooperate in international action against the transnational companies. From this perspective, he launched efforts to form international commodity organizations such as the International Bauxite Association. The Jamaican political sociologist Carl Stone argued that during the early phases of the island's modern party system the political parties were "captives of organized labor" (1986, 100). While this is an accurate statement about the sociological makeup of the mass base of the major political parties, it is not an accurate assessment of their major policies in government. Neither of the political parties passed any major laws in the interest of the workers during the period of internal self-government. Indeed, the single piece of major labor legislation passed was the Essential Services Law, which prohibited the labor movement from calling strikes in areas prescribed as essential services by the colonial governor.

The rank and file of the Jamaican labor movement organized itself into a union movement because it felt that the trade union organization was an instrument to fight for equality. This rank and file had hoped that the legacies of the old plantation master-slave relationship that existed in the workplace would be mitigated by trade union action. So within the workplace culture of the Jamaican economy, the historic task of the labor movement was to redefine social/class relationships, making them more equal. On this score, the Jamaican capitalist class refused to budge. In contemporary Jamaica, many workers still hold on to this historic task of the trade union movement, and the major complaints of Jamaican workers revolve around their treatment as human beings by management (see Carter 1997). These sentiments about the trade union's historic task have been expressed in the workers vernacular with expressions like "mi nuh slave" or "slavery days done." Manley's experiences in the sugar industry attuned him to this sentiment. His three-stage schema of labor-capital relationships was rooted in this deep sentiment of the Jamaican working class, and it was something that would preoccupy him for life—how to get the worker to be treated on human terms in the Jamaican postcolonial society. In the 1970s it would lead him and his government to develop social programs that attempted to address this issue.

The Manley Government and Labor

Michael Manley became Jamaica's prime minister on a reformist political platform. During the 1972 election campaign, he constructed an all-class alliance that demanded social change. Political currents like Black Power and strong leftist radicalism, which had begun to make their appearance on the island's political landscape, influenced the first Manley regime. During his election campaign, Manley had tapped into elements of these radical currents and, with his trade union experiences, had spoken directly to the issues that impacted on the social mind of the working-class Jamaican. As a consequence, leading figures in the radical Black Power movement such as D. K. Duncan were drawn to the PNP.[10] The entrance of these persons and Manley's political stance, which resonated with some of the central radical ideas swirling around the Jamaican political landscape, created the conditions for the renewal of the Jamaican two-party political system over the next decade.

In government, Manley moved quickly to repeal a set of laws that were the legacies of the island's colonial history of racial plantation slavery. One of the most odious of these was the masters and servants law, promulgated in 1838 by the local planter and colonial legislative assembly. This law was established to regulate the relationship between the newly freed black slaves and the white planter elite. The legislation gave the white planter elite all powers and authority of dismissal over the worker. The law was the embodiment of servitude and the social relationships between white planters and blacks in late nineteenth-century and early twentieth-century Jamaica. In mid-twentieth-century Jamaica, it was a bitter pill for the workers to swallow, although at that time it was mainly applied to nonunionized workers and female household workers.[11] In 1974 the law was repealed and replaced by the Termination of Employment Act. Manley claims that when he became prime minister in 1972, he already had in mind the repeal of this law. He stated that his trade union experience had given him an insight into how the Jamaican working class viewed the postcolonial state's legal codes. He claims that the Masters and Servants law was the most offensive to the workers and as such it was at the top of his list for repeal (Bogues 1996b).

The first Manley regime passed a slew of legislation, which attempted to redefine both the wages and status of the Jamaican worker. In 1974, a National Minimum Wage Act was passed, and there were exercises for the reclassification of public sector workers that gave them status and higher wages. In a critical phase of the regime, the government, with advice from the trade union movement, proceeded to centralize what had been numerous government post office accounts across the island into a financial entity called the Workers Bank. This bank was to marshal funds for workers and to develop sound banking polices more favorable to the working class than those of the regular commercial banks. In one of the frequent meetings with the leadership of the trade union movement that he held as prime minister, Manley was advised that housing continued to be a central difficulty facing workers. After a series of meetings, the union movement submitted a set of proposals for the establishment of a National Housing Trust that would be charged with the policy of developing affordable houses for workers.

All the evidence points to the fact that when confronted with changing the immediate status of the lowliest workers and attempting to meet some of the social requirements of the working class, the first Manley regime was successful. However, when it came to the issue of negotiating between the rights of employers and workers, Manley's attempts to reconcile these interests oftentimes led to conflictual positions. As well, the first Manley regime often had to be pushed leftward on questions that directly challenged the overall dominance of the elite. Two clear examples of this were the debates about new labor laws in the 1970s and the struggle of the sugar workers for control of sugar lands in the parishes of Westmoreland, St. Catherine, and Clarendon.

It has already been stated that one piece of legislation, which had been developed by the colonial and local political elite, was the Essential Services Act. The Manley regime of the 1970s set out to change this act and developed a series of proposals for what later became known as the Labor Relations and Industrial Disputes Act (LRIDA). In its first draft, the bill was modeled along the lines of similar pieces of legislation in England. In particular, it proposed the banning of strikes in essential services and then gave the responsible minster the power to declare which industries could be considered essential. The draft was not very different from the old legislation and caused an uproar in the island's labor movement. This led to a series of discussions between the labor movement and the government, and a year later a new bill was passed. The new bill attempted to assuage both employers and workers. It recognized the rights of trade unions to exist and to participate in representative polling at workplaces and the right to strike. It then made it obligatory for unions who were involved in disputes in the sectors defined as essential to engage in a series of dispute resolution mechanisms. During this process, the law made it illegal for workers to strike unless the dispute mechanisms had failed in a specified time period. In other words, the bill did not take away the strike weapon but delayed its application. Given his trade union background and his penchant for negotiation, Manley considered this piece of legislation an important modern mechanism for the resolution of industrial disputes on the island. The LRIDA over time became an omnibus piece of legislation, which attempted to reconcile union and management industrial relations practices.

Worker Participation and Worker Ownership

We have already noted that in the final stage of Manley's labor schema, labor participates in the decision-making process at the workplace. For Manley, this form of democracy was central to a model of participatory democracy that could broaden the traditional forms of liberal parliamentary democratic systems. Manley held the view that democracy at the workplace would erode (not overturn) the economic power of the capitalist class and shift the power balance both at the workplace and in the society (Bogues 1996b). With this in mind, the Manley regime of the 1970s attempted to develop worker participation schemes in different enterprises. To accomplish this, the government established a unit within a government ministry and sought to encourage both the trade union movement and the employers to buy into this project. However, the single largest and most radical attempt to develop a model of worker participation was initiated from outside the PNP government and by individuals who were critical of the regime.

By 1972, the multinational company Tate and Lyle had withdrawn from the sugar industry. When the PNP regime assumed the reins of government, it found in place plans to sell Tate and Lyles sugar lands to large landowners. On taking power, the regime did not formulate any alternative plans for the sale of the lands. However, a group of radical Catholic priests and social activists profoundly influenced by liberation theology began to organize the sugar workers on the different estates into a movement that demanded the sugar lands be leased to the field workers. This movement became the Sugar Workers Cooperative Council (SWCC). The Manley regime was at first reluctant to support the SWCC since even radical PNP elements viewed the SWCC with suspicion.[12] Because some of the key organizers were not supportive of the government and were politically closer to the independent Marxist-Leninist left, the PNP perceived that the SWCC was a potential base for the independent left. However, the government could not ignore the fact that it had publicly pledged its support for worker participation and that there was a growing movement among the field workers to take over the sugar estates. After months of negotiation between the SWCC and the sugar authorities representing the government, an accord was reached. From that moment, the PNP government claimed the movement and attempted to direct its development.

The SWCC took over the lands of the island's major sugar estates on long-term lease. However by the mid-1980s, the sugar cooperatives were in deep economic trouble and the JLP, then in power, began to return the lands to the traditional sugar companies. Commentators on this experiment in worker participation and ownership have suggested that the primary reason for the failure of the endeavor was the lack of responsible financial management practices of the enterprises (Stone 1981). Manley himself felt that the enterprises failed for this reason as well as the sugar industry's lack of international competitiveness (Bogues 1996b). But whatever the reason, the attempt is still regarded by many workers as an attempt to change the dynamics of the power relationships in the Jamaican workplace.

Later in his political career, Manley in the early 1990s would return to the issue of forms of democracy at the workplace. By then he had modified aspects of his political thought and pragmatically accepted the market economy as a foundation for economic activity. In this mode he began to think through different modalities for workplace democracy and subsequently became a supporter of employee share-owning schemes (ESOP) as a form of workplace democracy.

Economic and Political Democracy

The political ideas that emerged from Manley's involvement with the Jamaican labor movement are critical elements that allow us to distinguish his political thought from that of mainstream twentieth century social democracy in at least one major area. Social democratic political thought typically focuses on liberal democratic norms, the role of the state in redistributionist activities, and ignores the relationships within the economic productive domain of society (see Meyer 1981). Manley's immersion in the labor movement and that movement's drive for foundational equality in postcolonial Jamaica helped to shape his political thought, giving it a distinctive flavor that is not typically found in mainstream western social democracy. In his most conscious work of political ideas, *The Politics of Change*, Manley states, "that the ownership and control of capital by a small minority of the society arose largely from the nature of the society at the time" (1990, 110). He then argues that modern society had developed to a stage where education and knowledge made it incumbent for ownership structures to be broadened. So Manley's political thought, while distinctive in this aspect from social democracy, was also contrary to Marxist propositions. For Manley, the working class did not come to own the means of production because of their historic location in the relations of production but because of the ever widening circles of education, the growth of political democracy, and the attendant need for this to be accompanied by some form of economic democracy.

Noteworthy about this formulation is Manley's focus on economic democracy and his linkage of notions of economic and political democracy. However, a central problematic was that while in advanced capitalist societies such notions might not cause any flutters, in postcolonial Jamaican society, constructed as it was on the authoritarian relationships of race and class, such ideas sent chills of fear down the spines of the dominant economic elite.

In this group's perception, such ideas if implemented would erode their power. In the final analysis, this group's fear of the erosion of its social power moved it firmly into the political camp of active conservatism during the 1970s. Parenthetically this raises questions about the nature of reformist political change in Jamaican society and the extent of the local ruling class's ability and willingness to negotiate such changes.[13] For Manley, a central dimension of egalitarianism was creating the conditions for forms of economic democracy located at the workplace. This concern was intimately linked to his notion of a worker as a human being and not as a beast of burden. In the final analysis, it would mean that while preoccupied with redistributionist activity in the 1970s he would also focus on concrete forms of workplace organization.

Words, Power, and Manley's Political Thought

As stated earlier, Manley's sojourn on the Jamaican sugar estates was the critical ingredient shaping his mode of political communication. Political communication was at the heart of Manley's political practice. He writes that the tools of democratic participatory politics are "communication and dialogue, its method involvement and its purpose mobilization" (1990, 75). Linguistic studies have shown that language is an integral part of the system of culture (see Bourdieu 1994). In oral-dominated cultures, the power of the spoken word represents not only speech but also action (see Ricoeur 1991). This is different from a context where words and language only represent a form of a sign system. If we examine the meaning and function of political rhetoric in an oral society, then we may conclude that rhetoric is more than an ideological practice embedded within the public discourses of social and political practices. It is a speech act with a dual character. If we say that in oral cultures the power of words can constitute action, then within the context of political and social change political rhetoric has a dual character—it is communication and itself a site of political action that impacts upon hegemonic political discourse. This partly explains why, when the subaltern classes were dignified as equal human beings in Manley's speeches, consternation among the Jamaican elite became the order of the day.[14]

Manley himself felt that it was possible to renegotiate the terms of class relationships in Jamaican society by creating a public discourse of equality and brotherhood that was backed up with symbolic projects involving all classes (Bogues 1996b). One such project was Labor Day, which in the first few years of the regime was highly successful.

Manley had a view about the power of words and their capacity to influence and change Jamaican society. It is clear that he felt that he could use political rhetoric as an instrument to drive the reformist project in which he was engaged, to cajole those who resisted the project and to create the conditions for the project's success. One problematic, however, was that the word *equality*, from the standpoint of the Jamaican oppressed classes, had inscribed within it political values of freedom and economic opportunity that challenged the fundamental structures of the society, and its use could not be contained in a reformist project (see Bogues 1998).

In writing about an egalitarian society, Manley notes that "a society is egalitarian when every single member feels instinctively, unhesitatingly and unreservedly that his or her essential worth is recognized and that there is a foundation of rights upon which [their] interests can safely rest" (Manley 1990, 38). In the same text he further suggests that the social ranks, which are created by economic organization, should never be allowed to "harden into social classes." In Manley's political vision of an egalitarian society, doctors, street cleaners, workers, owners of large enterprises, and owners of small enterprises would all be able to see themselves as equal members of society. At the foundation of this idea is an understanding that society is a "group of people pursuing the common objective of survival" (Manley 1990, 17). Manley was acutely aware of the existence of classes in postcolonial Jamaica, but he believed that since these classes were a historical human construct then they could be dissolved by willful human action. This became one of his central political tasks of communication. His success in the Jamaican labor movement had convinced him of this possibility.

Labor and Socialism

Ten years after eschewing socialist ideology, the PNP in 1974 redeclared itself a democratic socialist party. This political shift meant that Manley's ideas about the role of workers now had to be fitted into an explicit ideological frame. With this in mind, Manley argued that the emergence of unions was the result of capitalism and that unions could do no more than mitigate the worst effects of the capitalist system. He also stated that traditional unions were a prop to capitalism since they accepted capitalist values. This was a different position from his earlier elaboration in which the unions had a fundamental role to play in the democratization of the economy and the society. In his later formulation, the role of change agent was now assigned to the mass democratic political party. In 1975 Manley limited the role of labor to reformist action in developing housing, dealing with wage differentials in the labor force, paying special attention to the problems of female employment, and worker education (Manley 1975, 212–15). While in government, Manley bemoaned traditional union rivalry and argued that the union movement needed to work out arrangements that would minimize conflicts and rivalry.

In his earlier labor schema, Manley had stated that the final stage of the labor movement was a struggle for democracy at the workplace based on the principle of human equality. While previously it seems that this issue could be separated from the nature of the economic system, it was not possible within the ideological framework of democratic socialism. As a consequence, Manley now believed that capitalism, as an economic system, could not facilitate democracy at the workplace, while on the other hand democratic socialism was capable of doing so. Socialism in Manley's political thought in 1975 became the climax of a series of historical evolutions in which the concept of equality gave birth to democracy, which in turn then "spawned socialism as a concept and method of social and economic organizations" (Manley 1975, 222).

However, what is distinctive about Manley's notion of socialism at the time was how it eschewed traditional socialist definitions that equated public ownership with socialism and worker democracy. Attempting to find a form for worker democracy at the workplace, Manley suggests that public ownership does not answer the question of inclusion "of the worker in the decision making process as a full and equal partner" (Manley 1975, 225). This is one of the central ingredients in Manley's political thought and was the brake on his advocating full state control of an economy. It also distinguished him from his acknowledged mentor Harold Laski, since one of Laski's major theoretical projects was to reconcile liberal democratic political values to Marxism (see Laski 1968). Manley however was preoccupied with searching for a form of society that would link human equality with liberal democratic forms and a form of economic democracy. An imposing state with economic and political dominance was therefore never an integral part of Manley's political ideas.[15] Because Manley did not favor such a state, he always attempted to develop ideas that would give workers "a voice at the workplace."

Assessment

When during the late 1980s Manley redefined his socialist project and admitted to what he considered to be the permanency of the capitalist market, a profound tension emerged within his political thought. This tension can be discerned in his own reflections on the 1980 electoral defeat and then the rapid advance of neoliberalism as the dominant political ideology in the world. As Manley began to feel that the market economic system was a better allocation of resources, his concern turned to how to tame the market, how to develop social institutions that would minimize the traditional inequalities of the capitalist market. This concern was even more acute since as a practicing politician in the 1990s Manley also had a tactical political objective of restoring the broken ties with the United States. Added to these tactical considerations was the problem of the ideological development of the party, for which he assumed ideological leadership. The concrete political problematic that he faced at the time was how to fit the tactical objectives and his rethinking of the nature of the market into a consistent socialist ideological framework, not upset Washington, and at the same time keep the PNP on an ideological track that would stop it from descending into the morass of Jamaican clientelistic politics.

All these factors combined to push Manley into a political elaboration that resulted into two things. First, although there was no hostility to workers and the labor movement, there was no fine-tuning of ideology in the way the doctrine of democratic socialism was fine-tuned in the 1970s. Second, Manley became more preoccupied with creating political stability and planning the terms of his own transition from political leadership. In his final days he had planned to begin work on redefining the political ideas that he felt would have been the best legacy he could have left the PNP. That work was never completed. Recognizing that his energy was running low because of his illness, Manley set himself the practical task of minimizing conflicts in the bauxite industry and of persuading the unions and employers that the concept of ESOPs was a worthwhile one.

How do we assess Manley's labor legacy? This legacy has two dimensions to it. The first is that Manley found in the labor movement a concern about human equality, which he attempted to implement. However, this implementation was stymied by the nature of the political unionism and subsequent union rivalry in the Jamaican labor movement. Manley himself was part of this political unionism. There is no doubt that he modernized collective bargaining techniques at the workplace and that in the bauxite industry, his work facilitated the emergence of mid-twentieth-century regionalism in the Caribbean labor movement. At the second level, there is his contribution to the labor movement conducted through the political process. Here the legacy is much more substantive in the laws, which repealed servitude status of the Jamaican worker.

But perhaps another way of assessing Manley's legacy to labor is to see how labor influenced his political ideas and practice. Manley's immersion for twenty years in the Jamaican trade union movement became the cradle for the development of his skills of political communication. It honed his talent for negotiation so much that negotiation was not a style but a substantive *form* of his political practices. He carried from trade unionism his abilities at negotiation and persuasion, believing that he could persuade the Jamaican oligarchy to give up some of its power and rearrange class relationships, which would make the ordinary black Jamaican equal. His talent for political communication and his political philosophy of human equality led him to create a public political discourse about human equality in a society that was shaped and organized by class, race, and color systems of domination. That many Jamaicans remember him today in a favorable way is testimony to the fact that while his efforts did not achieve their mark and were in some instances contradictory, they resonated with the ordinary Jamaicans' deepest aspirations.

In order to perceive the full significance of Manley to postcolonial Jamaica, it might be worthwhile for us to shift the site of analysis from its more traditional structural and institutional basis to the nebulous and problematic site of the subjective. One fundamental legacy of Jamaica's political history is how black Jamaicans as colonized racial subjects have been subjected to a language, ethos, vocabulary, and set of social relationships that denigrate them. From this frame, critical new sites of politics emerge as everyday indignities are suffered, and the humiliation and social relationships conducted through vocabularies and practices are contested. This type of analysis does not negate the central importance of structural forms of exploitation; however, it announces that in colonial-racialized societies there exists another level of domination that should be considered. Manley's conception of human equality resonated with some elements of the modes of resistance of the ordinary Jamaican. It deeply upset the local brown and white oligarchy and pushed them to actively organize against his regime in the 1970s. In his second regime, Manley accepted the tactical defeat of his quest for human equality. However, in the end, what Manley's political practice did was to place center stage in mainstream Jamaican politics the issues of human equality and the displacement of some of the legacies of white colonial plantation society. This was an active dimension of the deepest aspirations of the Jamaican working class. It was the most significant thing he had learned in the cauldron of the Jamaican labor movement.

Notes

An earlier version of this chapter was published in *Caribbean Quarterly* 48, no. 1 (2002). The author wishes to thank Geri Augusto, Norman Girvan, and the reviewers for their critical comments.

1. For a historical examination of the development of the labor movement in Jamaica, see Richard Hart, *From Occupation to Independence* (London: Pluto, 1998); and O. Nigel Bolland, *The Politics of Labor in the British Caribbean* (Kingston: Ian Randle, 2001). For an earlier historical account, see William H. Knowles, *Trade Union Development and Industrial Relations in the British West Indies* (Berkeley: University of California Press, 1959). Another account can be found in George E. Eaton, *Alexander Bustamante and Modern Jamaica* (Kingston: Kingston Publishers, 1975).

2. The labor rebellion of May 1938 swept the island and is viewed as a critical marker in twentieth-century Jamaican political history. For a detailed study, see Ken Post, *Arise Ye Starvelings* (London: Martinus Nijhoff, 1978).

3. For a biography of N. W. Manley, see Philip Sherlock, *Norman Manley: A Biography* (London: Macmillan, 1980), as well as Victor Reid, *The Horses of the Morning* (Kingston: Caribbean Authors Publishing, 1985). On Edna Manley, see Wayne Brown, *Edna Manley: The Private Years, 1900–1938* (London: Andre Deutsch, 1975), and Rachel Manley, ed., *Edna Manley: The Diaries* (Kingston: Heinemann Publishers, 1989).

4. Between 1992 and 1997, the unity of the island's labor movement became one of Manley's chief concerns, and he worked closely with the island's union leadership to develop a confederation of the Jamaican labor movement. Before that he had worked along with the island's trade union leadership to develop a central research and educational institution, the Joint Trade Union and Research and Development Center. This center then became the institutional frame that in 1994 created the Jamaica Confederation of Trade Unions. Today union rivalry in the Jamaican labor movement is at a minimum as the confederation often acts as a bargaining agent for some sectors of workers. Such a situation would have been unthinkable during the days of political unionism. It indicates that the Jamaican labor movement is becoming less dependent on its original linkages with the two major political parties and

developing its own independent stance. However the delinking process is by no means complete.

5. Typescript of speech in author's possession. I want to thank Dennis Daley for a copy.

6. Typescript of charges in author's possession due to the kindness of Dennis Daley.

7. It is interesting to note that in the 1970s when the leading Marxist-Leninist grouping in Jamaica, the Workers Party of Jamaica, was very active, several leading members were leading members of the University and Allied Workers Trade Union as well, confirming the political-union link. For many on the left, political unionism meant JLP/BITU and PNP/NWU links. There was however another current that was represented by some elements in the small radical Independent Trade Union Action Council.

8. Perhaps the most insightful critique of political unionism came from Joseph Edwards, a refrigerator mechanic who was a major worker-leader in the early 1970s. Edwards published a pamphlet titled *Union versus Management* (Kingston: Abeng, 1971) that detailed the way in which political unionism had turned the labor movement into an instrument of middle-class political practice. He also represented the current that eschewed party-union linkages.

9. The Jamaica Broadcasting Corporation was the government-owned media house. Initially modeled on the British Broadcasting Corporation, it has been the subject of much controversy, with charges of its editorial outlook being politically controlled. In the 1990s within the general frame of privatization, the station was placed into private ownership.

10. The major radical group that emerged in this period (1968–72) was Abeng. Organized around a radical newspaper, the group was highly critical of Manley and the PNP. However some members of the group, in particular D. K. Duncan, began to feel, after seeing and hearing Manley on the campaign trail, that Manley was representative of a progressive current within the country. Duncan joined the PNP, eventually becoming the leader of the radical left in that party during the 1970s.

11. One of the most intriguing untold stories about the development of the Jamaican working class is the emergence of domestic female labor in early twentieth-century Jamaica. It is a story of the oppression of women and the renegotiation of black Jamaican female identity. This is a story that badly needs telling.

12. As information officer of the SWCC, the author produced a video about the project that focused on the workers themselves telling their stories. As part of a plan to influence the PNP, the SWCC decided to show the video to elements of the PNP left to persuade them that the SWCC was worth supporting. To the amazement of the SWCC organizers who were at that meeting, the main comment of the PNP left who were present after the showing was that the video demonstrated the influence of communism.

13. Any discussion about the collapse of the radical politics of the 1970s in Jamaica has to face this critical question. So far it has not been answered with any profound examination of the nature of the social forces in the island and how hegemony has been constructed and is presently fragmented. I am grateful to my colleague, Anthony Harriott, who raised this point with me in discussing this article.

14. It is perhaps important here to note that while many authors have argued that Manley was charismatic, he himself was contemptuous of such analysis. In a 1996 interview with the author, Manley stated that the word did not explain how he had to be deeply involved in the lives of the workers in the movement, and that it was his willingness to listen and learn and to treat every worker with respect that gave him the ability to lead. I think Manley was unhappy with this description because it suggested that his followers would blindly allow him to lead them. Even though such blind faith might have been expressed in party songs like "Press Along, Joshua," the relationship between Manley and certainly the members of the PNP was sometimes a complicated one. The clearest example of this were the internal debates in the PNP in the 1970s about the role of the International Monetary Fund. For a discussion of charismatic political leadership in the Caribbean, see Anton Allahar, ed., *Caribbean Charisma* (Kingston: Ian Randle, 2001).

15. This is a point of controversy. Those who would disagree would point to the 1978 *Principles and Objectives,* in which the objective of state control of the commanding heights of the economy is elaborated. I would argue that *Principles and Objectives* should be studied as a tactical rather than a strategic/foundation document and was the result of struggles within the PNP at the time. As a tactical document, it marks the high point of the radical PNP left influence led by D. K. Duncan. As well I would suggest that the political thought of Manley can be studied textually from his numerous speeches and that the prime philosophical source for his ideas are to be found in his book, *The Politics of Change.* It is interesting that in the revised edition of this book, Manley states that he did not discuss socialism in the first edition. If indeed this text is the most accurate description of Manley's political thought, then it means that the so-called dramatic changes of the 1990s are not so dramatic after all. There is a methodological point about studying Manley's political thought that is important in general for the study of political thought. As a practicing politician, Manley's political ideas should be studied both from the textual point of view as well as from his vast political practice. When this is done, then adequate considerations can be given as to what is tactical and what is of philosophical political value.

References

Berlin, Isaiah. 1996. "Political Judgment." In *The Sense of Reality,* ed. Henry Hardy. London: Chatto and Windus.

Bogues, Anthony. 1996a. Interview with Hugh Small, November 14, 1996.
———. 1996b. Interviews with Michael Manley, June–September 1996.
———. 2002. "Nationalism in Jamaican Political Thought." In *Jamaica in Slavery and Freedom: History, Heritage, and Culture*, ed. Kathleen E. A. Monteith and Glen Richards. Mona: University of the West Indies Press.
Bourdieu, Pierre. 1994. *Language and Symbolic Power*. Cambridge: Harvard University Press.
Carter, Kenneth. 1997. *Why Workers Won't Work*. London: MacMillan.
Gray, Obika. 1991. *Radicalism and Social Change in Jamaica, 1960–1972*. Knoxville: University of Tennessee Press.
Laski, Harold. 1968. *Reflections of the Revolution of Our Time*. London: Frank Cass.
Manley, Michael. 1975. *A Voice at the Workplace*. London: Andre Deutsch.
———. 1990. *The Politics of Change*. [1975] Washington, D.C.: Howard University Press.
Meyer, Thomas. 1981. *Democratic Socialism in Thirty-Six Theses*. Bonn: FES.
Munroe, Trevor. 1992. *The Cold War and the Jamaican Left, 1950–1955*. Kingston: Kingston Publishers.
Ricoeur, Paul. 1991. *Text and Action*. Evanston: Northwestern University Press.
Stone, Carl. 1981. "An Appraisal of the Cooperative Process in the Jamaican Sugar Industry." In *Perspectives on Jamaica in the Seventies*, ed. Carl Stone and Aggrey Brown. Kingston: Jamaica Publishing House.
———. 1986. *State and Democracy in Jamaica*. New York: Praeger.

5

Colonialism, Political Policing, and the Jagan Years

JOAN MARS

The colonial police force played an important role in the early political career of Cheddi Jagan, particularly during the very turbulent preindependence years in Guyana's political history. Through various mechanisms the police force was made to operate as an extension of a repressive colonial state, and consequently helped in the destabilization of Jagan's Marxist-oriented government. This politicization of the Guyana police under colonialism has provided the foundation for its controversial role today, which may hold further implications for the future of an ethnically divisive country such as Guyana.

The governance of British Guiana during the Jagan years (1953–64) reflected a fundamental disjuncture between the attempts of the People's Progressive Party (PPP) at nation building and the interests of the British colonial authorities. Throughout his tenure of office during the colonial period, Cheddi Jagan and his PPP secured the mandate of the electorate, but he was without the means to maintain the stability and order upon which civil society rests. In scholarly analyses of the struggles that ensued, the main source of the colonial state's power and stability—the colonial police force—remains largely unexplored. Although some attention has been paid to the involvement of the police in containing racial and industrial conflicts (Danns 1982, Campbell 1987), the techniques used by the metropolitan power in the crafting of a political police for the maintenance of colonial rule have not been investigated. An analysis of police history elucidates not only the political instability and social turmoil that plagued British Guiana during the Jagan years, but also the enduring consequences of the distortion of the police role for the furtherance of statist goals.

Theoretical Framework

Many attempts have been made to describe the role of politics in policing, ranging from the assertion that all policing is political (Turk 1982, 115; Huggins 1998, 9) to the recognition that politics can play a calculated role in the creation and operations of police forces (Bayley 1977, Chevigny 1995). A distinction should, however, be made between the recognition of the inherently political character of the policing function to the extent that it helps to fulfill the requirements of the social contract in the Kantian sense, and the capability of the police to be used *covertly or overtly* for expressly political purposes. In the first instance, the recognition of an inherently political function for the police lies in the expectation that it would play a role in fulfilling the state's duty to maintain a well-ordered society. In this context, the police enable the state to protect its citizens from acts of injustice, to keep the people's peace, and, along with civil society, "to be a cooperative association for the prevention of crime" (Alderson 1998, 28). The covert or overt use of the police for expressly political purposes, on the other hand, involves the harnessing of the coercive capacities of the state primarily for the furtherance of statist goals. Such goals may include suppressing political dissent, protecting and promoting the interests of the dominant classes, and keeping selected individuals, groups, and classes in their place.

Among the array of countries that engage in covert political policing from time to time, the United States, to a lesser extent Britain mainly during the twentieth century, and Canada provide some colorful examples. In these cases, political policing has been conducted under the guise of traditional law enforcement functions. These police forces are not created primarily to be used as political weapons in the hands of the government and ruling class, but are mobilized by the ruling authorities to deal with perceived or actual threats to the hegemony of the dominant social order. These perceived or actual threats may take the form of "dangerous" individuals, classes, or groups that question the status quo, and can range from an innocent influx of immigrants (Brown and Warner 1995), to civil rights activists involved in legitimate protest activities, to suspected terrorists and insurgents (Chevigny 1995, Enloe 1980, Turk 1982).

Examples of police forces that are wholly or partially designed and employed for overt political purposes are not hard to find (Jeffries 1952, Enloe 1980, Huggins 1991, 1996). Such forces have proliferated in Latin America and the English-speaking Caribbean and openly operate as political weapons in the hands of the holders of state power. This form of policing usually requires a disproportionate investment of resources and manpower in control rather than service functions, control that can be achieved through varying degrees of militarization of the force. In addition to the aggressive policing of public order, one can expect that such forces will place a great deal of emphasis on activities such as intelligence gathering, information manipulation, and internal surveillance (Turk 1982).

A significant feature that has been overlooked in the literature is that overt political policing not only involves politically motivated, coercive actions taken by police, or what might be called *acts of commission;* but also the failure to act when action is required in pursuance of the state's duty to maintain an orderly society and to protect the safety of individuals, or *acts of omission*. The Jagan years in Guyana's government during the colonial period provide a classic example of overt political policing through politically motivated acts of commission as well as omission. During this period, political policing involved not only the repression of legitimate resistance to oppression but also the deliberate dereliction of duty in furtherance of the national security interests of the British Empire and its allies. This type of political policing was facilitated by three factors: the maintenance of constitutional control of the police force, the militarization of the force, and the use of race and ethnicity to ensure the loyalty of the force to the colonial administration.

The Maintenance of Constitutional Control of the Police Force

From its inception in the nineteenth century, the police force in British Guiana was directly answerable to the executive branch of the government. Under Ordinance 13 of 1838, which provided for the establishment of the force, county inspectors reported to their respective county sheriffs, who received instructions directly from the governor who even authorized the payment of their salaries. The following year, when the administration of the force was centralized under a single inspector general of police for the colony (by Ordinance 9 of 1939), he was required to report directly to the governor.

The Guyana police force that existed at the time Cheddi Jagan took office in 1953 was still under the firm control of the British Colonial Office through the colonial governor, and remained so until independence from Britain was achieved in 1966. None of the constitutional arrangements permitting self-government relinquished control of the police force to the local representatives of the people. In fact, provisions were made to ensure the exact opposite. The Waddington Constitution of 1953, under which Jagan took office, provided for universal adult suffrage and wider participation of the elected representatives of the people. However, full responsibility for defense, the police forces, and information remained in the hands of the governor and, ultimately, the colonial chief secretary. Despite the PPP's elected majority in the House of Assembly and the Executive Council, responsibility for the maintenance of internal stability and security remained entirely in the hands of the British government.

The Waddington Constitution was suspended shortly after the PPP took office in 1953 and was replaced by an interim constitution, but no changes were made in the arrangements relating to the police until the promulgation of a new constitution, which took effect in 1961. A proposal by the PPP that a minister in the government should assume full control of the police was rejected by the colonial authorities. The new constitution only allowed for a transfer of limited responsibility for the maintenance and administration of the force to the Council of Ministers (the new name for the Executive Council). An attempt was subsequently made by the PPP government, in the Miscellaneous Enactments Bill, No. 10 of 1963, to transfer operational control of the force to the Minister of Home Affairs, but this bill was reserved by the colonial governor for the signification of Her Majesty's pleasure under article 74(3), proviso (a) of the new constitution and never became law (Shababuddeen 1978). The governor retained his power (subject to the overriding powers of the colonial authorities) to refuse to assent, inter alia, to any bill affecting the maintenance of law and order or the terms or conditions of service of public officers, including the police. Constitutionally, therefore, the commissioner of police (who was appointed by the governor), the governor, and ultimately the British authorities retained complete operational control of the police force. Under this arrangement, the commissioner of police vigorously resisted any interference by the PPP government in decisions regarding the day-to-day operations of the force.

The frustration experienced by the PPP government as a result of this state of affairs was poignantly described by Cheddi Jagan as follows:

> We were engaged in a running battle with the Governor and the Commissioner of Police to delimit the powers of the Minister of Home Affairs vis-à-vis the Commissioner of Police. We felt that the Minister could not adequately perform her responsibilities if the Commissioner,

as he felt, was solely in charge of operational control of the police force without reference to the Minister. We tried to make this clear in a Miscellaneous Enactments Bill, but the Governor refused to give his assent. Constant disagreements on this score finally led to the Minister's resignation in 1964. (Jagan 1997, 259)

This reluctance to relinquish operational control of the police persisted even after Jagan was ousted from office following the results of the 1964 general election. The colonial governor retained ultimate control over the police until the post of governor was replaced by that of governor-general, and a prime minister assumed full executive power under the independence constitution, which came into effect with the passage of the Guyana Independence Act on May 26, 1966. This was a huge step forward, but, constitutionally, the governor-general still played a role in the appointment of the commissioner and deputy commissioner of police, subject to the consent of the prime minister. The final tie was not severed until Guyana became a republic on February 23, 1970, and an elected president replaced the position of governor-general. Both the commissioner and deputy commissioner of police are now appointed by the president, after consultation with the Police Service Commission, and responsibility for the police force remains vested in the Minister of Home Affairs.

The Militarization of the Police Force

Although military influences have played a role in the organization and training of civilian police forces worldwide (Enloe 1980, Fogelson 1977, Manning 1977), traditional civilian policing can be clearly distinguished from various degrees of militarized policing that emerged in preindependence Third World nations and continue to survive today. The work of these militarized forces is somewhat similar to that of the relatively recent paramilitary police units that have proliferated in the developed world, such as state and local SWAT teams in the United States (Kraska and Kappeler 1997), and Britain's paramilitary specialist public order squads (Enloe 1980). What is significant about the militarization of colonial police forces, however, is that military tactics and methods were not merely localized in particular specialized units but penetrated the structure, organization, and training of the entire force.

Though also engaging in crime-fighting functions, colonial militarized police forces, like the state's army, were primarily concerned with suppressing challenges to the social and political order. Close examination of militarized colonial police forces reveals several distinguishing characteristics: a centralized command and organizational structure; an emphasis on military tactics, weapons, training, and the show of force; and social distancing of police from the public. Police forces that are intended to provide internal security tend to be centralized forces, directly responsible to the state, operating under a hierarchical chain of command, with the trappings of a military force, such as designations and uniforms. Absolute and unquestioning obedience to orders given by superior officers is demanded. Divisions are woven together under a central command, with or without specialized units. The force is heavily armed with the most sophisticated hardware available and especially antiriot and crowd-control tools. Training is not focused on the cop-on-the-beat type of policing but rather on crowd-control tactics, proficiency in the use of weapons, and field operations. Regular displays of their capacity for coercion take the form of battalion drills and other public events. The members of a military force are usually housed in special residences and barracks away from the rest of the population.

Such policies represent a distortion of the traditional police function, but they became an indispensable component of a lengthy colonial experiment, the results of which continue to influence current police practice and methods. It is therefore important to understand the development of colonial-style militarized policing in order to make sense of the challenges posed by police behavior during the Jagan years and the problems that continue to plague policing in Guyana today.

Internal security and the maintenance of the social and political order were of paramount importance to Britain in its dependencies worldwide but came with a high price: troops had to be maintained to be called into action in the face of, at one time, slave revolts and rebellions, and then labor protests, interethnic conflicts, and other civil disturbances. After the end of the slavery period, local police forces were a much cheaper means of domestic order keeping than military units, and the establishment of constabularies in the West Indian colonies tended to follow the highly militarized, antiriot model of the Royal Irish Constabulary (Jeffries 1952).

In the case of Guyana, however, despite the arguments advanced by Danns (1982) to the contrary, it appears that the "usual West Indian pattern" was not initially followed in the establishment of the police force there (Jeffries 1952, 63–64). There is little evidence that, in 1839 when the force was established, the newly freed slaves in British Guiana posed an immediate security threat to the colonial administration. Throughout the emancipation period, colonial governor Carmichael Smyth firmly resisted attempts to further expand the inherited Dutch police system and establish twelve district police stations (authorized by Ordinance No. 43 of 1834) on the basis that the newly freed slaves were respectful and law abiding (Campbell 1987). In any event, the British West India Regiment and the local militia, which had replaced the Dutch Burgher Militia, were available to deal with any threats to public order. According to Jeffries, who served as deputy undersecretary of state for the colonies, the civilian model was implemented in the colony, under the advice of the commissioners of the London Metropolitan Police (Jeffries 1952).

In the decades that followed, however, the force became increasingly relied upon to deal with local resistance to the injustices of the colonial system. Public protests, mainly in the form of labor demonstrations, strikes and work stoppages protesting unfair work conditions on the sugar estates, and interethnic conflicts caused by the divide-and-rule policies of the British (such as the 1848 Berbice Riots and the 1856 Angel Gabriel Riots), posed a constant threat to internal security. The police, assisted by the troops, were depended upon to repress these disturbances, and the shift toward militarization of the force became noticeable as early as 1884, when three members of the Royal Irish Constabulary were enlisted to serve in the force. In 1889, a military officer (Colonel R. Stapleton Cotton) assumed full command of the police force, and when the British troops (the First West India Regiment) withdrew from the colony in 1891, the force was officially reorganized to replace the military, with every member being armed to undertake responsibility for defense as well as the suppression of internal disturbances (Ordinance 7 of 1891). The police and the militia formed the defense forces of the colony, and from time to time thereafter, whenever the militia was disbanded for lack of funding, the police were the only line of defense. At the turn of the century, the inspector general in his annual report prided himself on the successful reorganization of "what was a purely civil into a semi-military force and at the same time promoting efficiency in police work" (Campbell 1987, 94). Organizationally, the force was brought in line with those already in existence in the other territories of the British West Indies, which were fully modeled after the Royal Irish Constabulary.

Considerable attention was placed on discipline and obedience to orders given by higher ranks, proficiency in the use of advanced weaponry, and the show of force. Martini Henri rifles were replaced with the more powerful Martini Enfield. Emphasis was placed on skill in arms, daily drill with arms and squad, company and baton drill, and sharpshooting and musketry. Guyana's police force quickly became the most heavily armed in the British West Indies. By 1902, according to Campbell, the force drilled as a battalion regularly, and on several occasions they drilled in brigade with the militia (1987, 91). In 1905 a Mounted Police Branch was formed, and open rifle competitions were held. A section of the officer corps (noncommissioned officers) was trained in field defenses including hasty entrenchment, shelter trenches, gun pits, and obstacles (Campbell 1987, 96). Social distancing was achieved by the compulsory housing of constables and gazetted officers in special barracks and residences within a compound, fenced and separate from the rest of the population. Noncommissioned officers, who were mainly local born, were rarely allowed to work in police stations in their own villages or home towns.

The force remained a semimilitary undertaking throughout the colonial period and thereafter. In 1948 a Special Branch/Constabulary was formed to provide a reserve force that would be on call if needed for the preservation of good order. It was the urban counterpart to the Rural Constabulary that had been formed for the same reason during the early years of the postemancipation period, starting in 1849. Despite various, primarily cosmetic changes over the years, the military capabilities of the force were affirmed by the Police Act of 1957, during Cheddi Jagan's term in office prior to independence. The act provided for the use of the police as a military force in the event of war or other emergency, whereupon members of the force would hold their police ranks as well as "such military ranks as may be determined" (Section 13[2] as amended).

Following the upsurge of industrial unrest, political violence, and racial conflict between the two major ethnic groups, East Indians and blacks, during the Jagan years, a Special Services Unit was set up by the governor consisting of subordinate officers and constables from the main police force (B.G. Special Services Unit Order, 11/64). The Special Services Unit was a highly trained, disciplined, and heavily armed police unit as well as a miniature army, and was mandated to suppress internal disturbances as well as perform military duties authorized by the governor. It later became the nucleus of the country's first full-time army, the Guyana Defense Force, which came into existence on November 1, 1965.

The Use of Race and Ethnicity to Ensure Loyalty of the Force to the Colonial Administration

The British have always relied upon the skillful use of ethnicity to maintain control over the culturally diverse polities they helped create. In order to successfully divide and rule, police and military institutions received special attention, and Guyana was no exception. According to Enloe, recruitment formulas are purposefully designed to "make the police (1) a more reliable agent of the state and (2) a more effective deterrent against challenges to the existing political structure" (Enloe 1980, 135).

From the time the force was established in 1839, the racial composition mirrored the concerns of the colonial government in promoting absolute loyalty and obedience. The officer corps (both commissioned and noncommissioned) was exclusively British, without any local connections or family ties. The rank and file consisted of whites, mulattoes (also called coloreds), and blacks mainly from foreign countries. In 1887, the majority of the constables (48.1 percent) were nonlocals, consisting of 249 Barbadians and 52 West Indians from other countries (Moore 1987). Police were recruited from the East Indian population but in far fewer numbers than blacks. Census data record 66 East Indian police in 1891, 24 in 1911, and 20 in 1921, but their numbers on the force remained significantly disproportionate to their representation in the population and formed the basis for allegations of racial discrimination that surfaced during the Jagan years (International Commission of Jurists 1965). As political instability in the colony increased, so did the numerical strength of the police and the expenditure of the colonial government for their maintenance, but little gains were made in the numbers of East Indians recruited. Locally born "Creoles" eventually replaced the constables from abroad but held few positions in the officer ranks during the remainder of the colonial period. At the time of independence there were still white expatriate officers in the force, and it was not until the following year, 1967, that the first Guyanese officer was elevated to the rank of commissioner, after having served some thirty-one years in the force (Campbell 1987).

Apart from the need to maintain social distance from the local population of mainly blacks and East Indians, the racial composition of the force reflected expectations of loyalty and reliability based on racial ascription that started to evolve as far back as the slavery period. Mulattoes were considered reliable and loyal to the interests of the metropolitan power, and therefore eminently qualified for the supervisory ranks they held in the police force. Their dependability corresponded with the creation of special accommodations, life opportunities, and social roles based on lightness of skin color during the slavery period. They were born free and soon became proud imitators of the white aristocracy. Some of them even owned their own slaves and "in practice, the whites depended upon them a great deal" (Smith 1980, 27). They were counted as whites for the purpose of fulfilling the security requirement of the Crown that a ratio of one white to every fifty slaves be maintained on a plantation (Demerara Ordinance of 1784). They also served in the regular slave patrols and were allowed to take up commissions in the militia (Shahabuddeen 1978).

The situation was not so clear-cut in the case of black and East Indian recruits, however, but over time, a certain degree of confidence developed with respect to expectations for obedience of the black rank and file in preference to East Indians. African slaves had been used for the policing of other slaves during the slavery period, but they were not allowed to take up commissions in the militia (Rodway 1891). After emancipation, in a society where social mobility was determined by a color-class system of social stratification, blacks quickly became assimilated to British culture and values. East Indian contract laborers and their descendants, on the other hand, remained a culturally distinct sector of the population for a much longer period. There was also an initial language barrier in the case of the latter, most of whom spoke Hindustani upon their arrival, whereas blacks by that time had become for the most part fluent in English. Occupational specialization among the racial groups also played a role. Blacks who were practically driven off the land that they tried to farm independently after emancipation tended to seek positions in the civil service, while East Indian contract laborers were initially given their own plots of land to farm and were encouraged to remain on the estates after the end of their period of indenture (Moore 1992). Additionally, entrance requirements for the police force, such as those for height and chest measurements and unmarried status, operated to exclude East Indians, who tended to be more diminutive in stature than blacks, and married at an earlier age (International Commission of Jurists 1965). Hence, a complex array of factors may have influenced what emerged as a preference for blacks rather than East Indians for the rank and file of the police force.

In January 1958, a cadet officer scheme was established that permitted locally born Guyanese to enter the officer ranks of the force, but most of the early appointees were light-skinned descendants of the colored class. The rank and file were kept in line under a severe disciplinary code that imposed strict penalties, including dismissal from the force, for failure to obey orders or for the dereliction of duty. By Force Order 12 of 1957, the disciplinary procedures were revamped to move the responsibility for imposing discipline on the rank and file from inspectors and constables to the hands of the commissioner, with the governor being the final arbiter in all appeals from the decisions of the latter. Only other members of the force were allowed to represent the accused ranks, and the disciplinary proceedings remained an internal matter, shielded from external review by the judicial system. This ended a long practice of permitting accused ranks to retain counsel for their representation either in the magistrate's court or during internal disciplinary proceedings.

Political Policing during the Jagan Years

Acts of Commission: Policing the "Communists"

The PPP's ideological commitment to a combination of nationalist and Marxist strategies for improving society was anathema to the political interests of the British government and its allies, especially the United States. In fact, by the time Cheddi Jagan had assumed office, the British government had already pledged itself to the defeat of all communist movements in the British Commonwealth (Shahabuddeen 1978, 527). After a mere 133 days in office, Cheddi Jagan's PPP was considered a formidable threat to British political interests in the region, and on October 4, 1953, the Waddington Constitution was suspended. On October 8, 1953, the governor declared a state of emergency and made emergency regulations enabling the removal of the portfolios of the elected ministers. A commission was appointed to recommend changes for a new constitution and an interim government was constituted. The colonial government then turned its attention to the police, the first line of defense against any resistance from the PPP and its supporters.

Despite assurances from the governor of the loyalty and reliability of the police force, the colonial government was concerned about the presence of PPP supporters in the force and the negative effect this could have on its dependability should there be public resistance to the course of events (St. Pierre 1999). British troops were considered necessary in order to ensure internal security, and on October 8, 1953, a battalion of British troops landed in the colony to assist in the maintenance of law and order in the event that there was violent resistance. Under emergency orders giving the police expanded powers of arrest, detention, and search, the police were openly deployed for purely political purposes, designed to neutralize and contain the Marxist revolutionary potential and the popularity of the PPP. Political meetings throughout the country were banned. PPP violators of the emergency regulations banning public meetings and demonstrations were arrested by police and imprisoned. The headquarters of the PPP and the homes of PPP leaders were constantly raided by police in search of communist materials (Jagan 1997).

Thirteen PPP leaders identified as potential "troublemakers" were arrested and detained without trial. After they were eventually released, they and many other PPP leaders, including Cheddi Jagan, were placed under constant surveillance, and their mobility was restricted to the districts in which they lived. Some of them were required to report daily to the police, upon pain of imprisonment. Jagan was arrested by the police for traveling 35 miles out of his restricted area (Georgetown) to work at the branch dental surgery that he operated in Mahaicony. He was later imprisoned for five months on this charge. The restrictions on his mobility lasted for three years (Jagan 1997). The police cast a wide net that included not only the PPP leaders but any of their supporters who happened to be present, and as a result many innocent people were unjustly arrested and imprisoned. Jagan characterized the country during this period as a "police state," and even the anticommunist media were loud in their condemnation of police tactics during this period (Jagan 1997, 149–52).

Acts of Omission and "Soft Tolerance": The Policing of Public Order (1962–1963)

The British government attempted to alleviate the political crisis created by the suspension of the Waddington Constitution by holding national elections under a new constitution in 1957, which resulted in a resounding victory for the PPP. Cheddi Jagan, however, was laboring under significant constitutional limitations. During the interim period, a split had taken place in the PPP and the party was now divided along racial lines with the African-dominated section, led by L. F. S. Burnham, becoming the main opposition force in the country. That breakaway segment of the PPP eventually changed its name to the People's National Congress (PNC) and contested the 1961 elections, which were again won by Jagan's PPP. Jagan was expected to lead the country to independence, a matter that troubled the British authorities greatly. The PPP now had to contend with both the colonial government and the PNC.

In 1962 antigovernment riots erupted as a result of opposition to the socialist-oriented economic policies of Jagan's PPP. Public demonstrations and a major general strike called by the Trade Union Congress (TUC), including the Civil Service Association, crippled both the private and public sectors of the economy. Members of the opposition political parties (the PNC and United Force [UF]) took to the streets and called for the resignation of the PPP government (HMSO 1962). On the morning of February 15, the government issued a proclamation (under Section 6 of the Public Order Act of 1955) banning public meetings and assemblies in designated areas around the capital, Georgetown, where the public protests were taking place.

The decisions taken by the governor and the commissioner of police regarding the deployment of the police during this period stand in sharp contrast to those made to enforce the emergency regulations during the period of the suspension of the constitution and the removal of Jagan from office in 1953. On the same day that the 1962 proclamation went into effect, the leader of the People's National Congress, L. F. S. Burnham, and the leader of the United Force, Peter D'Aguiar, openly defied the law and led processions through the restricted areas of the city. Despite a warning from Assistant Commissioner Phoenix, the two opposition processions met outside the government buildings, ignoring the riot squad and other senior officers who were present. No attempt was made by the police to arrest the opposition leaders or to take any punitive action against them (HMSO 1962). It soon became clear that the police were demonstrating their approval of the behavior of the anti-PPP strikers by practicing "soft tolerance." Cheddi Jagan, on the other hand, considered such an open defiance of the law to warrant the intervention of the army, but the colonial governor would have none of it (Jagan 1997).

Predictably, the restraint and calm exercised by the police emboldened the demonstrators, who became more assertive in their defiance of the police and their apparent determination to oust the Jagan government from office through undemocratic means. There is no question that the heavily armed, militarized police were capable of enforcing the proclamation, but no such orders were forthcoming from the colonial governor or the commissioner of police. Instead, the governor appealed to the two opposition leaders to "use [their] influence and advise the people to desist from acts of violence and to

... ask the people to leave the streets." Both of the opposition leaders replied that they could not comply with this request (HMSO 1962).

On February 16, which came to be known as "Black Friday," crowds were allowed to gather outside an electricity power plant where scabs were suspected to be working, and they were joined by a group who had attended a meeting at the parade ground held by one of the opposition leaders, Peter D'Aguiar. They stoned the building and jeered the riot squad who came on the scene. The crowd was allowed to disrupt attempts by an officer to arrest a stonethrower, who was promptly set free. Eventually the police used tear gas in an attempt to disperse the crowd, but the crowd's acts of defiance were not yet over, and they became incensed when a rumor circulated that a child had died from smoke inhalation. (In fact, the child had been only slightly injured and had been rushed to the hospital by police.)

Angry crowds converged on the headquarters of the PPP, shattering windows with bottles, stones, and other missiles. Police reinforcements were called out but were met with automatic rifle fire from snipers, which injured two officers (one of whom later died from his injuries), two corporals, and a constable. The police exchanged shots with the snipers but no definitive attempt was made to restore order. The crowds quickly realized that they had the upper hand and surged forward, overturning cars, extracting gasoline and setting stores and businesses on fire. The disorder spread throughout the business center of the city. Firemen were attacked and some of their hoses were cut as they attempted to put out fires. Looters emptied stores while the police looked on, unwilling to intervene. It was only after it became clear that the disturbances threatened to engulf the entire city that the decision was made to request the assistance of British troops in order to restore order. At the end of the episode, one superintendent of police and four demonstrators were dead, forty-one persons had been injured, several vehicles belonging to the police and members of the public had been damaged, and property damage caused by arson and looting totaled in excess of $11 million (Jagan 1997, Reno 1964, HMSO 1962).

On April 18, 1963, the Trade Union Council again called a general strike, this time against the introduction of the Labor Relations Bill by the PPP government. The Civil Service Association joined the strike, which lasted eighty days and was supported by the opposition political parties. During the strike, workers engaged in various protest activities, conducted demonstrations, and squatted in front of government offices and homes of government officials. A state of emergency was again declared, and the police resorted to using tear gas grenades that were sometimes promptly hurled back at them by crowds (Campbell 1987). Jagan records many instances where he prevailed upon the commissioner of police to disperse riotous crowds, and implement the proclamation to restore order, all to no avail (1997). Several requests were made for the assistance of the British army in restoring order, but they were rebuffed by the colonial governor, who suggested that the withdrawal of the Labor Relations Bill was the only way that the disturbances would end. Crowds repeatedly assembled around the government buildings where the office of Premier Jagan was located, and on several occasions, despite Jagan's pleas, the commissioner of police was unable to disperse them. During one incident, a government minister was savagely beaten and Jagan, along with the police and bodyguards escorting him from his office, was stoned by angry mobs. Under the watchful eyes of the police, demonstrators armed themselves with weapons (galvanized pipe, sticks with nails embedded in them, and motorcycle chains) and defied the emergency regulations prohibiting public processions and meetings. Incidences of rioting, beatings, looting, arson, and even bombings became commonplace. When the strike was eventually called off on July 6, 1963, the police reported that nine murders, forty-three bomb incidents, thirty-six cases of arson, and seventeen cases of attempted arson had taken place (Campbell 1987). In addition, many strikebreakers and East Indian citizens and government officials had suffered beatings at the hands of the protesters (Jagan, 1987).

Policing the 1964 Race Riots

In 1964 the Guyana Agricultural Workers Union (GAWU) called a strike in pursuance of union recognition for workers at Plantation Leonora. The sugar planters recruited mainly Africans from Georgetown to replace the striking East Indian workers, and it was alleged that the African scabs were transported by the predominantly African police, who "cooperated with the African vigilantes in terrorizing the strikers who squatted at strategic points" (Jagan 1997, 306). Persistent race baiting that had taken place between the leaders of the PPP and the opposition PNC throughout the period of protest against Jagan's economic policies had fueled ethnic rivalry between the supporters of the East Indian–dominated PPP and the African-dominated PNC. What started as an industrial dispute took a violent turn when a bomb was thrown into a bus transporting scabs to Plantation Albion, where workers were also on strike, and two laborers were killed.

Racial tensions exploded into open warfare between blacks and East Indians, starting on the west coast of Demerara and spreading throughout the country. Homes and businesses were bombed and blacks and East Indians beaten, raped, tortured, and murdered openly in attacks and counterattacks. In spite of the chaos that prevailed in the country, there is no evidence of any concerted action by the police to restore order. An attempt was made, however, to reduce the number of weapons in circulation with the enforcement of emergency regulations requiring the surrender of all arms. Searches were conducted on the homes of both PPP and PNC activists, and in the case of the latter, one such search resulted in the seizure of a large quantity of arms and ammunition (Jagan 1997, Campbell 1987). As far as police activity toward the maintenance of public safety, scrutiny was focused on East Indian strikers who were picketing the estates where they worked. Jagan cites examples of the East Indian squatters and striking workers being teargassed, beaten, arrested, and even shot while little attention was paid to developing a strategy to neutralize rioters engaged in reprisal attacks (1997). Nor was any assistance forthcoming from the colonial governor, who constantly refused the PPP government's requests for the assistance of British troops to restore order and instead advised Jagan to resign (Jagan 1997.

One of the worst incidents of discriminatory treatment by police occurred in the Mackenzie/Wismar area, a predominantly black mining town, where almost all of the businesses were owned and operated by East Indians. A motor launch owned by one of the few black Mackenzie businessmen, the *Sun Chapman*, was bombed a few miles from its destination on its journey from Georgetown to Wismar, resulting in the death of over forty persons, most of whom were of African descent. In the angry reprisal attacks that followed, all the East Indians (about 1,800 persons) were violently driven out of Mackenzie/Wismar by blacks, and their homes and businesses were looted and burned while black police stood by and witnessed the murderous rampage, largely refusing to intervene. It was the most blatant case of police apathy and racially motivated dereliction of duty during the disturbances. The Minister of Home Affairs laid the blame for the tragic course of events squarely on the shoulders of the commissioner of police, who despite her repeated requests refused to send police reinforcements and/or British troops to Mackenzie/Wismar, even after she informed him that the situation "had gone beyond control" (Jagan 1997, 309). Without operational control of the force, the minister could do nothing, and she subsequently resigned in protest.

Race-based reprisals continued after the Mackenzie/Wismar incident, and when the disturbances finally ended after more than three months of ethnic violence, 176 people had been killed and 920 injured. An estimated 15,000 persons had been forced to move from their homes and resettle in ethnic communities of their own kind, and damage to property was estimated at several million dollars (Jagan 1997, 311). The police have never taken responsibility for their failure to take action where action was required during the disturbances. Their dereliction of duty was politically motivated and deliberately executed without regard for their responsibility to protect human life and prevent the destruction of property. The events that took place during the 1964 riots demonstrate the grave consequences that can result from a negative act, or an act of omission, in the policing of public order.

Conclusion and Recommendations

Political policing during the Jagan years took the form of the deliberate neglect of one of the basic functions of the police, the maintenance of public order and safety, in order to force a democratically elected government out of office. Jagan fully understood that the colonial office was responsible for his inability to exercise operational control over the security forces in the country, but he clearly underestimated the consequences of decades of politicization of the police force. Even if the PPP had been given operational control of the police, a command may not have been sufficient to reverse the effect of decades of loyalty to the metropolitan power and the consequences of racial cleavages that were fostered by racial imbalances in the force.

In order to be effective with the police, the PPP would have had to find strategies to overcome the allegiances of a white commissioner and deputy commissioner of police and white and colored officers whose loyalties were most likely with the Colonial Office. With regard to the rank and file, there is little evidence that the government would have fared any better. During the 1962 disturbances, the police had threatened to join the strike against the PPP government's budget proposals. In addition, several members of the predominantly black force had refused to take up arms against the demonstrators in Georgetown (who were mostly of African descent) when ordered to do so by senior ranks, and were subsequently subjected to disciplinary action (Jagan 1997, Campbell 1987). Similarly, it is extremely unlikely that the predominantly black rank and file would not have felt sympathy for their own kith and kin who were being attacked and murdered by East Indians during the race riots of 1964. It was only after the riots ended that a commission of inquiry was appointed to investigate racial problems in the public service, including the police force (International Commission of Jurists 1965). By the time its report was released in 1965, the PPP was out of office.

Political policing in Guyana did not end with the termination of Jagan's term in office after the 1964 general elections. It continued during the entire period of postindependence governance under the PNC led by Forbes Burnham. The force will remain a potential political weapon to be used in pursuance of unpopular statist goals unless fundamental changes are made in the definition of the role of the police, and there is a return to traditional civilian policing practices and methods. Decades of politicization cannot be easily reversed, but attention can be paid to resolving the current crisis in police-community relations, especially in relations with the East Indian community. Urgent measures also need to be taken to redefine the role and function of the police. These measure would neutralize the antagonistic, power-driven "us versus them" control subculture of militarized policing in pursuance of a more cooperative, public service orientation that recognizes the role of citizens as coproducers of police services.

The experience of Guyana provides an example of the special challenges faced by police operating in multicultural communities. Police forces in such communities need to develop the capability to mediate and resolve the intergroup conflicts that can result from ethnic, religious, or cultural differences and the competition for scarce economic resources. In Guyana, conflict between East Indians and blacks was both the result of historical factors and the exploitation of ethnic differences by the two major political parties (PPP and PNC) in their quest for political power. The ability to manage the resulting conflict is a crucial part of the peacekeeping function of the police (DeGeneste and Sullivan 1997), and attention must be paid to developing strategies to prevent intergroup conflict from degenerating into ethnic warfare. In order to be able to achieve these goals, the police must bridge the gap that divides them from the communities they serve, and replace the distrust and fear that separates them from the community with the confidence and security that comes from respect for the rights and dignity of all citizens and their entitlement to protection and fair treatment under the law. In pursuance of this objective, urgent attention needs to be directed toward first, correcting the ethnic imbalance in the police force and second, reforming the current community policing initiatives to implement tactical and organizational measures that can result in improved police-community relations.

Correcting the Ethnic Imbalance in the Force

The police force has always reflected a significant underrepresentation of East Indians compared to their numbers in the general population. In 1965, East Indians comprised only 18.4 percent of the force although their percentage in the population was estimated at around 50 percent in 1960; meanwhile, blacks comprised 74.9 percent of the force although they made up only about 30 percent of the population at that time (ICJ Report 1965). The underrepresentation was also significant in the higher ranks. In a multicultural society such as Guyana, it is imperative that the police reflect and respect the racial diversity of the communities that they serve. As a general principle this is well recognized, but it is an absolute necessity in communities where ethnic polarization is pervasive. Although no public opinion polls are available, the level of distrust and fear of the police in the East Indian community of Guyana is likely to have a negative effect on the ability of the police to form partnerships with the community for conflict resolution and problem solving.

In its report, the International Commission of Jurists made several recommendations for increasing the intake of East Indians in the force (1965), but the imbalance appears to have persisted. In 1995, the Minister of Home Affairs agreed that there was still a significant underrepresentation of East Indians in the force and further stated that there was no official policy to increase the number of East Indians by the use of racial quotas or other such measures. The minister also confirmed that members of the force were still being selected on the usual competitive basis from the pool of applicants received, regardless of race. The Guyana government needs to take affirmative action to increase the representation of East Indians in the force. An affirmative action plan should be based on the degree of underrepresentation of East Indians, which could be determined by conducting a census of current employees in the public service in general. Positive steps must then be taken to attract more East Indians to the force and to promote East Indians to higher ranks in greater numbers. As the ICJ report suggested, it may be necessary to use racial quotas until the imbalance is corrected. This method has been used either as a court-ordered remedy or a voluntary measure to correct the underrepresentation of minorities in several police departments in the United States, and it was found to be very successful (Walker 1999).

Reforming Current Community Policing Initiatives

The Guyana police force has maintained community policing groups for several years and at the end of 1996 reported that there were 434 volunteer community policing groups. These groups operate in divisions and "provide (d) service within their own communities by maintaining effective patrols with Police Ranks" (Guyana Police Force 1996, 17). No further information concerning the activities of the community policing groups is provided in the *Annual Reports*, but they have been accused repeatedly of operating like vigilantes, without being subject to the liabilities of regular members of the force. They are allowed to carry arms and have been involved in shooting deaths and other acts of excessive force and violence, such as the chopping and beating of citizens, sometimes in the presence of police officers (Guyana Human Rights Association 1994 and 1999). They have also been accused of attacking opposition political activists (Guyana Human Rights Association 1999). Instead of improving community-police relations, this type of community policing will result in more distrust of the police and a widening of the rift between the police and the community.

In addition to the need to put an end to what is apparently criminal and illegal behavior by community policing groups, the Guyana police force needs to reform its entire program to incorporate concrete initiatives that could bridge the gap between the police and the community and inspire confidence in the force. This would necessitate a reversal of the "control" mode and the cultivation of an entirely new philosophy of policing that is based on the delivery of services to the community as a whole. On a tactical level, the police must seize opportunities for positive interaction with citizens, and create partnerships and joint projects with the community that would develop problem-identification and problem-solving skills. Solutions must be obtained by including all members of the community. The police must also be willing to collaborate with community organizations or other service providers when necessary. Despite ethnic or cultural differences, citizens have similar needs for safety and protection, and the police can find common interests around which to organize collaborative community participation.

The organizational dimension requires changes to be made in the structure and management of the force to facilitate the ability of officers to deliver services to the community. The current rigid hierarchical structure would need to be "flattened" in order to provide some freedom in the use of staff and resources to accomplish long-term goals. Management duties should include not only continuous strategic planning, but also the supervision and mentoring of junior officers with emphasis placed on ethics, respect for cultural differences, human rights, and the rule of law. Interracial teams of officers should be used to conduct problem-solving exercises or implement projects whenever possible.

Cheddi Jagan's People's Progressive Party was successful in the national elections in Guyana in 1992, and has repeatedly expressed its commitment to maintaining the independence of the force and addressing the problems facing the police establishment. Foremost among the concerns were the depoliticization of the force, correcting racial imbalances, and fostering better police-community relations. Jagan adopted an open policy with regard to entertaining suggestions regarding the improvement of police operations, but he passed away before any concrete steps could be taken to improve the record of the Guyana police force.

References

Alderson, John. 1998. *Principled Policing: Proecting the Public with Integrity.* Winchester, Mass.: Waterside Press.

Bayley, David M., ed. 1977. *Police and Society.* Beverly Hills, Calif: Sage.

British Guiana Constitutional Report of 1951. The Waddington Report.

British Guiana Constitutional Report of 1954. The Robertson Report.

Brown, M. Craig, and Barbara D. Warner. 1995. "The Political Threat of Immigrant Groups and Police Aggressiveness in 1900." In *Ethnicity, Race, and Crime: Perspectives across Time and Space,* ed. Darnell F. Hawkins. Albany: State University of New York Press.

Campbell, John. 1987. *History of Policing in Guyana.* Georgetown, Guyana: Guyana Police Force.

Chevigny, Paul. 1995. *Edge of the Knife: Police Violence in the Americas.* New York: Free Press.

Danns, George K. 1982. *Domination and Power in Guyana: A Study of the Police in a Third World Context.* New Brunswick, N.J.: Transaction, Inc.

DeGeneste, Henry I., and John P. Sullivan. 1997. *Policing a Multicultural Community.* Washington, D.C.: Perf Publications.

Enloe, Cynthia H. 1980. *Police, Military, and Ethnicity: Foundations of State Power.* New Brunswick, N.J.: Transaction, Inc.

Fogelson, Robert M. 1977. *Big City Police.* Cambridge: Harvard University Press.

Guyana Human Rights Association. 1994. "Press Release: Police Encourage Shootings." Georgetown, Guyana: Guyana Human Rights Association.
———. 1999. "Press Release: Community Policing Must Be Politically Impartial." Georgetown, Guyana: Guyana Human Rights Association.
Guyana Police Force. 1996. *Guyana Police Force Annual Report.* Georgetown, Guyana: Guyana Police Force.
Her Majesty's Stationary Office (HMSO). 1954. *Robertson Commission Report.* London: Colonial Office.
———. 1962. *The Wynn Parry Commission Report.* London: Colonial Office.
Huggins, Martha K. 1991. *Vigilantism and the State in Modern Latin America: Essays on Extra-Legal Violence.* Westport, Conn.: Praeger.
———. 1998. *Political Policing: The United States and Latin America.* Durham: Duke University Press.
International Commission of Jurists. 1965. *Report of the British Guiana Commission of Inquiry, Racial Problems in the Public Service.* Geneva, Switzerland: ICJ
Jagan, Cheddi. 1997. *The West on Trial: My Fight for Guyana's Freedom.* St. John's, Antigua: Hansib Caribbean.
Jeffries, Sir Charles. 1952. *The Colonial Police.* London: Max Parrish and Co.
Manning, Peter K. 1977. *Police Work: The Social Organization of Policing.* Cambridge: MIT Press.
Moore, Brian. 1987. *Race, Power, and Social Segmentation in Colonial Society: Guyana after Slavery, 1838–1891.* New York: Gordon and Breach Science Pub., Ltd.
Reno, Philip. 1964. *The Ordeal Of British Guiana.* New York: Monthly Review Press.
Rodney, Walter. 1981. *A History of the Guyanese Working People, 1881–1905.* Baltimore: Johns Hopkins University Press.
Rodway, James A. 1891. *A History of British Guiana from the Year 1668 to the Present Time.* 3 vols. Georgetown: J. Thompson.
Shahabuddeen, M. 1978. *Constitutional Developments in Guyana: 1621–1978.* Georgetown: Guyana Printers, Ltd.
Smith, Phillip Thurmond. 1985. *Policing Victorian London: Political Policing, Public Order, and the London Metropolitan Police.* Westport, Conn.: Greenwood Press.
Smith, R. T. 1962. *British Guiana.* London: Oxford University Press.
———. 1980. *British Guiana.* Westport, Conn.: Greenwood Press.
St. Pierre, Maurice. 1999. *Anatomy of Resistance.* London: Macmillan Education, Ltd.
Turk, Austin. 1982. *Political Criminality: The Defiance and Defense of Authority.* Beverly Hills: Sage.
Walker, Samuel. 1999. *The Police in America.* Boston: McGraw-Hill.

PART II
Labor-Politics Nexus

6

Guyana, Jamaica, and the Cold War Project: The Transformation of Caribbean Labor

HILBOURNE WATSON

The cold war project can be treated as a strategy orchestrated and directed by the United States in the international political economy for restructuring the material, economic, geopolitical, ideological, and national security foundations and processes of world capitalism. As a "project," it involved much more than East-West ideological conflict, more than geopolitics, and more than military realignments and competition. At its core, it was the project that energized Franklin D. Roosevelt's "fifth freedom" into a U.S.-centric definition and that orchestrated a national security right to "enjoy unimpeded access to labor, land, resources, and markets" on a world scale (Landau 1988, 40). It assumed the status of an idea beyond reality that legitimated and articulated an American notion of freedom that was designed to elicit worldwide resonance. It was the crowning principle for postwar American hegemony. The United States normalized the "right" to dominate and exploit by extolling the rhetoric of democratic freedoms, thereby masking the real substantive intent of Roosevelt's fifth freedom.

The real nature and purpose of the strong American state has largely been hidden from view. Actually, Americans have habituated themselves to a view of their government (and therefore of desirable governments) as embodying the Lockean notion of the depoliticized, neutral, civil (domestic) state, while the real American state has operated in the world as a hegemonic state. The American state is a globally embedded capitalist state that employs a variety of means to get the rest of the world to consume all manner of U.S. exports, including U.S. forms of political organization, trade union models, and culture (see Cummings 1998, 49). All of this has been backed by a vast coercive military capability and the economic and financial mechanisms for extracting surplus value and accumulating capital within and outside its borders, in order to dictate to the world (Wallerstein 1983, 56–57). The "project" of the cold war masked this reality, stressing the moral idea and purpose of freedom beyond materiality, much like the idea of the abstract universality.

Class and social-class relations of production, within which organized labor is included in this essay, have been central to the relationship between the cold war and the former British West Indies (BWI) and the Commonwealth Caribbean countries. In arguing that BWI labor was transformed into an agent of cold war globalization, it is necessary to take the issue of labor beyond its generic meaning to its social-class composition in the contradictory capital–wage labor relation in which the working class is reproduced.

Under capitalism labor power is commodified, and capital harnesses labor power to facilitate its own organization and reproduction: the normal organization of capital necessitates the disorganization and control of the working class. Capital and the state have a direct interest in disorganizing the working class due to the historical necessity of exploitation for capital accumulation. The accumulation of capital requires the "extended reproduction of labor power," which calls for a wage rate that presupposes the existence of a state to mediate the "procreation of labor power" (Rueten and Williams 1989, 89). Labor politics and the trade union movement can be examined to see how the capital–wage labor relation mediates the labor process and class struggle in social reproduction. The state is itself deeply implicated in this mediation process, for the state, like capital, has a direct interest in the exploitation of the working class. It is appropriate to go beyond the bureaucratic relationship between the BWI and CARICOM labor movement and organized labor in the United States, and specify the larger American strategy for reorganizing the territorial spatial relations in the productive base of world capitalism, along East-West and North-South trajectories.

The postwar experiences of countries like Guyana and Jamaica can be used to denaturalize experience relating it to material conditions and locating it in the labor relations within historical capitalist relations of production. The United States used Guyana under the late Cheddi Jagan and the People's Progressive Party (PPP) from 1953 to 1964, and Jamaica under the late

Michael Manley and the People's National Party (PNP) from 1972 to 1980, as two sites where it tested its cold war national security doctrine and strategy. Examination of key aspects of the larger BWI twentieth-century experience shows how those colonies were targeted for, and integrated into, cold war globalization decades before independence.

National states can be viewed as particular historical political formations that manage the heterogeneous geography of the global economy. States do more than extract surplus value, monopolize means of violence, and make societies pay for their own domination as protection; they also reproduce themselves by processing world capitalist social relations of production, largely via the agency of sovereignty, for which there already necessarily exists an international system of states. The essay ends with an analysis of the deepening of the integration of CARICOM trade unions into neoliberal globalization, which I see as part of the restructuring of the cold war project.

Restructuring the Cold War Project

The end of certain military, geopolitical, and ideological aspects of the cold war has produced a deafening neoliberal rhetoric: that the cold war favored national security concerns, defined in military and geopolitical respects, while the "end of the cold war" means a new focus on markets, trade, civil society, and democracy. Such an argument has the effect of masking the real nature of the cold war project of world capitalism and stifling theoretical analysis. In order to demystify such a claim as it relates to the Caribbean, the role of Latin American and Caribbean (LAC) states in the cold war project, as defined under the Inter-American Treaty of Reciprocal Assistance (Rio Treaty) of 1947, should be examined. The Rio Treaty defined very broadly national security threats to American republics. Article 6 of the Rio Treaty defines a national security threat as "an act of aggression that is not an armed attack . . . or any other fact or situation that might endanger the peace of America." The Rio Treaty asserted the primacy of the property rights of international capital, starting with U.S. capital, and capital's right to property income. In that context, the Rio Treaty defined as a national security threat any act by a state, political party, labor organization, or other group that the United States might deem inimical to world capitalism and its geopolitics. From the angle of the working class, the Rio Treaty posed a mortal threat to revolutionary nationalist or socialist strategies of transformation.

Bloomfield argues that the United States did not envisage

> a direct armed military intervention by the Soviet Union but rather the installation in one of the American republics of a regime friendly to the Soviet Union. In the years that followed, the United States response to political movements that looked to the Soviet Union for support or seemed to be headed in that direction, or that Washington deliberately and maliciously characterized thus . . . was to try to prevent them from coming to power, or, if they succeeded in doing so, to overthrow them. (1998, 123)

The Rio Treaty inscribed the first antidemocratic and antiproletarian feature of the U.S. national security project to reinforce the integration of all the American republics into postwar capitalism. The Rio Treaty was tested in Guatemala in 1954, when the United States got the Organization of American States (OAS) to resolve that the "domination or control of the political institutions of any American state by the International Communist Movement would endanger the security of the hemisphere" (Bloomfield 1998, 123). The United States had a similar attitude toward Guyana and the Cuban revolution.

In 1991, the OAS adopted Resolution 1080 (Santiago Commitment) as part of the restructuring of the cold war project in the Americas. OAS Resolution 1080 requires the OAS and its member states to defend against "threats" to state sovereignty and democracy in any American republic (Bloomfield 1998, 126) in ways that are reminiscent of the Rio Treaty strategy. If the Rio Treaty legitimated the cold war project in the LAC region, then OAS Resolution 1080 marked the restructuring of the cold war project in the region. This is happening with the restructuring of the Western hemisphere political economy, including the further integration of national states via economic integration, their production systems, markets, labor forces, financial and communications systems, and geopolitical and military arrangements. The restructuring of the cold war now brings into the open national security issue areas like drugs (see Griffith, this volume), the environment, and human rights that were there all along but were eclipsed by the way ideology-conditioned cold war national security thinking about the world. Ideological conditioning was also shaped by realist views of the relationship between the inside and outside of national states.

OAS Resolution 1080 stresses reciprocal collective security and puts left-wing groups and revolutionary regimes like Cuba's on notice. Resolution 1080 places the burden on Caribbean states to protect capitalism, bourgeois democracy, and national sovereignty at a time when neoliberal capitalism accelerates the shifting of key areas of national decision making to the hemispheric and global levels. This shift signals the deepening of capitalist globalization, which also intensifies the necessary decomposition of national states and their societies. Resolution 1080 makes the protection of capital's interests and rights the primary focus of national sovereignty. The idea that economies, markets, and democracy have moved into higher priority over cold war national (military) security is an ideological deception, for the cold war project was never constructed around any dichotomies between national (military) security and economies or markets. The cold war project always has been a characteristically antiproletarian imperialist project, whose ideological representation has had the effect of masking the true class nature of capitalism, largely on account of the dominance of ideological interpretations of world change.

Bourgeois democracy is antiproletarian; yet representative democracy is renewed by popular contention from among the working class. The bourgeoisie cannot be committed to participatory (direct) democracy because of the implications for the ownership of the means of production. Representative democracy is convenient for the bourgeoisie because it fits neatly with the inevitable deepening of the socialization of capitalist production, although indirect representation is contradicted by the deepening of the private character of the appropriation of surplus value. Hence, the bourgeoisie will endorse indirect democracy (see Tilly 1997, 193–244 passim) so long as it does not undermine private appropriation, capital accumulation, and bourgeois class power in state and society. In effect, it is a form of deception to suggest that there was/is any dichotomy between the cold war, in relation to national security, and the end of the cold war, in relation to markets and civil society. In reality, all state-market relationships under capitalism reflect specific historical forms of state regulation to reproduce bourgeois economic power and political rule (see Gramsci 1971, 160).

The experiences of Guyana and Jamaica demonstrate that the United States has practiced different forms of low-intensity warfare along the lines of the Rio Treaty to shape outcomes in global geopolitics and protect global capitalist accumulation. Historically, American leaders have been conscious of the fact that the survival of capitalism at home is directly dependent on securing capital accumulation on a world scale: herein lies the secret behind Roosevelt's "fifth freedom." The United States carried out low-intensity warfare against Guyana (1953–64), Jamaica (1974–80), Grenada (1979–83), and Nicaragua during the Sandinista revolution. Low-intensity warfare has been broad in scope, ranging from psychological and economic warfare to outright counterrevolutionary activities against progressive and revolutionary regimes or groups with the aim of restructuring the internal political and social balance in a targeted country. Tactics have included blockade, embargo, sabotage, and media propaganda, as well as providing military training, weapons, and material support to counterrevolutionary forces and even direct military action with the aim of giving the United States a strategic advantage.

Low-intensity warfare aggravates the instability that is inherent in capitalism, and it is unsatisfactory to suggest that instability is a function of explicit acts of "destabilizaton" the way Mars (1984), Kaufman (1985) and Stephens and Stephens (1986) have, though there is plausibility to their assertions. But so-called destabilization tends to aggravate the instability that is already present as a function of the anarchical and contradictory nature of the fundamental capitalist process mediated by market forces, which are themselves socially constructed and deeply conditioned by politics. Kaufman (1985, 185–89) and Stephens and Stephens (1986, 135–37, 250) stress the role of internal forces, including opposition parties, business interests, the police and military, trade unions, religious organizations, the media, and other interests in producing destabilization in Jamaica under Michael Manley (1972–80). Manley (1982), Maurice Bishop, and Cheddi Jagan (Searle 1984, 121–52) also defined destabilization as part of an imperialist design to control the Caribbean, by undermining and/or overthrowing governments by means of political, ideological, and propaganda measures. By treating destabilization as a subset within the context of the Rio Treaty, it is possible to understand its place in the cold war project of world capitalist restructuring and hegemonic assertion by the United States in the LAC region.

During the 1980s, the concept and strategy of "wars of low-intensity conflict" was introduced and emerged within U.S. military and intelligence circles to inform shifts in the national security doctrine, with special reference to the Third World. The low-intensity conflict concept encompassed a broader array of activities and conditions than assumed under the "destabilization" concept (NACLA 1986; Jaramillo 1987; Manley 1982, 210–12). The U.S. military defined low-intensity conflict as "all out war at the grassroots level" in the cold war competition and confrontations in the Third World. The Pentagon described low-intensity conflict goals and objectives as follows: "Our range of activities at the lower end of the conflict spectrum includes support to nations facing insurgent threats and to groups resisting communist aggression, peace keeping operations; peace time contingency operations; and counterterrorism efforts" (Carlucci 1989, 21). Manley informed PNP cadres that the methods of the low-intensity conflict strategy involved "Psychological operations [that] are actions destined to influence foreign nations" and are carried out in "peace time or in places other than war theatres . . . to influence the feelings, attitudes, behavior of foreign groups in a manner favourable to the achievements of the policies of the United States" (Manley 1982, 210–11; see also U.S. Army Joint Low-Intensity Conflict Project 1986, Morelli and Ferguson 1984, Hosmer 1987). The U.S. position is that its national security interests are globally configured and call for a multifaceted strategy with multidimensional programs that blur the lines between the national and international in all areas of life in the affected countries. Clearly, the material and social context of low-intensity wars lies in global capitalism and capital accumulation and the necessary configuration of imperialist geopolitics.

Historical Basis of U.S. Intervention in BWI Working-Class Struggles

The United States began to interfere in the internal affairs of the former BWI colonies soon after the republic was founded (see Garcia-Muqiz and Borges, 1998). Statements by Thomas Jefferson and Theodore Roosevelt have conditioned the ideology of Manifest Destiny and expansionism around the sovereignty-of-violence paradigm that depicts realist ideology, which girds capitalist imperialism. Manifest Destiny formed part of a U.S.-invented tradition about human nature, war making, state making, surplus extraction for capital accumulation, and legitimation in terms that call to mind Charles Tilly's concept of state making as "organized crime" (Tilly 1997, 165–91). The United States began to flex its economic, financial, and political muscles in the Caribbean at a time that was more or less coincident with the decline of Britain. Soon after, businesses in the BWI began to sense that closer economic ties with the United States would be in their interests (Joseph 1973, 24–30; Pratt 1951; Baptiste, 1978, 16–17; Garcia-Muqiz and Borges 1998).

Between 1846 and 1989, the United States intervened in several LAC countries for a total of seventy intervention years, with a view to projecting its national security (capitalist and geopolitical) interests. From the outset, the exercise of sovereignty by LAC states "meant asking U.S. permission before making changes in economic or foreign policy" (Landau 1988, 17). The Cuban revolution violated that understanding reiterated in the Rio Treaty. LAC states are the unambiguous expression of national states that use sovereign autonomy to process the property relations of global capitalism (Watson 1998b). Former U.S. Marine Corps general Smedley Butler summed up his role and experience as a gangster-racketeer and muscle man for U.S. imperialism and American capital in the LAC region. He said:

> During [my thirty-three years in the Marine Corps] I spent most of my time being a high-class muscle man for Big Business, for Wall Street and for the bankers.... I was a racketeer for capitalism.... I helped make Haiti and Cuba a decent place for the National City Bank.... I helped purify Nicaragua for the international banking house of Brown Brothers in 1909–1912. I brought light to the Dominican Republic for American sugar interests in 1916. I helped make Honduras "right" for American United Fruit Companies in 1903. (Landau 1988, 19)

These and other such activities gave the United States a tacit protectorate over the region.

Clearly, the seventy intervention years in LAC countries from 1846 to 1989 shows that communism was not a precondition for U.S. intervention (Baptiste 1978, 37; Joseph 1973, 46–53). By the early twentieth century, U.S. capital had established a presence in bauxite in Guyana; in petroleum in Trinidad, the Dutch Antilles, Venezuela, and Colombia; and in civil aviation (Pan American Airways), agricultural production and shipping (United Fruit Company), trade, and military bases throughout the region (Baptiste 1978). After World War II, the U.S. presence intensified through the Anglo-American Caribbean Commission, which gave birth to the Puerto Rican model of postwar capitalist restructuring, that deepened the integration of the BWI into the U.S. political economy (Watson 1975).

Foreign military service by the West Indian Regiment in World War I exposed black military personnel to imperialism, and led to resistance movements in the BWI via trade unions and political parties, for example. Black anti-imperialist and revolutionary ideas in the BWI colonies attracted the attention of American diplomatic personnel. For example, the U.S. embassy in London informed the state department that the Communist International (COMINTERN) might have been "sending funds for the purpose of exploiting the labor disputes which had . . . occurred in Trinidad and Jamaica via the Communist Party of America's headquarters in New York" (Baptiste 1978, 37). The U.S. secret service also investigated the extent to which black American communists might have been involved in developing ties with black radical intellectuals and working-class groups in the BWI. The internationalization of the Marcus Garvey movement was also a trigger point in the development of black nationalist ideas and strategies among West Indians in the colonies and in the United States. A key theme that cannot be developed here is how the sojourn of West Indians in the United States conditioned their proletarianization and how U.S. imperialism responded to that proletarianization outside and in the connections back home (see James 1998).

The U.S. state department and the Central Intelligence Agency (CIA) gathered information about ties between the BWI trade union and workers movement and the black radical and Communist movements in the United States. The state department investigated the role of the U.S.-based National Negro Congress (NNC), which it described as "a united front organization . . . dominated by Communists and . . . the successor to the Communist League of Struggles for Negro Rights" (Naison 1988). The NNC had supported the struggles of diaspora blacks and had stressed issues of working-class consciousness and solidarity in the international working-class movement. In 1942, J. Edgar Hoover, director of the Federal Bureau of Investigation, informed Assistant Secretary of State Adolf Berle that the PNP was promoting "communist activities in Jamaica" with plans for a socialist Jamaica based on public ownership of essential means of production. Hoover stressed that the activities of the PNP were of interest to the United States, insofar as they bear on "American communistic organizations which have been closely allied to the PNP, the most prominent of such organizations being the Jamaica Progressive League and the West Indies National Council" (Manley 1984, 163).

Munroe argues that

> between 1940 and 1950, Marxism had developed in Jamaica beyond the mere theory to a practical movement with which the colonial state and local oligarchy had to actively contend. . . . The cold war gave Britain and the US added support to try to eradicate communist influence in

> the national and colonial movements in . . . the West Indies. In Jamaica, the offensive . . . opened up a new stage in the reconciliation of the Jamaican National Movement with imperialism. (1978, 69–70)

Monroe's argument confirms that the PNP and JLP adopted consensual strategies for governing and moved Jamaica squarely into the cold war camp in the transition from colonialism to neocolonialism (see also Mills 1988, 4: 1–24).

Very early in the postwar period, BWI business interests, the new political parties, most of the trade unions, and the core of the BWI intelligentsia became witting or unwitting agents of cold war globalization. They sought to control the BWI masses and refashion the anticolonial aspirations of the working class, the trade union movement, and other political formations that were emerging around them. Such was the environment in which Cheddi Jagan and Michael Manley came into trade union organizing activities and party politics in their respective countries.

American Organized Labor and BWI Labor Movement

The cold war project played a strategic role in triggering a number of crises in the BWI labor movement in the formative postwar period. Since World War II, the bureaucratic leadership of corporate unionism in the United States supported the militarization of the American economy by the state and corporate capital via the military-industrial complex (MIC), and helped to shape and direct cold war labor foreign policy and politics around the globe (see Herod 1997). The Taft-Hartley Act of 1947 normalized corporate unionism in the American labor movement (Radosh 1969, 452) via an alliance of organized labor, the U.S. government, and corporate capital that was buttressed by cold war ideology. Corporate unionism has advanced the interests of the leadership of the American trade union movement, and helped to execute a relentless and protracted cold war offensive against revolutionary forces of organized labor and working classes around the globe. Largely, American organized labor has portrayed communist and/or socialist regimes as irrational and alien forces in the international labor movement. American organized labor defined itself against the world working class, with a chauvinistic design and zeal to subject global labor to cold war imperialism and capital accumulation (Radosh 1969).

A number of postwar developments strengthened organized labor's role in the American strategy of containment and counterrevolution against communism that marked the Truman Doctrine. Kurzman argues that the American Federation of Labor (AF of L) and its successor the AFL-CIO developed their "own private network of ambassadors, administrators, and intelligence agents. Labor attachés or their assistants in key countries are often more loyal to the AFL-CIO than their diplomatic superiors. Many of [its] agents are believed to work closely with the Central Intelligence Agency" (1966, 29). Organized labor influenced the distribution of Marshal Plan funds in Europe and European colonies. European unions, including socialist and communist unions that belonged to the World Federation of Trade Unions (WFTU) faced a relentless attack from the AF of L and the CIA. The United States played a strategic role in creating the International Confederation of Free Trade Unions (ICFTU) to marginalize the WFTU (Lens 1965, 13; Radosh 1969, 304–47).

The Taft-Hartley Act of 1947 was yoked to the National Security Act to buttress the Truman Doctrine. This linkage made it easier to carry out the counterrevolutionary programs of the AF of L and later the AFL-CIO against workers around the world. Taft-Hartley serves as the battering ram of the American state and corporate capital against the American working class. McCarthyism legitimated the institutionalization of repressive tolerance against the working class to embed bourgeois hegemonic designs and consolidate the politics and geopolitics of capital accumulation. Lens agues that the leadership of the trade union movement helped deepen the integration of the working class into imperialism between 1945 and 1965, such that the AFL-CIO's international practices could be called "outside subversion. . . . [T]hey have . . . interfered in the internal affairs of sovereign states without being accountable for their acts to Congress, the . . . people, or . . . the American working class" (1965, 10). As a rule, the antiworking-class stance of the AFL-CIO in the cold war tended to be more strident than the state department's.

The AFL-CIO could do "what the U.S. Government does not do directly, because it would be flagrant meddling with the internal affairs of other nations, and what the CIA cannot do because it is suspect" and this allows the AFL-CIO to throw "its weight toward the making and unmaking of governments with the hope of instilling abroad the phobic anticommunism that has become entrenched at home" (Lens 1965, 11). The AFL-CIO employed similar strategies to desired effect in Guyana between 1953 and

1964. The United States used its hegemonic position to promote sovereign autonomy in the Third World under the United Nations system, but with the aim of broadening and deepening the global reach of American capital. Broadly, economic militarization, mass production, the internationalization of the dollar, credit expansion, and the export of capital and commodities complemented the strategy for deepening of the integration of the American working class in the cold war project along the lines of "Fordism" (see Gramsci 1971, 279–81, 310–13).

Military pacts such as the North Atlantic Treaty Organization (NATO) and the Inter-American Defense System (via the Rio Treaty) were designed to project U.S. military power and protect capital accumulation. The "UN Model" of sovereign independence was automatically yoked to economic dependence to protect the global scope of capital's right to property and property income. The U.S. government, American capital, and the AFL-CIO collaborated in building strong alliances with the oligarchs and dictators in the LAC region against revolutionary working-class organs and many trade unions, but could not stem the erosion of hegemony. Shortly after his 1972 inauguration, Richard Nixon confirmed that "the postwar order of international relations, the configuration of power that emerged from the Second World War" had passed, along with "the conditions which ... determined the assumptions and practices of United States foreign policy since 1945" (Landau 1988, 102). Nonetheless, American hegemony was still sufficiently strong to keep most Caribbean states, societies, businesses, and trade union movements yoked to cold war globalization.

The deepening crisis of the capital-wage labor relation that was aggravated by the Great Depression also influenced the BWI working-class revolts of the 1930s. Those revolts fueled the demand for political, economic, and constitutional reform and strengthened the trade union movement in the BWI, and made possible the rise of the Caribbean Labor Congress (CLC) in 1945. Some of the colonial intelligentsia that emerged as leaders of the new labor organizations and political parties were unreconstructed Anglophiles whose thinking never matured beyond the myth of the British Empire as a "moral idea of freedom."

In July 1945, the CLC celebrated its inaugural meeting in Barbados. Delegates like Grantley Adams (Barbados), Norman Manley and Richard Hart (Jamaica), Albert Gomes (Trinidad), Hubert Critchlow (Guyana), and others advocated the creation of a socialist Caribbean commonwealth to deal with the BWI economic, political, and social problems (Jagan 1967, 89). In

1948, Grantley Adams addressed the U.N. General Assembly and defended Britain and its moral idea of freedom (Watson 1975). Adam's action before the United Nations signaled the rapid pace at which the BWI trade union and political movements were being integrated into the cold war project. Adams and many of the others were colonial loyalists, whose class and political interests and sensibilities converged with the Anglo-American cold war interests in the Caribbean. Their pragmatic approach to West Indian self-government shared a structural compatibility with the moral logic of the British Empire and the American cold war project. Britain, having already acknowledged her own decline, guided the BWI fully into the American cold war project.

Britain and the United States demanded the withdrawal of BWI trade unions from the WFTU and pressured them to join the American-inspired ICFTU. Grantley Adams, who headed the CLC, proposed that the CLC be disbanded if total and unconditional compliance was not forthcoming. Jagan in Guyana and Richard Hart and a few others in Jamaica were the main recalcitrants. In Jamaica Norman Manley and the PNP expelled the Marxist left from the party and the trade union movement: they weakened the Trade Union Congress (TUC) and created the National Workers Union (NWU) in 1952 as part of their accommodation with the cold war. In those circumstances, there was going to be little or no sympathy from Manley, Adams, and the West Indian intelligentsia for Jagan or his plan for a revolutionary Guyana. The United States had brought the cold war into the heart of the decolonization process in the BWI and had obtained broad cooperation from the nationalist leadership in the trade union and political movement (see Baptiste 1978, Munroe 1978, Mills 1988). The cold war made a decisive impact and left a profound imprint on the strategy of modernization and independence in the BWI.

The Cold War Offensive and the Jamaican Working Class

The problems Michael Manley and the PNP encountered with the cold war project in the 1970s had incubated in the specific relationship the PNP had helped to construct within the cold war project decades earlier. Around World War II, the material and techno-industrial base of BWI capitalism operated on a relatively primitive techno-industrial base, with sugar, bauxite, and oil as the leading industries in the main colonies of Jamaica, Trinidad, and Guyana. There was no activity in modern science and technology or the research and development and capital goods industries that facilitates the development of a modern capitalist class and/or industrial proletariat with highly skilled, professional, and technical cadres of workers. Services associated with commerce, distribution, governmental activities, and domestic service coincided with plantation agriculture in the largely merchant capitalist culture.

The BWI intelligentsia helped to pave the way for American organized labor to influence the direction of the BWI labor movement and working-class politics. By the middle of the 1950s, the American Federation of Labor intensified the integration of Caribbean labor into the cold war project via CADORIT, the Caribbean subsidiary of Latin-American Regional Organization of Workers (ORIT), the CIA's surrogate in the Latin American labor movement. The British Guyana labor movement and working class bore the brunt of the offensive against the BWI labor movement between 1953 and 1964 (Jagan 1968, Spinner 1984). The main goal of the dominant tendencies within American organized labor was to undermine or neutralize any approach that was sympathetic to working-class struggle and promote alternative policies based on the corporate unionism strategy that characterized capital-wage labor relations in the United States (Radosh 1969, 304–47). Lens notes that AFL-CIO groups interfered in the internal affairs of Guyana to depose Cheddi Jagan (1965, 13). They supported right-wing labor leaders in the Dominican Republic, where they also participated in the overthrow of Juan Bosch in 1965–67. They worked with the military in Brazil to overthrow Goulart in 1964. They openly supported U.S. militarism in the region and helped to select "Meany-type" labor attachés for U.S. embassies in the LAC countries, in line with the American national security strategy of the Rio Treaty.

The financing of labor organizations and the training of labor leaders in LAC countries has been done under AFL-CIO auspices since the 1950s. The AFL-CIO labor foreign policy in the LAC region rested on the cold war constructs of "collective self-defense" against "foreign aggression" and "internal subversion" (Dietz 1984, 8). There is a certain resonance here with the OAS Resolution 1080 in relation to the protection of sovereignty and democracy. U.S. alarm about communist influence in Jamaica was also framed by and through the Jamaican press. The editor of the Standard Newspapers labeled PNP leaders "avowed Communists" and "half-baked intellectuals" (Manley 1984, 106). The moderate social democratic orientation of the PNP alarmed the British authorities, which blocked the implementation of the PNP Party Programme in 1942, when communists were elected to the party's General Council. The decision to preempt the consolidation of the left within the PNP hierarchy involved placing the PNP left-wing heads of departments into detention to ensure that "the party programme as approved by the Executive was never carried out because the major personnel in charge of the programme . . . had restricted orders placed against them" (Manley 1984, 203).

On September 3, 1941, the governor of Jamaica, Sir Arthur Richards, remarked in a memorandum to Lord Moyne that extreme elements were gaining control of the PNP; he accused Norman Manley of making concessions to the extremists by moving further to the left. Paul Blanshard, who served as senior economic analyst at the U.S. consulate in Kingston at the time, argued that Alexander Bustamante was collaborating with the Colonial Office by launching vicious attacks against the PNP. There was a confluence of interests between Whitehall and Washington over the security implications of the social democratic orientation within the PNP, though "there was far to go in using that Party (PNP) as a vehicle in establishing the preconditions for a socialist Jamaica" (Post 1987, 70). Governor Richard's preoccupations aside, Norman Manley was confident that the left could be expelled if they failed to act "responsibly" (Manley 1984, 163, 171, 201–3).

The U.S. intelligence agencies gathered information and monitored developments in Jamaica with reference to the relative strength of the political left, center, and right; the frequency and duration of meetings; the issues that were addressed; the strengths and weaknesses of Norman Manley; and the influence of the left in the trade union movement, among other considerations. In a 1942 memorandum, the FBI director wrote as follows to Assistant Secretary of State Adolf Berle: "With the infiltration of the People's National Party into Labor organizations, it would appear that the groundwork is being laid for mastering the Island's forces for a slowdown. The only saving feature of the present situation is that Bustamante and his Bustamante Industrial Trades Union is on the side of the Government and may prove to be the balancing factor and prevent any serious difficulty."

Bustamante had strong support among Jamaican capitalist interests who were elated by the victory of the JLP in the 1945 general election. Blanshard reported that, in spite of Bustamante's "eccentric dictatorship," the newspapers were relentless in their antiManley attacks while they overlooked "the obvious unfitness of Bustamante for serious governmental control." According to Blanshard, "the conservatives excused themselves for their tolerance of Bustamante by saying that he believed in capitalism and the British Empire and Manley did not." The alliance between the JLP and the capitalist interests in the Jamaica Democratic Party in 1945 showed that the JLP was clearly representing the interests of capital while claiming to be the party of labor. Blanshard argued that it was left to Jamaica's traditions and safeguards for freedom of speech to prevent Bustamante's incipient alliance with the upper classes from transforming Jamaica overnight into a "fascist dictatorship." Bustamante's approach to trade unionism and labor politics was based on organizing labor along nonproletarian lines, which was tantamount to disorganizing the working class to aid and abet the organization of capital in the postwar years, thereby influencing the neocolonial transition in Jamaica.

While cold war capitalist restructuring promoted industrial change and the making of a postwar working class, it constrained the democratization of life in the colonies (see Tilly 1997, 210–13). The BWI bourgeoisie was far more interested in organizing oligarchic and dictatorial power than promoting democratization. Wherever capitalism and democracy coexist, there exists a contradictory relationship, considering that capitalism reproduces the working classes by intensifying the socialization of production and deepening the private character of appropriation. Thus the working class is forced to struggle for democracy under conditions that can never make democracy a foregone conclusion under any type of capitalist system. Thus for the working class, democracy amounts to a continuous plebiscite, a point that, according to Tilly, is not fully appreciated by Rueschemeyer and Stephens and Stephens (1992, 43). Tilly notes that Rueschmeyer et al. "do not quite recognize their argument's implication: not capitalism itself, but proletarianization constitutes the crucial conditions for democratization. To the extent that proletarianization occurs by noncapitalist means . . . it still promotes democratizaton" (Tilly 1997, 210–11). Guyana from 1953 to 1964 offers a compelling case of how the United States, Britain, corporate capital, and fractions of the working class collaborated in undermining proletarianization and democratization, and shaped the conditions under which BWI colonial subjects would eventually become citizens.

Cheddi Jagan and Cold War Strategies, 1953–64

When Cheddi Jagan's PPP won the 1953 general election in Guyana, the key areas of the country's economic life were dominated by British capital in sugar and shopkeeping and by North American capital in bauxite. When Jagan lost power in 1964 under an Anglo-American national security electoral strategy of proportional representation, little had changed in that regard. Jagan and the PPP had placed the capital–wage labor relations at the center of the struggle for working-class economic, political, social, and cultural rights on an ontological basis, beyond mere bourgeois abstract universality.

The Rio Treaty was designed to preempt or overturn strategies like Jagan's. Restructuring the capital–wage labor relation within postwar capitalism involved adjusting the "relation between the national state and global capital" to produce "a significant change in the forms of global capitalist domination" (Holloway 1995, 134). The U.N. model of sovereign autonomy and the cold war project dovetailed around the principle of making sure that "political decisions taken at the level of the national state *would become* directly integrated into the global movement of capital." Postwar capitalist restructuring has intensified the "subjection of the national state to the global movement of capital," and has rendered "more difficult the national decomposition of society." Working-class resistance and struggles around the world aggravate the "the violent restlessness of capital" and confirms "capital's incapacity to subordinate the power of labor on which it depends" around the world. The Truman Doctrine sought to broaden the reach of Roosevelt's fifth freedom partly by checking the "power of the insubordination of labor" (Holloway 1995, 134, 135).

Jagan's Labor Relations Bill was the main plank in the PPP's government reform programs in 1953. The Labor Relations Bill sought to legalize trade union recognition and introduce representation of workers at the point of production under the Guyana Industrial Workers Union (GIWU). Bookers Company and Lionel Lukhoo's Man Power Citizens Association (MPCA) strongly opposed the bill (see Reno, 1964; also see St. Pierre, this volume) on the grounds that it was communist oriented, and they moved to disorganize the working class and stymie trade union democracy in Guyana. During the 1953 elections, the Guyanese electorate had voted for the PPP on a broad pan-ethnic basis (Greene 1974). The United States, Britain, corporate capital, and a fraction of the Guyanese working class collaborated around anticommunism to exploit ethnicity and undermine trade union democracy and the prospects for working-class unity and political democracy in Guyana. Ethnic identity was treated as a timeless marker of cultural difference, and shared historical experiences that cut across ethnic lines were discounted. Minor differences between Afro-Guyanese and Indo-Guyanese that resulted largely from the contradictions of capitalist development were elevated to the status of absolute differences between the two groups (see Rodney 1981, 162–81).

The labor opposition organized a general strike that was "inspired by a combination of CIA money and British Intelligence" (Lens 1965, 12). British troops were sent into Guyana to maintain colonial "law and order"; Britain suspended Guyana's constitution and dismissed Jagan and the elected legislators. Whitehall justified its action on national security grounds, contending that "the constitution of British Guiana must be suspended . . . to prevent communist subversion of the government . . . [because] the faction in power has shown that they are prepared to go to any length, including violence, to turn British Guiana into a Communist state" (Radosh 1969, 395; see also Spinner 1984). Britain's actions represented a clear confirmation of the assertion of U.S. hegemony and the ongoing erosion of her own power in the BWI in the postwar period.

The Man Power Citizens Association had withdrawn from the WFTU and joined the ICFTU and CADORIT. GIWU had defied the AF of L and the CLC by refusing to withdraw from the WFTU and join the ICFTU. The class, labor, and ethnic questions in Guyana became a cold war problem. Serafino Romualdi, a socialist-turned-communist who played a strategic role in building CADORIT's activities, admitted to CIA involvement in Guyana's politics and labor matters from as early as 1951 (Romualdi 1967, 346; Singh 1988, 32–33). The general strike was a political move to derail Jagan's labor bill, which sought representation for 20,000 MPCA members (Lens 1965, 12). The CIA and CADORIT contributed to the food benefits and other programs for striking workers for almost three months. A formidable group of U.S. trade unionists from the AFL-CIO, the Newspaper Guild, Retail Clerks, the Steel Workers, the Electrical Workers Union, and others from Latin American unions participated directly in the strike.

Nevertheless, the PPP won the general election in 1957, the year Forbes Burnham left the PPP and created the People's National Congress (PNC). Again, imperialism and the AFL-CIO cited the PPP's electoral victory as a national security threat. The Rio Treaty took precedence over the fact that Jagan's victory was based on free and fair elections. The AFL-CIO continued to send representatives to Guyana to oppose Jagan and the PPP. Bookers and the MPCA held out against GIWU. Corporate capital (Bookers-McConnell and the North American bauxite companies), Anglo-American imperialism, the AFL-CIO and its agents, and the CIA were actively restructuring the trajectories of politics along lines of class, ethnicity, labor, and trade unionism in Guyana. The political crisis enveloped the working-class movement, and the racialized politics of ethnicity began to cast a long and ominous shadow over the class struggle, the trade union movement, party politics, parliamentarization, and decolonization. The cold war project turned Guyana's self-determination struggle into a battle between U.S. national security priorities and the colony's self-determination.

But the cold war project did not oppose all forms of sovereign autonomy or democracy throughout the LAC region. Rather, Washington used the Rio Treaty to condition the definition of self-determination and democracy. Having failed to prevent Jagan and the PPP from winning free and fair elections in Guyana between 1953 and 1964, the United States and Britain sought to overthrow them at the polls through ostensibly constitutional means (see Bloomfield 1998, 123). Jagan expressed his dismay thusly: "Our local government reforms came from the United Kingdom, our Labor Relations Bill from the USA, our land law from Puerto Rico, an American colony" (Birbalsingh 1996, 150). His policy initiative to lay the base for unifying politics (sovereign autonomy) with economics (capital accumulation) went against the grain of the cold war project.

By the early 1960s, the Cuban revolution had repulsed a challenge by American imperialism in the Bay of Pigs fiasco. The BWI became more deeply integrated into the cold war project, with the left-leaning Caribbean Labor Congress (CLC) giving way to the cold war–oriented Caribbean Congress of Labor (CCL). The CIA-dominated American Institute for Free Labor Development (AIFLD) replaced ORIT and CADORIT under the Alliance for Progress. In 1961, Jagan and the PPP won their third general election with 42.7 percent of the popular vote and 20 of 35 seats to the PNC's 41 percent and 11 seats; a third party, Peter D'Aguiar's United Force (UF), won four seats. Richard Ishmael of the MPCA accused Jagan and the PPP of strengthening political ties with Cuba and the USSR, and called on the ICFTU to increase its support for his union (Radosh 1969, 399).

Between 1961 and 1964, the International Trade Secretariats (ITS) and the London-based Public Services International (PSI) operated in Guyana as labor fronts for the CIA. As in 1953, the central issues from 1961 to 1964 revolved around the struggle over the wage labor–capital relations and the right of the majority of the working class to choose the trade union they wanted to represent them in collective bargaining and related matters. In 1963, CIA-supported forces facilitated another workers strike in Guyana. The PSI paid the salaries of the MPCA full-time staff and civil service union leaders. AIFLD mobilized a number of its graduates in the service of the MPCA and the TUC against the PPP, its trade unionists, and their supporters. Bookers locked out their sugar workers. The PSI-AIFLD offensive constituted a form of low-intensity warfare against the PPP and the Guyanese working class. Still, only 2,000 of Guyana's 20,000 sugar workers joined in the CIA-backed MPCA challenge against the PPP program.

The economic, political, and social consequences of the 1963–64 crisis were devastating, with a toll of about $10 million in property damage or loss, and around 170 fatalities and a large number of injuries (Radosh 1969, 303–4; Sheehan 1967; Spinner 1984). Ethnicity, politics, trade unionism, national culture, and working-class politics were heavily racialized (see P. Mars, this volume). The PPP was working from a position of major disadvantage on several counts. The opposition was better off in terms of organization and funding, with the big guns of Anglo-American labor and intelligence on their side. The split in the PPP weakened its popular base and created a chasm in Guyana's ethnic, political, and cultural configuration. The PNC and the UF formed an anti-PPP alliance with imperialism. The racialization of ethnic and cultural politics; the tenuous level of the development of the working class and trade union movement as a whole; the social power of American money capital, which funded the trade union opposition; and the PPP's own embrace of the racialized politics of ethnicity and culture contributed to the success of the cold war project in Guyana.

The CIA had spent between U.S.$50,000 and U.S.$130,000 per week in pursuit of the national security goal of removing Jagan and the PPP from power, and in 1964, Britain and the United States instituted proportional representation to that end (Lens 1965; Radosh 1969; Meisler 1964; Sussman 1983; Herod 1997, 178–80). Proportional representation hardens political cleavages, works against proletarianization and, by extension, democratization, and tends to consolidate and normalize the despotism of bourgeois pluralist ideology. Proportional representation rises upon myths of ethnic and cultural primordialism, fosters national decomposition with negative consequences for trade union democracy in the labor movement and working-class solidarity, and privileges gender inequality and the retrospective illusion of ethnic primacy. The effects of the cold war are still evident across the spectrum of social existence in Guyana today.

Michael Manley, Global Capitalism, and Social Democracy

The cold war project had been based on the "postwar order of international relations" and "the configuration of power that emerged from the Second World War." Nixon acknowledged the decline of American postwar hegemony (Landau 1988, 102). Michael Manley's strategy for "democratic socialism" in Jamaica was constructed in the environment of hegemonial erosion, but the PNP and JLP had done much in earlier decades to undermine the prospects for making democratic socialism work in Jamaica. The high point of the Bandung "bourgeois national" project of nonalignment crystallized in the call for a New International Economic Order (NIEO) in the 1970s (see Amin 1994, Singham and Hune 1984, Watson 1998a). The NIEO strategy and democratic socialism were unveiled under the auspices of nonalignment to respond to the crisis of the postwar model of world capital accumulation. Both expressed the outlook of the "bourgeois national project" in a way that confirmed the extent of the crisis of the postwar order, but represented very little of any bold initiative to reinvent the world.

Thus the coincidence of the erosion of American hegemony and the launching of democratic socialism by Manley calls for further elaboration. Manley and the PNP did not have a strong material, industrial, economic, and working-class base for building socialism in Jamaica. When Manley won the 1972 general election, the PNP and JLP had long worked out a collaborative strategy for sharing political power to facilitate colonial and neocolonial capitalist accumulation. Both parties were explicitly anticommunist and antiproletarian, and they had done much to constrict the public space available for Marxism and revolutionary democratic working-class agendas to develop in Jamaica (see Munroe 1978). The JLP–Bustamante Industrial Trade Union (BITU) alliance, and the PNP–National Workers Union (NWU) alliance kept the "Marxist Left" isolated from mainstream party politics and organized labor. Gunst draws out the political class implications of the rationalistic and performative aspect of Michael Manley's consensualist politics during the 1970s, with reference to how his populist politics glossed "over the viciousness that has turned his country into a battlefield for the past twenty years" (1996, 240). Although the Jamaican ruling class, the political elite, and trade union aristocracy had already accommodated to the cold war project, the United States viewed Manley's moderate social democratic initiatives as inimical to its national security doctrine as defined by the Rio Treaty.

Yet the 1970s produced radical experimentation in the Third World in the throes of the ignominious defeat of U.S. policy and strategy in Southeast Asia. Examples include the national liberation revolutions that came to power in Africa, and the PNC's attempt at what seemed like a radical program in "cooperative socialism" in Guyana. Also Moscow and Washington were advancing toward détente, although détente was not designed to apply to the Third World, as Chile (1973) was to make unambiguously clear (Landau 1988, 103–6).

A number of left-oriented formations emerged in Jamaica, such as the Workers Liberation League (Workers Party of Jamaica), the University and Allied Workers Union (UAWU), the Communist Party of Jamaica, and others. Their presence and political work among the working class confirmed the radicalization of social and political consciousness at a certain level, but this was not necessarily widespread or well received across the working class. Nor did it confirm that Jamaica was ripe for a revolutionary transition. Manley and the PNP did not organize or lead any revolutionary movement or social forces in Jamaica. Manley and the PNP openly distanced themselves from Marxists and Communists and made it quite clear that their foreign relations with Cuba and other revolutionary states did not signal any affinity with Marxism or Communism. Jamaica's involvement with the Group of 77, which underscored NIEO and the Bandung "bourgeois national" Project of Non-Alignment, was quite consistent with U.N. initiatives around the NIEO project. Therefore, Jamaica's international assertiveness was an attempt to exploit the space that was afforded by the erosion of American hegemony without necessarily denying agency to Jamaica by implying that its international role was strictly a product of America's decline. More to the point, the PNP, the bourgeoisie, and broad social forces across the class spectrum were not committed to making a revolutionary transition in Jamaica from world capitalism.

The opposition JLP, the business community, elements in the police force, the army, and the CIA were among the main protagonists in the anti-PNP destablization campaign. Concrete acts of destabilization, including capital flight via illegal transfers abroad of large sums of money, were intended to protect the profit base and accumulation (Manley 1982, 197–202; Kaufman 1985, 187–189; Stephens and Stephens 1986, 234–41). The JLP-led opposition forces, including the *Gleaner* newspaper, practiced political violence against the PNP with malicious statements and stories about the PNP and its relationship with Cuba, and the influence of Cuba and the Soviet KGB in the PNP and its government (Stephens and Stephens

1986, 135–37, 350; Kaufman, 1985, 191). Widespread violence, including numerous murders and other criminal acts, weakened capital's confidence in Jamaica as a safe investment site and tourist destination. The inability of the PNP to implement its reform program aggravated capitalist instability. Capital flight, smuggling, black market exchange rates, double invoicing of imports, and hoarding by merchants yielded a combined effect of low-intensity commodity and financial terrorism. Some of the major effects included artificial scarcity and inflation, rising unemployment, and loss of productive labor time by large numbers of white- and blue-collar working-class consumers.

The bourgeoisie was not monolithic. Manley's democratic socialist initiatives were designed to promote new strata within the national bourgeoisie that the PNP could rely on. Elements in the bourgeoisie joined imperialism in opposing the reforms the PNP initiated, including a land reform program, sugar cooperatives, a national minimum wage, a literacy program, expansion of public education, gender sensitive equal pay legislation and maternity leave, and the State Trading Corporation. Manley had lamented the unresponsiveness of the political system to the dire situation of broad masses of working-class people dating back to the late colonial period (see Watson 1998a). Neither sovereign autonomy nor democratic socialism was sufficient to turn around the material and social condition of the mass of the working-class people.

Low-intensity warfare was stepped up to sabotage the PNP's reforms. To this end steps were taken to shift the balance in the security apparatuses of the state. In 1980, the Jamaica Defense Force (JDF) was implicated in a coup attempt that led to the arrest of thirty-three JDF personnel and implicated them in a right-wing plot to kidnap the chief of staff and capture the prime minister and force him to resign (Kaufman 1985, 188–89). The JDF broke up a PNP election campaign meeting in 1980, in spite of protest from the prime minster and the PNP general secretary who were at the meeting. (Stephens and Stephens 1986, 238–41; Manley 1982, 200–202). More than 2,000 people were killed in Jamaica between 1977 and 1980; many of them were victims of the "tribal" politics of the PNP and JLP gunmen (Kaufman 1985, 185; see Gunst 1996, xiii). Party-aligned violence helped to demobilize and disorganize the working class and has worked against working-class interests. Such violence suggests that the PNP and JLP have been far more interested in their own survival than in the emancipation of the working class.

There are several other reasons why the PNP's social democratic reforms were targeted for low-intensity warfare. It is necessary to consider the collaboration of the two political parties and union bureaucracies with the cold war project, and the state of the productive forces in Jamaican capitalism that keeps the working class structurally weak and insecure about the conditions of its own reproduction. Certain provisions of the Labor Relations and Industrial Disputes Act (LRIDA) alienated certain workers, trade unionists, and capitalists. Worker participation was anathema to capital. State acquisition of private property, such as hotels and sugar plantations that were in a state of disrepair, and the formation of producer cooperatives smacked of socialist collectivism to some. The PNP's anti-imperialist foreign policy and its adoption of government-to-government relations with states such as Cuba led some to think Jamaica's foreign policy was being restructured away from the West with negative implications for the Rio Treaty. Jamaica's leadership in the formation of the International Bauxite Association (IBA), and its support for NLRs in Africa also incensed the Jamaican right wing and Washington.

The Nixon Doctrine (Landau 1988) sought to stem the erosion of U.S. hegemony by raising the cost of Third World internationalism. Jamaica's historical integration into the American system, the subsumption of Jamaica's national trade union movement and political parties under cold war imperialism, and other weaknesses and divisions in the working class, suggested that democratic socialism began from a very fragile base, even under the conditions of an eroding American hegemony. In sum, democratic socialism was less of a strategic attempt to restructure the fundamental social-class relations of production in Jamaica than a way of exploiting the conditions of hegemonial erosion to introduce moderate social reform. Manley hoped the international conditions would have favored subduing the cold war (East-West) Leviathan to perform Bandung (North-South) surgery on its internal organs within the norms of a reformed capitalism (see Hart 1997). This was tantamount to a petit bourgeois flight of romantic fancy.

Global Neoliberalism, CARICOM Trade, and the Union Movement

Catherine Sunshine's depiction of the nature and extent of AIFLD's involvement with the Caribbean Congress of Labor (CCL) during the 1980s is relevant to the so-called post–cold war (Sunshine 1985, 109; see also Cos 1996, 34). In the neoliberal context, cold war institutions like AIFLD and USAID have worked through the trade union movement and grassroots organizations in the LAC countries to intensify the disorganization of the working class. Neoliberalism aggravates the crisis of neocolonial democracy, partly by intensifying the decomposition of national states and their societies. This involves increasing the distance between the working class and parliamentary institutions, and rolling back the social borders of the state via state restructuring (see World Bank 1997, Gill 1998, Panitch 1998). The neoliberal reform strategy of AIFLD and USAID is to convince organized and unorganized workers to purchase a future based on deliberate class strategies that privilege the rights and power of capital over those of the working class. Part of their tactic involves defining society as disjointed continua, like rich and poor, rather than as a social system based on the capitalist organization of the means of production, and distribution of income, wealth, and power.

AIFLD and USAID operate strategically at the grassroots level to intensify the separation of politics from economics and national states from the global economy in order to bring the notion of national states into closer conformity with the motion of global capital. AIFLD draws on the deep financial pockets of the AFL-CIO to deliver resources to certain Caribbean groups in vital areas of community development and worker socialization. The ICFTU and AIFLD have been the CCL's main source of funding, including funding for the construction of labor training and community centers, medical clinics, and housing development projects in a number of Caribbean countries. Capitalist inequality is one way capital and states disorganize the working class.

AIFLD has been the primary enforcer of low-intensity warfare on the labor front against Caribbean working classes. The social power of money from AIFLD and the ICFTU reinforces the power of capital and imperialism over the trade union movement while these agencies seem to stand outside the social relations of production. The social power of money shows its brashness by separating its technical functions as a medium of exchange or a store of value from its social-class function as purveyor of the power of capital. This is where money mesmerizes all and sundry, possessor (capitalist or state) and propertyless (worker). The social power of money engenders "a certain asymmetry . . . those who have it use it to force those who do not to do their bidding. This power asymmetry in social relations ineluctably connects to 'other asymmetries in order' . . . to dominate . . . people." It is the "lack of any moral judgment inherent in the money from itself [that] can liberate the individual from direct . . . social constraints" and foster the notion that "the market is by far the best mechanism yet discovered to realize human desires with a maximum of individual freedom and a minimum of social-political restraints" (Harvey 1996, 155, 151).

In fact, the market produces concrete political effects without seeming to represent any political agenda or preferences. The social power and asymmetry of money, and the suggestion that the market is the "best mechanism . . . to realize human desire" normalize experience in bourgeois societies without being capable of explaining it. AIFLD has used its political and social-financial power to pressure unions to isolate or exclude progressive and/or revolutionary trade unionists in line with the goals of the cold war project (Sunshine 1985, 109). Since AIFLD superceded CADORIT in the 1960s, it has trained numerous CCL trade unionists. AIFLD targets organized labor in key areas such as dock, transport, electrical, and communications workers. By the early 1980s, AIFLD had affiliates in fourteen CARICOM countries, the Dutch and French Antilles and Suriname. The professional mobility of many CARICOM trade unionists has hinged on the ideological socialization, training, and opportunities AIFLD has provided. AIFLD works to reinforce the deontological basis of social, economic, and cultural rights along class, gender, and ethnic lines in Caribbean societies.

It is necessary to grasp how AIFLD's role facilitates providing foreign capital with nonunionized low-wage labor, and how measures to control or weaken the unions converge with AIFLD's labor foreign policy in the Caribbean. Under neoliberal capitalism, Caribbean states have been socializing financial insolvency by shifting the cost onto the working class, with the explicit aim of freeing capital of social obligations to the state and working classes. It is in the interests of Caribbean workers to understand how AIFLD's project dovetails with the antiproletarian strategies of the IMF and World Bank. The World Bank deliberately rationalizes "the regressive shift in taxation from corporate and personal income taxes, and trade taxes, toward consumption-based taxes like VAT as an inevitable consequence of the global integration it advocates" (Panitch 1998, 15). The cold war project was designed to strengthen the global base of postwar capitalism; the transformation of Caribbean trade unions into agents of globalization has been an integral part of that strategy.

Above the argument was made that the OAS Resolution 1080 of 1991 makes states responsible for protecting sovereignty and democracy to reinforce the empire of capital through which the rights of private capital gain primacy. OAS Resolution 1080 masks a broader security agenda, namely to intensify the deontological nature of human rights for the working classes. In other words, social and political legitimacy is being redefined along neoliberal lines to legitimate the erosion of the social borders of the state. The relationship between government and capital is becoming closer while that between unions and their members seems to be deteriorating to the detriment of both, and this is quite in keeping with AIFLD desires.

Trade union democracy is conditioned by the norms of capital accumulation and representative government; it thrives on the idea that economics and politics inhabit two distinct spheres with government as administrative caretaker of depoliticized public interests. This helps the bourgeoisie cover over its political interests in the market, away from public scrutiny, so to speak. This way corporate capital can actually increase its influence in setting the agendas of political parties, as popular alienation from the political parties increases in the face of the contraction of the social borders of the state. Unions, political parties, and parliamentary institutions seem to be suffering from popular alienation. In addition to corporate capital, technocrats are gaining influence over the political process and right-wing populism seems to be on the rise (see Bryan 1998, 39–40). Civil society, as bourgeois capitalist society, cannot help but reflect these seething contradictions. This is not a matter of mere displacement, for displacement is itself a form of preservation. The phenomenon is more pronounced toward the global level where capital accumulation takes place.

It is fitting to reintroduce Holloway at this point: global neoliberal restructuring confirms a significant increase in the pace at which "political decisions taken at the level of the national state are now more directly integrated into the global movement of capital." This integration renders "more difficult the national decomposition of society" and intensifies the class struggle in ways that expose "the violent restlessness of capital." Not only does the process confirm "capital's incapacity to subordinate the power of labor on which it depends," but it also shows that despite "appearances, the restless movement of capital is the clearest indication of power of the insubordination of labor" (1995, 134, 135).

Conclusion

The underlying theme in this argument has been that national states are delimited by the specific "social relations of a particular type of society"

(Rosenberg 1994, 2). In order to "recover the history of the international system, past and continuing," we must understand that "geopolitical systems are not constituted independently of, and cannot be understood in isolation from, the wider structures of the production and reproduction of social life" (Rosenberg 1994, 4, 6). Thus the decolonization process leading up to national state sovereignty should not blind us to the fact that sovereignty expresses the mediation of bourgeois property relations on a global scale. It has been difficult to grasp this simple point because the geopolitical habit of seeing sovereignty as a conflict between national particularity and world universality is intended to obfuscate reality.

In 1980, following the defeat of the PNP by Edward Seaga and the JLP, Manley said he regretted that his democratic socialist strategy had underestimated the importance of the "free market" to democracy and economic development in Jamaica. In 1991, Cheddi Jagan iterated that a PPP/Civic electoral victory did not imply a viable socialist option in Guyana in the era of global neoliberalism. Jagan said he had no choice but to adopt neoliberalism while holding to the "socialist utopia" to protect the interests of the Guyanese working class (Watson 1998a). Unlike Manley, Jagan continued to advocate the possibility of ending class society. Manley's aspirations were limited to using democratic socialism as a way to promote a viable national bourgeoisie and capitalism without its key contradictions in Jamaica. Both strategies proved unacceptable to the cold war project: though democratic socialism would not have limited the effective reach of global capital, it would seek to redistribute surplus value away from capital. Jagan's project from the 1950s sought to roll back capitalism. He was far more acceptable to imperialism after 1992.

Since 1980, the JLP and PNP have moved Jamaica along the neoliberal path. When the PPP/Civic came to power in 1992, Guyana had undergone at least five years of neoliberal restructuring that the PNC had facilitated from around 1987 under the direction of the World Bank Group, European Union member states, the United States, and Canada (see Murray 1992). The neoliberal projects in Jamica and Guyana are designed to restructure the productive and capital accumulation bases to accelerate the integration of those societies into global capitalist production and accumulation.

Neoliberalism seeks to normalize a number of myths about the "end of history," the ultimate victory of capitalism and markets over history and the left, and the natural origins of inequality among humankind. Neoliberal ideology also asserts that the struggle for socialism goes against human nature;

the highest purpose of national states is to mediate inequality, rather than seek to abolish it. Neoliberalism affirms the boldness of the bourgeoisie and demands a rethinking of class-struggle strategies. The historical record shows that the cold war project of world capitalist restructuring and geopolitical respatialization posed deep paradoxes for decolonization in the Caribbean. It subordinated the U.N. model of sovereignty (politics) to the priorities of economics (global capital accumulation) in order to reconfigure the subjugation of the working classes worldwide. The strategy of American organized labor to control the labor movements in the Caribbean was based on a clear understanding that the survival of capitalism in the United States depended on securing Roosevelt's fifth freedom around the world. The U.S. strategy for winning over key sections of Caribbean labor to the cold war project and anticommunism began with getting the support of members of the intelligentsia. Those individuals (of the intelligentsia) fought for bourgeois trade union democracy, which called for undermining the progressive and revolutionary elements in the trade union movement and the political parties. Their opposition to proletarianization meant opposition to working-class democracy, which placed them on the side of the United States' global antiworking-class strategy. This explains why the AFL-CIO and AIFLD and its predecessors were so active in the LAC region.

Capitalists, in seeking to extend the global reach and scope of their accumulation drive, find it necessary to combat attempts by states and working classes to gain or increase their control over surplus value, which is indispensable for capital accumulation. National states in the advanced region of world capitalism have generally supported capital in this resistance. Yet the fact that all national states are integral parts of the prevailing social relations of production means this point must be located at the core of social analysis of class issues. The cases of British Guyana and Jamaica help to demystify the cultural logic of state sovereignty in the Caribbean and reveal that the methodologies that treat space and place as finished objects, as opposed to expressions of particular forms of social relations, impede prospects for arriving at rigorous explanations of social reality.

The AIFLD and the AFL-CIO have worked with the American state to oppose political strategies for giving working classes popular control of their organs and institutions by keeping politics separated from economics, with an emphasis on the abstract universality of formal political and juridical equality. This separation is necessary for normalizing social and economic inequality, thereby keeping class society subordinated to the imperative of capital accumulation. This is partly why the bourgeoisie has to saturate working-class consciousness with the norms and practices of bourgeois two-party politics, corporate unionism, trade union democracy, economic insecurity, racism, and other phenomena that reinforce individualist fragmentation. The key ideological container for individualist fragmentation is cultural pluralism, which is apt for market society. Its core methodological techniques are phenomenological and philosophical individualism that reduce humanity to a mass of individuated "competition subjects," all equally propelled by a logic of rational (market) calculus. The market can assume the semblance of something standing apart from politics, society, conflict, and even contradiction. But this is only the apparition of the market, since the real market is an instrument of class power and a site of acute class struggle. The view that human progress comes from competition, conflict, and struggle for domination and superiority among individuals, societies, and states works to the advantage of bourgeois notions of the market. It does so by abstracting both the market and the state from society and politics and conjuring up the myth that economic competition and exploitation are natural. The key lesson is that democracy has to be subjected to vigorous class analysis as a strategy and a political form of the organization of state power.

Even before neoliberalism, CARIOM states, political parties, and trade unions have privileged features of the marketization of society by emphasizing those factors that fragment social life in bourgeois society and that keep the majority from active political participation. In reality, the political model and constitution found in CARICOM states such as Guyana and Jamaica contain already the "antinomies of the modern democratic state" and considering that "representative governments are themselves built upon the exclusion from political life of the majority of citizens" (Yuval-Davis 1997, 20). In other words, national citizenship is built on certain exclusions, as such the national state does not provide a reliable basis for negotiating ethnic nationalism (see also Fine 1994, 441). The transformation of the Caribbean labor movement into an agent of cold war globalization offered strategic venues for working-class subversion through low-intensity conflict warfare at the level of trade unions. CARICOM states have been directly complicit in this process. Indeed, those states transited from colonialism to neocolonialism, conditioned by the reality of limited state sovereignty.

It would be remiss to ignore the seminal fact that Caribbean workers have experienced their own reproduction at different moments of historical capitalist restructuring dating back to slavery. The motion of capital has summoned vast numbers of Caribbean workers to Central America, North America, and Europe where they have reproduced themselves with new employment opportunities, new skills, higher labor productivity, and have deepened the socialization of their production experiences. Basch, Schiller, and Blanc's 1994 designation of Caribbean nations as "nations unbound" is more than apt. Capitalist accumulation has rendered migration central to the reproduction, disorganization, and deterritorialization of Caribbean nations. Capitalism robs Caribbean societies of prospects of the means to become effective containers for reproducing cultural life for Caribbeans, a reality that has been clouded by the ideology of sovereign autonomy. But this is due to the nature of capitalism, rather than the result of a conspiracy. State sovereignty came to the CARICOM states already stripped of the key means for asserting economic autonomy, without which no state can make good on national integration or provide human rights with any concrete ontological foundation. It is proletarianization that produces democracy, and proletarianization emerges from within the proletariat!

The cold war project in the Caribbean, Cuba apart, successfully isolated the Marxist and communist movement from the political and economic mainstream, and conditioned the class struggle by sanitizing the terms of political competition and normalizing the rules for building strategies for sharing state power within bourgeois norms. The transition to neocolonialism in places like Guyana and Jamaica was based on the grand political compromise with the cold war project. The class struggle has attempted to break the seams of the compact with imperialism, as was achieved in Cuba, but unsuccessfully attempted in Guyana and Jamaica.

In the neoliberal era, the survival of the left demands a fight for a real alternative to the right (see Anderson 1998, 81). Given that neoliberalism is based on the abiding right-wing assertion that inequality is the natural and inevitable human condition, what are we to make of Manley's and Jagan's embrace of neoliberalism? Neither Manley nor Jagan can be evaluated as isolated figures. They simply did not have the most favorable conditions and social forces to make socialism. Manley was not interested in anything beyond social democracy. Jagan's formalistic approach to Marxism and his addiction to Sovietism hampered his understanding of the domestic and international situation. Clearly, any leader who opts for the neoliberal solution will not be in a position to rock any boats! Could Manley and Jagan have simultaneously embraced neoliberalism and pursued full employment, income redistribution, capital market regulation, public ownership of the means of production, or any other key principles of the welfare state? Hardly! Manley seemed to have reached a point of wanting capitalism and the free market without the inevitable contradictions. If Manley was confused theoretically, he knew where his class interests were grounded. My own sense is that Manley's and Jagan's apologia for neoliberalism pointed to a convergence against the insubordination of labor and what remains of the left in those countries. Jagan's relationship with the Working People's Alliance (WPA) in Guyana was always an uncomfortable one. Jagan was never at home with any left formation that held a different worldview than his, and he relied on the notion that Indo-Guyanese were the real majority from which the working-class majority sprung (Watson 1998a).

The crystallization of global capitalism demands new working-class strategies on an explicit transnational and postnational basis. I have argued that there were key differences between Jagan and Adams and the Manleys. Therefore, without attempting to equate them in retrospect, I think there are good reasons for concluding that in the neoliberal era, neocolonial parties like the PNP and PPP shifted to the point of becoming an admixture of the "technocratic Right" and the "populist Right" (see Bobbio 1998, 87–88). This is where Jagan's rhetoric about adopting neoliberalism while holding to the socialist utopia unfolded, although Jagan preferred to say Washington would not allow anyone to choose a socialist option. This is plausible, but one must consider that the question of socialism for the left is not to be decided by Washington. Where does the working class feature in this scenario?

OAS Resolution 1080 strengthens the antiworking-class bulwarks, suggesting that the bourgeoisie has not found a way to negate the insubordination of labor. Manley and the PNP felt buoyed by the support from the Socialist International and its disdain for class struggle. Jagan remained highly traditional in his ideas about race, ethnicity, and culture. Hence his approach to issues of class and class struggle did not reflect any sophisticated understanding of those concepts and their relationships in class struggle. Also his submissiveness to the official Moscow notion of "socialist orientation" along so-called noncapitalist development did much to compromise his political strategies at home and undermined his attempts to build genuine relationships with left formations such as the WPA (see Hinds 1998, Watson 1998a).

All strategies to restructure and reproduce global capitalism produce undeniable contradictions for the working classes around the globe, that only the working class can work to resolve by transforming themselves into classes for themselves. Considering that the role of the Caribbean labor movement as an agent of cold war globalization reinforced the reproduction of the working class for itself, the future course must not repeat past legacies. Appreciating what this statement means requires a close reflection on capitalism's net record on human development. As a system based on the accumulation of capital—that the bourgeoisie defines as freedom and progress—the bourgeoisie has taken the moral high ground of normalizing this contradictory system. Actually, capitalism, by equating itself with all that is positive while blaming its historical contradictions on human nature, actually wastes human energy, forces society to finance its own domination, treats inequality as a natural human condition, and organizes production not to maximize human cultural potential but rather to facilitate bourgeois hegemony. The record is clear: the cold war project imposed a very heavy price on working classes in North America, the LAC region, and other parts of the world, and the time has come to set the record straight so as not to repeat the past. Neoliberalism is the latest attempt by the bourgeoisie to hoodwink history, and the left must work against such an eventuality.

References

Amin, Samir. 1994. *Re-Reading the Postwar Period: An Intellectual Itinerary.* New York: Monthly Review Press.

Anderson, Perry. 1998. "A Sense of the Left." *New Left Review,* no. 231: 73–81.

Baptiste, Fitz A. 1978. "The United States and West Indian Unrest, 1918–1939." *Working Paper,* no. 18, Mona: Institute of Economic and Social Research, University of the West Indies.

Basch, Linda, N. Glick Schiller, and C. Szanton Blanc. 1994. *Nations Unbound: Transnational Projects, Postcolonial Predicaments and Deterritorialized Nation-States.* Langhorne, Pa.: Gordon and Breach Science Publishers.

Bobbio, Norberto. 1998. "At the Beginning of History." *New Left Review,* no. 231: 82–90.

Butler, Stuart, M. Sanera, and B. Weingold, eds. 1984. *Mandate for Leadership II.* Washington D.C.: Heritage Foundation.

Carlucci, Frank. 1989. Secretary of Defense, Annual Report of the Congress Executive Summary, Washington, D.C. Department of Defense.

Cox, Kevin, ed. 1997. *Spaces of Globalization: Reasserting the Power of the Local.* New York: Guilford Press.

Cox, Robert W. 1996. "Influences and Commitments." In *Approaches to World Order,* by Robert W. Cox with Timothy J. Sinclair. Cambridge: Cambridge University Press.

Cummings, Bruce. 1998. "The Korean Crisis and the End of 'Late' Development," *New Left Review,* no. 231: 43–72.
Dietz, James. 1984. Introduction to "Destabilization and Intervention in Latin America and the Caribbean," *Latin American Perspectives* 11, no. 3.
Draper, Theodore. 1985. "The Dominican Crisis." *Commentary* 40, no. 6: 30–65.
Fine, Robert. 1994. "The New Nationalism and Democracy: A Critique of Pro Patria." *Democratization* 1, no. 3: 423–43.
Garcia-Muqiz, Humberto, and Jose Lee Borges. 1998. "U.S. Consular Activism in the Caribbean, 1783–1903, with Special Reference to St. Kitts–Nevis' Sugar Depression, Labor Turmoil, and Its Proposed Acquisition." *Revista Mexicana del Caribe* 3, no. 5: 32–79.
Gill, Stephen. 1998. "New Constitutionalism, Democratization, and Global Political Economy." Unpublished essay. York University, Toronto.
Gramsci, Antonio. 1971. *Selections from the Prison Notebooks of Antonio Gramsci.* Ed. and trans. Quintin Hoare and Geoffrey Noel Smith. New York: International Publishers.
Greene, Edward. 1983. "Cooperativism, Militarism, Party Politics, and Democracy in Guyana." In *The Newer Caribbean: Decolonization, Democracy, and Development,* ed. Paget Henry and Carl Stone. Philadelphia: Institute for the Study of Human Issues.
Gunst, Laurie. 1996. *Born Fi Dead.* New York: Henry Holt and Co.
Harrod, J. 1962. *Trade Union Foreign Policy.* Garden City, N.Y.: Doubleday.
Harvey, David. 1996. *Justice, Nature, and the Geography of Difference.* Boston: Blackwell.
Herod, Andrew. 1997. "Labor as an Agent of Globalization and as a Global Agent." In *Spaces of Globalization: Reasserting the Power of the Local,* ed. Kevin Cox. New York: Guilford Press.
Hinds, David. 1998. "Authoritarianism and Popular Protest in Post-Colonial Anglophone Caribbean Politics: The Case of Guyana." Ph.D. diss., Howard University, Washington, D.C.
Holloway, John. 1995. "Global Capital and the National State." In *Global Capital, National State, and the Politics of Money,* ed. W. Bonefield and J. Holloway. New York: St. Martin's Press.
Holwill, Richard N., ed. 1982. *The First Year: A Mandate for Leadership.* Washington, D.C.: Heritage Foundation.
Hosmer, Stephen. 1987. *Constraints on U.S. Strategies in Third World Conflicts.* New York: Crane Russak.
Jagan, Cheddi. 1966. *The West on Trial: The Fight for Guyana's Freedom.* London: Michael Joseph.
———. 1980. *The West on Trial.* Berlin: Seven Seas Books.
———. c1984. *The Caribbean: Whose Backyard?.* Georgetown, Guyana.

Jarmillo, Isabel. 1987. *Low-Intensity Conflict: A Puzzle for Assembling.* Havana, Cuba: Centro De Estudios Sobre America.

Joint Low-Intensity Conflict Project Final Report Executive Summary. 1986. Prepared by the Joint Low-Intensity Conflict Project, United States Army Training and Doctrine Command, Fort Monroe, Virginia, August.

Joseph, Cedric L. 1973. "The Strategic Importance of the British West Indies, 1882–1932." *Journal of Caribbean History* 7 (November).

Kaufman, Michael. 1985. *Jamaica under Manley: Dilemmas of Socialism and Democracy.* London: Zed Books.

Kennan, George. 1956. "Overdue Changes in Our Foreign Policy," *Harper's Magazine,* August, 27–33.

———. 1985. "Containment: Then and Now," *Los Angeles Times,* December 29.

Kurzman, Dan. 1966. "Lovestone's Cold War: The AFL-CIO Has Its Own CIA." *New Republic,* June 25, 17–22.

Lens, Sidney. 1965. "American Labor Abroad: Lovestone Diplomacy." *The Nation,* July 5, 10–16.

Lewis, Linden. 1988. "State Control of the Labor Process in the Commonwealth Caribbean. Ph.D. diss., American University, Washington, D.C.

Manley, Beverly. 1984. "The Programmatic and Ideological Platform of the People's National Party (1938–1944)." MSc. thesis, University of the West Indies, Mona.

Manley, Michael. 1982. *Jamaica: Struggle in the Periphery.* London: Third World Media/Writers and Readers Publishing Cooperative.

Mars, Perry. 1984. "Destabilization and Socialist Orientation in the English-Speaking Caribbean." *Latin American Perspectives* 11, no. 3: 83–110.

Marx, Karl. 1977. *Capital: A Critique of Political Economy.* Vol. 1. Trans. B. Fowkes. New York: Vintage.

Marx, K., and F. Engels. 1952. *The Manifesto of the Communist Party.* Moscow.

Meisler, Stanley. 1964. "Dubious Role of AFL-CIO Meddling in Latin America." *The Nation,* February 10, 133–38.

Mills, Charles W. 1988. "Red Peril on the Green Island: The Communist Threat to Jamaica in Genre Fiction, 1955–1969." *Caribbean Studies* 20, nos. 3–4.

Morelli, Donald R., Major General, U.S. Army (ret.), and Major Michael P. Ferguson. 1984. "Low-Intensity Conflict: An Operational Perspective." *Military Review* 65 (November).

Morris, George. 1967. *CIA and American Labor.* New York: International Publishers.

Munroe, Trevor. 1978. "The Marxist Left in Jamaica, 1940–1950." *Working Paper* No. 15. Mona: Institute of Social and Economic Research, University of the West Indies.

Murray, Winston. 1992. Deputy Prime Minister of Guyana. Presentation at the Seminar Guyana at the Crossroads, North-South Center, University of Miami, November 1991.

NACLA Report on the Americas. 1986. "The Real War: Low-Intensity Conflict in Central America," 20, no. 2.

Naison, Mark. 1988. *Communists in Harlem during the Depression.* New York: Grove Press 1985.

Payne, Anthony. 1995. *Politics in Jamaica.* New York: St. Martin's Press.

Post, Ken. 1981. *Strike the Iron. A Colony at War: Jamaica, 1939–1945,* vol. 1. Atlantic Highlands, N.J.: Humanities Press.

Pratt, J. W. 1951. *Expansionists of 1898.* New York: Peter Smith.

Radosh, R. 1969. *American Labor and United States Foreign Policy: The Cold War in the Unions from Gompers to Lovestone.* New York: Random House.

Reagan, R. 1988. *National Security Strategy of the United States.* Washington D.C.: Pergamon-Brassey's International Defense Publishers.

Reno, P. 1964. "The Ordeal of British Guiana." *Monthly Review* 16, no. 3.

Reuten, G., and M. Williams. 1989. *Value-Form and the State: The Tendencies of Accumulation and the Determination of Economic Policy in Capitalist Society.* London: Routledge.

Rodney, W. 1981. *A History of the Guyanese Working People.* Baltimore: Johns Hopkins University Press.

Romualdi, S. 1967. *Presidents and Peons: Recollections of a Labor Ambassador in Latin America.* New York: Funk and Wagnalls.

Searle, C. 1984. *Grenada: The Struggle against Destabilization.* London: Writers and Readers Publishing Cooperative Society.

Sheehan, N. 1967. "CIA Men Aided Strikes in Guiana." *New York Times,* February 23.

Singh, C. 1988. *Guyana: Politics in a Plantation Society.* New York: Praeger Publishers.

———. 1998–99. "Master Speculator" Issue. *Rolling Stone,* no. 802/803: 133–37.

Stephens, E., and J. Stephens. 1986. *Democratic Socialism in Jamaica: The Political Movement and Social Transformation in Dependent Capitalism.* Princeton: Princeton University Press.

Stone, C. 1980. *Democracy and Clientelism in Jamaica.* New Brunswick, N.J.: Transaction Books.

Sunshine, C. 1985. *The Caribbean: Survival, Struggle, and Sovereignty.* Washington, D.C.: EPICA.

Sussman, M. 1983. *AIFLD: U.S. Trojan Horse in Latin America and the Caribbean.* Washington, D.C.: EIPCA Special Report.

Thomas, C. Y. 1984. *The Rise of the Authoritarian State in the Periphery.* New York: Monthly Review Press.

Tilly, C. 1977. *Roads from Past to Future.* Lanham, Md.: Rowman and Littlefield.

Virtue, E. 1997. "I Was Never a Die-Harded PNP, Says D. K. Duncan after Thirty Years in the Party," *Jamaican Gleaner,* Sunday, July 20.

Wallerstein, I. 1983. *Historical Capitalism*. London: Verso Books.
Watson, H. A. 1975. "The Political Economy of Foreign Investment in the Commonwealth Caribbean since World War II." Ph.D. diss., Howard University, Washington, D.C.
———. 1998a. "An Assessment of the Contributions of Michael Manley and Cheddi Jagan in the Global Political Economy Context." Unpublished Paper. International Relations Program, Bucknell University, Lewisburg, Pa.
———. 2000. "Global Finance: The Role and Status of the Caribbean." In *The Political Economy of Drugs in the Caribbean*, ed. Ivelaw Griffith. London: Macmillan Press.
Wells, S. F., Jr., ed. 1984. *Economic and World Power: An Assessment of American Diplomacy since 1789*. New York: Columbia University Press.
Yuval-Davis, Nira. 1997. *Gender and Nation*. Thousand Oaks, Calif.: Sage Publications.

7

Globalization, Economic Fallout, and the Crisis of Organized Labor in the Caribbean

CLIVE THOMAS

Cheddi Jagan and Michael Manley were leading figures in the worldwide struggles against colonialism and imperialism and for the advancement of working-class interests everywhere. They performed many roles in these struggles, as writers, social activists, labor leaders, politicians, and heads of government in Guyana and Jamaica. They are widely recognized as among the foremost Third World figures to emerge from the Caribbean in the second half of the last century. As demonstrated in their lives, organized labor has played remarkable roles in molding the contemporary English-speaking Caribbean. In the broadest sense, it has been the standard-bearer of all the great social movements of the twentieth century, playing leading roles in the struggles against colonialism and for independence, national sovereignty, democracy, peace, and social justice. The labor movement's role in promoting Caribbean unity has also been distinctive. Credit should also be given for its contributions toward raising the levels of social consciousness and awareness among Caribbean peoples, promoting the diversification of regional economies away from their traditional colonial bases of primary production, raising the standard of living of the population at large, as well as promoting the modernization and change of Caribbean society and culture. In addition, organized labor has also produced a significant portion of the political leadership of our times (including Jagan and Manley), earning for itself in the literature the label of *political unionism*, which is portrayed as a distinctive feature of Caribbean trade unionism (see Eaton 1988).

Given the scope of its involvement, not all the endeavors of organized labor could have been successful. There have been important failures. Thus we find that its distinctive brand of political unionism has been both a source of strength and weakness. As Thomas observes, its strength has lain in the political consciousness of the workforce it promoted and the strong commitment to the ideals of liberal democracy, which it also encouraged (Thomas 2000). Through organized labor's democratic efforts, it was able to secure legislative support for the removal of the civil-criminal conspiratorial view of trade union activity, consolidate the legality and legitimacy of unions, promote workers' rights and "immunities" in the law, and advance their expectations as regards pay and conditions of work. Thus labor legislation was passed setting minimum levels of pay; controlling working conditions, especially in areas of health and occupational safety; preventing the use of child labor; securing gender protection through equal pay for equal work; providing opportunities for training; and ensuring national schemes of social security for the workforce.

However, in several territories, political unionism has also led to a considerable separation/disjuncture between the trade union leadership and its rank and file. This has occurred most frequently when the union leadership embroils the unions in national political conflicts that have led to a shift in trade union priorities away from the particular interests of the membership to broader national political issues. Negative outcomes have also occurred where, despite the practice in the region of individual trade union affiliation to a national umbrella organization, serious conflicts and rivalries have nevertheless developed among individual unions. These conflicts have often been complicated by the legal situation in the region, whereby laws governing trade union recognition are outdated, and where the practice of "voluntarism" and "gentlemen's agreements" prevail over codified labor contracts under an integrated labor code. Negative outcomes have also occurred because many unions are organized at the industrial level while negotiations with employers typically take place at the firm level. In this situation, the umbrella organization plays no significant role in industrial negotiation unless there is a major breakdown and a crisis erupts during the negotiation.

At times organized labor has also become embroiled in destructive political and racial conflicts. In particular in Jamaica during the Manley period, this can be seen in the growth of "garrison politics," which directly affected trade union political affiliation and access to jobs. In Guyana during the Jagan period, this can be seen in the prevalence of race-based political organizations and the existence of significant occupational segmentation of the workforce along racial lines.

Over the years organized labor has suffered its fair share of criticisms for these negative outcomes. Indeed it became fashionable in the late 1960s and early 1970s to call workers in the leading sectors of the economy, such as petroleum, mining, and export agriculture, all of which were then owned and operated by transnational companies in the region, an "aristocracy of labor." These sectors had high levels of unionization of the workforce and were frequently among the most militant, with the result that these workers were able to command a significant wage premium over other areas of employment. Since that time, however, differential employment/wage changes have drastically eroded this premium, as new sectors like tourism and financial services, which are less amenable to trade union organization of their workforce, have emerged as leading sectors. Today it is more frequent to hear trade unions described as "archaic and antediluvial institutions," out of place in the modern age of liberalization. These criticisms mount when industrial conflicts occur, causing inconveniences for those affected and the wider society.

The criticisms that have been made of organized labor in the region are harsh and somewhat unfair. Generally, organized labor, strongly guided by figures like Jagan and Manley, has never turned its back on any of the great popular challenges of our times—including the recent fallout from globalization and liberalization, the social and economic degradations that accompanied policies of structural adjustment pursued in many countries of the region and in particular Guyana and Jamaica since the 1970s, the erosion of human and social rights since independence, and the balkanization and external domination of the region. Indeed, without organized labor the prevailing market ideology that supports (and also has supported) globalization would have by now removed concerns like socioeconomic reform, social justice, and the protection of national economic interests entirely from the agenda of urgent regional issues.

Having pointed to all these positives, however, it is nevertheless fair to say that organized labor faces a crisis of unprecedented magnitude—a crisis that stems in considerable measure from the impact of fundamental global changes on the region. This essay seeks to explore these global changes, mainly with reference to Guyana and Jamaica in tribute to the legacies of Cheddi Jagan and Michael Manley. Some of the major international currents that contribute to the crisis situation facing the labor movement will be identified. The discussion then turns to the impact of Guyana and Jamaica's economic and social performance on labor in a broader regional (CARICOM) context during this period. And finally, indicators for a way forward are identified.

International Currents

To fully understand the crisis that presently faces organized labor in the region, it is necessary to locate the region in the broad international context, which plays a leading role in the performance of its economy and shapes its national economic policies. With a population of only 6 million people and a combined GDP of U.S.$15 billion, the economic integration arrangement of the English-speaking Caribbean, CARICOM, represents a very small region in a very large world. If comparison is made with the western hemisphere alone, we find that the grouping accounts for only 0.6, 0.8, and 0.2 percent respectively of the hemisphere's land area, population, and GDP. All the territories in the region are very "open," in that the bulk of their employment, income, foreign exchange earnings, and tax revenues are generated out of the export of primary agricultural products (sugar, bananas, rice, and citrus and tree crops), minerals (bauxite-alumina, petroleum, natural gas, and gold), services (tourism, offshore finance, and educational institutions), foreign direct investment (in all sectors), and concessional capital flows from bilateral donors and multilateral agencies. Its commodity exports in particular are high cost and uncompetitive when traded in open global markets. This, however, rarely occurs, as most of the important crops (sugar and bananas) benefit from nonreciprocal preferential trade arrangements with Europe and North America, in force for most of the period since independence. The consequence is that today the CARICOM region remains one of the most preferences-dependent economic regions in the world. It goes without saying, therefore, that in circumstances as described above, the global environment is crucial to the economic survival of the region.

Turning to that environment, we find that at present far reaching global changes are severely impacting the region's economy and confronting organized labor with some of its most profound challenges. Of these, perhaps the most important is the unprecedented growth in global trade (which has exceeded growth in global output, incomes, consumption, and investment) and the shift in international economic policy that has accompanied this. This shift has been away from trading regimes based on special protection, subsidies, the national regulation of production and trade, and other such "nonmarket" considerations, to a more open, deregulated, liberal, rules-based trading regime with strong enforcement capabilities, under the aegis of the World Trade Organization (WTO). This shift constitutes a sea change in trade policy and is progressively undermining the special preferences on which the region's economies have traditionally depended. As this occurs, the region's workforce faces heightened risk and grave threats to its standard of living.

A second fundamental global change is that the increasing globalization of output, trade, and investment that has been taking place has been markedly uneven. Most current global foreign direct investment (approximately 60 percent) is concentrated among the developed economies, and flows to the developing economies are concentrated (80 percent) in about twenty countries. At the height of the cold war, however, the region's geostrategic location within the U.S. security zone had encouraged particular U.S. attention to its economic interests. A number of measures were put in place then, such as the Caribbean Basin Initiative designed to promote U.S.-Caribbean trade and investment, which was of considerable benefit to the workforce. With the end of the cold war, the region had expected to benefit from the "peace dividend," but this has not occurred. Instead, official concessional capital flows to the region as a percentage of its GDP has fallen dramatically to about 40 percent of the levels of its earlier peaks.

A third change has been the increasing global inequalities of income and wealth, and the widening gaps in production potential (including scientific and technological capacity) between countries, that have accompanied globalization. Thus United Nations Development Programme (UNDP) data show that the disparity between the richest and poorest country was 44 to 1 in 1973 and today it is close to 80 to 1. The competitive pressures of globalization also place a premium on knowledge, science and technology, research and development, innovation, and human development. This has led to a profound reconfiguration of the work process and labor markets worldwide—a process that has not escaped the region. Thus there have been marked changes in the skill requirements of the workforce as well as a growing economization in the use of labor—the latter leading to the phenomenon of "jobless growth" and concerns about persistent unemployment. As an example, the skill content for ordinary clerical work in the region has changed dramatically with the advent of the computer, and so have the number of persons required to perform simple routine tasks at comparable occupational levels. The result of technological innovation is that transnational firms, including those operating in the region, have been undertaking far reaching restructuring of their organizations through mergers and acquisitions, downsizing, and indeed changes to the very nature of firm competition, as they resort to practices like "contracting out" and focus on "core activities." All of these changes arising from globalization profoundly affect economic activity in the region, and consequently the opportunities for its labor force.

One consequence of the inequalization of growth has been a growing differentiation among the developing countries themselves. And as they have become more heterogenous, and marked gaps in their capacity in science, technology, and R&D emerge, South-South cooperation, which the region's trade union movement had strongly supported as a means of extending the leverage of developing countries in the global economy, and which figures like Jagan and Manley were identified with internationally, has receded. Indeed, earlier causes such as the struggle for a new international economic order (NIEO) that both Jagan and Manley championed have all but disappeared from the agenda of the South. Today we find that the transnational corporations, which organized labor had vilified in the 1960s and 1970s as agents of neocolonial exploitation and contributors to their impoverishment, are now promoted as the standard-bearers of economic modernity, progress, innovation, and change.

The sea change in trade policy identified above has been generalized into a sea change in global economic policy. The previous primacy, which figures like Jagan and Manley had advocated should be given to the national determination of economic policy and to state-led growth strategies as an expression of independence, has given way to market liberalization, the divestment of public assets, and an emphasis on private sector-led strategies of growth and development. There still remains, however, some residual tension in the region between, on the one hand, such canons as free trade, unrestricted markets, deregulation, divestment, and privatization, and on the other, the older practices of protection, state management of a country's strategic economic interests, and a special role for organized labor. The sea change in global economic policy has also led to the considerable dismantling of the welfare-oriented state worldwide, and this process has also advanced considerably in the region. While up to the 1970s the trade union movement under the influence of Jagan and Manley had championed the idea (and it was universally accepted) that certain social services such as housing, health care, education, and social security were entitlements for citizens, today these services are falling increasingly within the provenance of the marketplace, through such state "modernizing" policies as contracting out, privatization, user fees, and the removal of nontargeted subsidies.

This marketization of welfare provisions has been accompanied by a number of political developments that also severely impact on the situation of labor in the region. In the context of structural adjustment programs (but also in situations without this external pressure), we have witnessed major policies of downsizing and restructuring of the state. Downsizing of the state has led to large layoffs in public sector employment. Thus, for example, in Guyana between the mid-1980s and 2000, public sector employment has fallen by more than one-half, from approximately 76,000 persons to 36,000 persons. In the central government, the current establishment is about one-third (10,000) what it was in 1985 (29,000). Restructuring of the state has led to the contracting out of public services and the creation of semiautonomous agencies that perform functions formerly provided by government departments. For example, revenue collection authorities in Guyana and Jamaica have been introduced to replace Inland Revenue Departments operating out of line ministries. Overall, these changes reflect new concepts at work in the redefinition/reconceptualization of citizenship and individual rights, the reevaluation of governance and the roles of political elites in society, and some restructuring of the legal/economic framework under which organizations of civil society (nongovernmental organizations and community-based organizations) operate.

Finally, at the global level one other change of great moment is that several of the great abuses of the past, which organized labor had fought resolutely against, have reemerged, and often with unimaginable ferocity and savagery. This is especially true of racial, ethnic, cultural, religious, ancestral, and territorial conflicts, where unspeakable barbarisms are now routine. Some new abuses have emerged as well, in particular the threat of or actual breakup of states (including some within the Caribbean), threats to the global natural environment from pollution and mismanagement of natural resources, and the plight of indigenous and other minority populations in many countries. Many old issues have also turned up in a new guise: jobless growth, the marginalization and exclusion of certain social groups, and economic dependence.

It is a truism that workers in the region have never believed that their interests were confined solely to wages and conditions of service at the workplace. Policies and programs at the international level were always interpreted as impacting on their welfare. While the cold war had been a primary source of global tension, its coming to an end, along with the disintegration of socialism as a world system has not, however, noticeably reduced the intensity of national competition at the global level. Indeed, as globalization has proceeded, opportunities for progress (for example, scientific advancement) continue to coexist with an intensification of conflicts that threaten the global pursuit of peace, security, and economic advancement. However, the fundamental reality is that because of its small size, the region is in no position to reciprocate the influence these global economic factors have on it. The region is therefore justifiably fearful that its small size could lead to its marginalization. So far the response of authorities at international fora has been to make the case for small-size developing economies being afforded "special and differential treatment" because of their vulnerability. This response is the basis for the plea for special financial aid, technical support, and longer adjustment periods before its compliance is required for the implementation of changes to the international financial architecture and WTO-type trading standards.

Economic Performance: Guyana and Jamaica

As international figures advocating working-class struggles worldwide, global economic reform, and development of the South, Jagan and Manley stood out in the region. It is somewhat ironic, therefore, that since independence, Guyana and Jamaica have been the two worst economic performers among the English-speaking Caribbean. This has had profound implications for the welfare of ordinary workers in these two countries. Jamaica's average annual per capita growth during the decades of the 1970s, '80s, and '90s has never exceeded 1.5 percent. Guyana's annual average per capita growth in the 1970s was only 1.6 percent, and in the '80s it was negative (minus 3.5 percent). This growth rate, however, recovered to 6.5 percent per annum during the 1990s (table 1). (Cheddi Jagan was president of Guyana from October 1992 until his death in March 1997). The result of this poor performance was that the per capita GDP of Guyana and Jamaica in 1997 was U.S.$947 and U.S.$2,631, respectively—well below that of other CARICOM countries like Antigua and Barbuda (U.S.$8,484), Barbados (U.S.$8,212), and St. Kitts and Nevis (U.S.$6,095). In the 1999 UNDP Human Development Report, Jamaica

Table 1 Average Annual Growth Rate

Growth rate (%)	1970–80		1980–90		1990–97	
	Guyana	Jamaica	Guyana	Jamaica	Guyana	Jamaica
Per capita GDP	0.8	–1.2	–3.5	0.4	6.4	0.4
Population	0.8	1.3	0.5	1.1	0.9	0.7
Urban	1.1	2.8	1.1	2.6	2.6	2.9

Source: Inter-American Development Bank (1999)

was ranked at 82 and Guyana at 99 out of 174 countries. These were the two lowest rankings in the region, with Barbados, the Bahamas, and Antigua-Barbuda reaching the ranks of 29, 31, and 38 respectively, allowing them to be classed as achieving high levels of human development.

In both Guyana and Jamaica economic conditions have been so bad, combined with political and social unrest, that "push" factors have led to high rates of external migration. For the three decades since the 1970s, the population increase in Guyana has been below one percent per annum. In Jamaica it was 1.3 and 1.1 percent in the 1970s and 1980s, but it declined to 0.7 percent in the 1990s (table 1). At the same time, the urban population grew at more than twice the rate of the total population, displaying strong declines in the rural workforce. This growing urbanization has been a factor in the growth of open unemployment, as prior to this rural underemployment masked the full extent of the underuse of the labor force. The unemployment rate in Guyana and Jamaica was recorded at 12 percent in 1992 and 16 percent in 1998 (see table 2).

Other data show that this unemployment is heavily concentrated among two sections of the labor force: youth and women. Although rural underemployment has given momentum to the urban growth depicted above, in the urban areas as well, underemployment in the form of low-productivity, informal, low-wage jobs has grown dramatically. Indeed underemployment has grown to such an extent that a significant category of the "employed poor" now exists. Recent estimates of poverty in the two territories show a head count of the absolute poor as 36 percent for Guyana (1999) and 16 percent (1998) for Jamaica.

Apart from the "employed poor," other important categories of poor have also emerged in these two territories. One is the *systemic poor*, or hard core of persons whom Thomas has described as "born poor and remain poor

Table 2 Unemployment, Poverty, and Income Distribution

	Guyana	Jamaica
GNP per capita (Atlas method) U.S.	770 (1998)	1680 (1998)
Population in poverty (%)	36 (1999)	16 (1998)
UNDP ranking (HDI)*	99	82
Unemployment rate	12 (1992)	16 (1998)
Gini coefficient	0.423 (1993)	0.372 (1998)

*This ranking is based on 174 countries (United Nations Development Programme, 1999).

over their lifetime, mainly because of the manner of their insertion into the system of production and asset ownership" (1997). There is also a group of "newly poor." This group is substantial in the two countries, and has come about because of massive and persistent macroeconomic imbalances, which resulted in the two countries undergoing long, drawn out structural adjustment programs with the IMF/World Bank. Under these programs there were cuts in public employment and wages (referred to above), cuts in public services like education, health, housing, and pensions, and the removal of subsidies. Many workers in traditionally middle-class jobs, such as teaching, nursing, and civil service, consequently found themselves unemployed. There was also a liberalization of import policy, which led to the gutting of embryonic indigenous economic sectors such as clothing, food production, woodworking, and services such as restaurants and entertainment that governments were trying to promote after independence with the aid of tariff protection and subsidies. The hardships for these industries contributed to the failure of the private manufacturing sector to generate an adequate number of jobs as government employment contracted.

There is also in both these countries a large number of "transient poor." These are persons who move in and out of poverty in response to the seasonality of economic activity in the two countries and fluctuations in the levels of economic activity. The former comes about because of the dependence of these economies on seasonal industries like tourism and agriculture. And the latter is more often than not associated with falling commodity prices and natural disasters (for example, flood and drought). Trade in relation to GDP in Guyana and Jamaica is high, 151 percent and 175 percent, respectively. As a general rule poverty and income inequality are usually closely linked and this holds true for Guyana and Jamaica. The Gini coefficient for Guyana is 0.423 (1993) and Jamaica 0.372 (1998).

With low incomes, poverty, and inequality so prevalent, social problems abound and certain systemic weaknesses in the fabric of these two societies have become very pronounced. A good example of this is that the rigid colonial hierarchal social structures that were inherited at the time of independence, although showing some signs of social mobility and flexibility, have also encouraged conflictual and confrontational styles of social interaction. The trade union movement and its struggles in both these countries exemplify this tendency. Another example is the violent political cleavages that have occurred in both countries during the Jagan and Manley years. In Jamaica this has led to the virulent spread of "garrison politics" and political/tribal conflicts to the point where the 1980 national election year witnessed a thousand deaths due to violence. In the case of Guyana, this manifests itself in repeated race-based political conflicts and division. In both these countries crime and civil disorder have been worse than in any other in the region, save possibly for Trinidad and Tobago.

To organized labor there is a well-established connection between the opportunities for work and the welfare of workers' families and households. Labor markets and their functioning are therefore of great importance to trade unions. Unfortunately, in both Guyana and Jamaica, despite the efforts of Jagan and Manley, labor markets face very serious limitations. We have already referred to the presence of significant unemployment and underemployment and their concentration among youth and women, as well as the impact of state contraction on public sector employment. These apart, the following negative features also characterize the job markets in the two countries:

- The inadequate growth of private sector employment as a means of bridging the gap between the demand and supply of labor.
- The growing informalization of the workforce operating outside formal markets, and in low productivity, low wage, low quality jobs with no legal protection of wage payments, health and safety.
- In both countries, lack of education is the single most important indicator of the likelihood of being poor, out of work, or engaged in low quality, unremunerative work. Yet the bulk of the employed labor force has a minimal education. Thus in Guyana, 11 percent of the labor force in 1992 had no schooling or schooling below the primary level. The largest category of the workforce had only primary schooling (55 per-

cent) with as many as 86 percent of those in agricultural jobs with primary level training alone. Secondary training accounted for 20 percent of employed labor, and university training only 4 percent.
- Gender discrimination in pay and employment is still quite significant in both countries. Female workers are overconcentrated in the caring and nurturing sectors where, as a result of economic difficulties in the two countries, waged salary payments have slipped relative to other sectors.
- Although led for many years by such prominent trade union leaders as Jagan and Manley, the unionization of the workforce in Guyana and Jamaica is far from that which the trade unions desire. Thus, in Guyana, less than one-quarter of all workers are unionized.
- The inequality in income distribution highlighted earlier is mirrored in a wide wage/salary spread in employment. Thus in Guyana the spread between the bottom and top of the "official" pay scales in the central government is about 1 to 14. This does not take into account those at the top who serve under special contracts, which can themselves be three to five times the "official top of the scale." In the private sector the spread is about 1 to 18.
- In Guyana and Jamaica, the Ministry of Labor is the government agency responsible for monitoring and superintending the labor market. In general, in both countries, it remains ill equipped for these purposes. Thus there is either none (Guyana) or a very rudimentary labor market information system. In Jamaica there are regularly conducted surveys and analyses of the labor market, but in Guyana there is none. There is no effective nationwide counseling and guidance service, especially for new entrants to the labor force in either of the two countries. The enforcement of labor market violations is lax, and many employers, including the government, routinely violate occupational, health, environmental, and safety requirements.

The Way Ahead

The analysis of the situation of labor in Guyana and Jamaica has helped to reveal the nature of the crisis facing organized labor, and it may be useful at this stage, therefore, to ask a number of questions: Is there a way out? Is the situation retrievable? Are there lines of fruitful advance still open to organized labor? It would take a great deal of optimism, if not foolhardiness, to answer any of these questions confidently in the affirmative. Nonetheless, as tribute to Jagan and Manley, I shall conclude by directing attention to some elements of a way forward.

First, despite Jagan and Manley's leading of governments and commitment to worker interests, organized labor in the region still suffers from basic legislative and organizational deficits, which urgently need remedying. Here I would single out in particular those handicaps that follow from the absence of an integrated labor code, the uncertain legal standing of collective bargaining agreements, and the role and relationship of individual unions to their national and regional umbrella organizations. Thus, for example, Guyana's labor laws are very ad hoc. Like those in the rest of CARICOM, these were originally modeled on British common law, custom, and legislation, and were framed in the early periods of the industrial revolution, when the presumption was that trade unions were civil-criminal conspiratorial associations designed to restrict an employer's lawful business activities. As Antoine has observed: "The very nomenclature 'Master and Servant Act' betrays the obsolete, class stratified, narrowly capitalistic identity of a labor law system. Yet sadly, such archaic legislation is still evident in Commonwealth Caribbean statute books" (1999).

There have been improvements to this original model, particularly in the postindependence period, with in some instances legislation that takes as its line of departure the preservation of worker interests and rights. Often this reflects citizens' rights enshrined in the independence constitutions. The general feeling in legal circles, however, is that law and legal policy have not kept pace with modernizing developments in the region. Not infrequently, also, judgments in the courts have led to the reversal of worker gains in social and economic areas. The obvious solution to this is the consolidation and integration of labor laws, practice, and custom into a unified code. There is a regional project (the CARICOM Harmonization Project) whose goal is to have omnibus legislation for each country in the region that systematizes, harmonizes, and modernizes its labor laws. Much of the inspiration/impetus behind this comes from the International Labor Organization (ILO), which has helped by drafting model laws that incorporate ILO standards. In this regard, therefore, definite timetables for action and targeted dates for the implementation of specific legislation should be matters of priority. This is a necessary, if not sufficient, condition for reenergizing the labor movement in the region.

Second, one consequence of the many crises facing the labor movement is that it has become obvious that no one social grouping is capable of resolving these crises on its own. This, therefore, gives special urgency to the requirement of forging social partnerships between labor and other major stakeholders in the society. Indeed, this may be considered a strategic imperative, if the crises are to be resolved in favor of the broad masses of Caribbean society, and if labor is to emerge from the process without being mortally wounded. Modern experience indicates that such partnerships will not develop without conscious effort to promote them, or in the absence of the systematic creation of networks and alliances whose aim is to define/redefine existing relations. In the case of organized labor, efforts to form alliances with such social partners as NGOs and CBOs are clearly priorities. So too is the need to put the labor-government-private business relationship on a new footing, one that is more in keeping with the realities of our time.

Third, the systematic pursuit of such networks, as well as the redefinition of relationships they entail, would require that the trade union movement take on a more proactive mantle than it has at the moment. Indeed, it often appears as if many trade union leaders are not fully aware of the extent to which some of the recent phenomena discussed in this chapter, such as globalization, privatization, IMF/World Bank structural adjustment programs, and membership of international (for example, United Nations, IMF/World Bank, and WTO) and regional groupings (for example, NAFTA) have already produced irreversible changes in the role of the state and the structures of civil society of which the unions are a part.

Fourth, in undertaking these responsibilities the trade union movement should be guided by definite principles of social practice. The most important of these is the need to continuously deepen the involvement of its own membership in the activities of the movement. Members' rights in relation to their unions require considerable improvement before the test of "natural justice and reasonableness" can be said to apply fairly. The division of unions sharply along party lines and their continued dependence on governmental patronage are no longer desirable attributes. Trade unions in Guyana and Jamaica, and indeed in the wider Caribbean, need to come out in fuller support of efforts directed at the decentralization and deconcentration of both the public and private economic sectors. This is necessary if organized labor is to be put in a position where it can fulfill its duty to protect and promote the democratic state as the ultimate expression of sovereignty and the embodiment of the popular will, without the partisan political relations or political unionism of the past.

Fifth, because of the fundamental importance of "survival" issues among its rank and file, the trade union movement has the responsibility to crusade against the twin evils of (1) jobless growth and growth without prosperity for the masses, and (2) the untenable separation of social adjustment from the pursuit of macroeconomic and financial equilibria when this becomes necessary, as has been practiced in the region in the past. Experience to date supports the view that without full all-around human development, the mobilization of all social classes and groups, the integral treatment of social and economic reform, and a recognition of the fact that social resources are not only inexhaustible but multiply in significance with usage (for example, acts of solidarity, self-help, social innovation), there can be no social advance.

Sixth, while it has been the case that historically the labor movement has taken root among persons who have no assets but their labor-time to sell, today it is important for labor organizations to reexamine the potential of the resources at their direct command. The potential of the trade union movement as asset owner, producer of goods and services, as well as an organization where tremendous human resources and skills are located, needs to be explored far more vigorously than it has been so far.

Seventh, experience has proven that poverty and social exclusion of groups and individuals can only be seriously reduced if policies are substantially based on the expansion of productive employment at a fair and living wage, recognizing at the same time the importance of self-employment and access to resources for achieving this. Organized labor's interest in jobs, therefore, reaches beyond securing the position of its members. It lies also in ensuring that job expansion and/or increasing self-employment at a living wage lies at the heart of economic policies and programs pursued in the region.

Finally, the legacies of history, size, and geopolitical circumstances make it inconceivable that permanent solutions to the dilemma of labor can be achieved within existing national frameworks. The sheer weight of the international situation makes separate national solutions unlikely and advances the urgency of regional cooperation. Regrettably, the model of integration that CARICOM incorporates is inherently incompatible with present policies that focus on structural adjustment, open trade systems, reduced roles for the public economic sector and public bureaucracies, deregulation, foreign investment, and export-led growth. The leading organizational modes and actors of our present era are very different from those enshrined in CARICOM's economic model. Although at the formal level CARICOM's functional programs require periodic involvement of "other" actors such as NGOs, labor, farmers organizations, private businesses, consumer associations, and professionals, their roles remain essentially subsidiary and subject to institutional direction from above.

All the suggestions made above are consistent with the basic principles from which Jagan and Manley formulated their ideas and advocated policies. In practice both fell well short of achieving them or even setting the processes in place for their eventual implementation. Both were, however, operating in environments over which they could not exercise exclusive control and under the pressure of public events they could not anticipate. It is nevertheless regrettable that even today neither the constitution of Guyana nor Jamaica upholds the *rights* of labor per se. Instead the laws grant "immunities" from civil/criminal process for legitimate trade union activities. Guyana's constitution makes reference to "the right to work" but this is a nonjusticiable right; it is declaratory, since the individual can obtain no remedy in the courts if it is violated. Workers whose rights depend not upon legislative enactment but collective agreements are under great hazard. Labor rights enshrined in law are the necessary starting point for the advancement of workers' interests in the region. At the moment, one of the greatest threats to labor rights is the foreign investment flows into the region in such areas as sweat shops, export-processing zones, and other similar types of offshore activity, which reject unionism as unprofitable for their ventures. It does not serve the legacy of Jagan and Manley well for this to continue—even if it occurred during their lifetimes.

References

Antoine, Rose-Marie Belle. 1999. "One Hundred Years of Labor Law." *Caricom Perspective* (June): 46–52.

Eaton, G. 1988. "The Concept and Model of Political Unionism." Caribbean Labor Series, *Caribbean Institution of Social Formation (CARISFORUM)*, no. 13.

Inter-American Development Bank (IADB). 1999. *Economic and Social Progress Report, 1998–99*. Washington, D.C.

Thomas, C. Y. 1994. "The Future of the Labor Movement in the CARICOM Region," feature address presented at the Fiftieth Annual Conference of Delegates of the Oilfield and General Workers Union, San Fernando, Trinidad, October.

———. 1995. Report on Restructuring the Labor Movement in the Caribbean, prepared for the Caribbean Congress of Labor.

———. 2000. "The Guyana Trade Union Movement in the New Millennium." *Transition* 29: 98–110.

United Nations Development Programme. 1999. *Human Development Report, 1999*. New York.

8

Ethno-Politics and the Caribbean Working-Class Project: Contributions of Cheddi Jagan and Michael Manley

PERRY MARS

Working-class solidarity was viewed by Cheddi Jagan and Michael Manley, particularly during the 1960s and '70s, as necessary for the realization of national economic and social transformation in their respective territories. International cold war politics soon destabilized and derailed their working-class political agendas. This investigation seeks to determine the extent to which ethno-political divisiveness in both Guyana and Jamaica, particularly in the context of highly contentious cold war international politics, undermined the working-class project (that is, efforts toward working-class mobilization, solidarity, and development) championed by these two Caribbean leaders. A further objective of this essay is to address how the destabilization of the working-class project impacts the future development of labor-political relations in the English-speaking Caribbean region as a whole.

In Caribbean labor-political relations there is an apparent contradiction between an observed labor militancy at the economic level, that is, agitation and demand for better wages and working conditions, and a persistent cynicism or even apathy on the part of the working and subordinate classes at the level of political and ideological struggle. How Jagan and Manley grappled with this dilemma, that is, their efforts to bring trade unionism in line with what they regard as genuine working-class interests, is a principal focus here. Their efforts toward these ends represent perhaps the most significant dimensions of their historical legacies, particularly as they affect such critical issues as democratization, political conflict, and conflict resolution in Caribbean societies as a whole.

A major part of the explanation of what appears to be the failure of the political radicalization of the Caribbean working classes, despite the best efforts of a Jagan or Manley, resides in the recurrent tendency at critical historical junctures for ethno-political cleavages to supersede class-oriented politics in countries such as Guyana and Jamaica where ethnic or tribalistic loyalties often define democratic political life. However, unlike the position of a variety of Caribbean social theorists following M. G. Smith (1964, 1965), the fundamental sources of ethno-political cleavages and conflicts that threaten to upset class-interested projects do not necessarily or solely reside in the fundamental character of the groups themselves. The argument here is that the more fundamental sources of ethno-political conflicts in peripheral capitalist countries like Guyana and other ethnically plural Caribbean societies inhere in the relationship between these ethno-political groups on the one hand and external forces primarily interested in hegemonic political and economic pursuits on the other. The two most significant external forces in this respect relate, firstly, to the increasing globalizing interests of foreign capital and internationally hegemonic states, and secondly to the derivation of political and trade union leadership from the usually foreign-dependent and contentious middle classes in Caribbean polities.

Both Jagan and Manley, in their efforts at making a difference historically, appeared themselves to have been unwitting pawns in larger historical processes outside their control. In their pursuit of political power, and their unavoidable location within middle-class leadership structures, it would seem inevitable that they would themselves have contributed to the very contradictions that ultimately undermined their quest for the realization of working-class unity and development. In both their albeit innovative approaches to the ethno-political situation in their respective countries, and to the forces that shape foreign and international political relations, Jagan and Manley ultimately succumbed to hostile global and historical forces. In short, their theoretical and ideological preferences for working-class unity often gave way to historical pressures toward conformity with the demands of economic globalization and the ethno-political realities within their respective domestic environments.

The Working-Class Project

The idea of "the working-class project" derives from the focus of leftist political and social forces in the Caribbean and elsewhere in the Third World on the struggles of labor and the working and subordinate classes to gain a better stake in the economic and political system. Both Cheddi Jagan and Michael Manley were to varying degrees products and initiators of leftist politics in the region (see Mars 1998). An objective of leftist political participation is the fulfillment of the aspirations of the working and subordinate classes, which in the Caribbean context is represented to varying degrees in the organizing and mobilizing patterns of the major left political parties and movements in the region, particularly during the 1970s. Both the People's Progressive Party (PPP) led by Cheddi Jagan in Guyana and the People's National Party (PNP) led by Michael Manley in Jamaica represent different poles within the leftist political spectrum, with the former being originally Marxist and the latter relatively more moderate (that is, democratic socialist) in ideological outlook. This initial ideological variation between the two parties and their leaders is also reflected in their approaches to the realization of working-class objectives. Nevertheless, there are common elements in their conceptualization of, and ideological adherence to, class politics in general and working-class politics in particular.

The working-class project involves, principally, ideological or political-philosophical adherence to five basic assumptions about political and power relationships: (1) that class relations ultimately supersede race, ethnic, or cultural considerations in the conduct of political struggle, (2) that unity among the working and subordinate classes is necessary for successful power struggles and ultimate social transformations, (3) that workers' organizations and trade unions facilitate working-class unity and the necessary politicization of the workforce through organic linkages with political parties, (4) that both class unity and successful power struggles are facilitated by international class solidarity through the development of close links with like-minded trade union and political movements abroad, and (5) that the primary objective of working-class political and ideological struggles is the attainment of some form of socialism in which the working and subordinate classes play a more elevated role—whether in the form of what the moderates term "worker participation" or the Marxists term "worker control"—in both economic and political processes in the particular political system.

Cheddi Jagan talking among the crowd at Bourda market, Georgetown. © Nadira Jagan-Broncier

Within this perspective, the Caribbean working classes as a whole are broadly defined to include, principally although not exclusively, the relatively few urban industrialized workers (particularly in the sugar industry, mining, manufacturing, and construction). Also included in this conceptualization are the largely rural semipeasants (that is, poor landless farmers, inclusive of those who work part time on the sugar plantations), the lumpen proletarian elements comprising the usually large numbers of urban unemployed throughout the region, and the lower echelons (basically the salaried service sector) of the middle classes (see Thomas 1988, Beckford and Witter 1980). In fact the full range of membership of these subordinate classes constitute what Rodney and others refer to as the "working people" of the region (Rodney 1981). Here, also, are assumptions: firstly, of homogeneity of interests among these seemingly disparate categories that make up the Caribbean working people, and secondly, of an essential conflictual (although not necessarily antagonistic) relationship between these perennially subordinate classes and the economically dominant (capitalist) classes, whether of the domestic or foreign variety.

Where Jagan and Manley differ in their conceptualization of the working-class project is mainly in terms of strategies toward the empowerment of these disadvantaged classes. Manley, for example, conceptualized his strategy in terms of his party's original platform of democratic socialism, meaning that class political struggles should be conducted within the ambit of Westminster electoral processes inherited from British colonialism (Hart 1989, 142). Within this context the relationship between dominant and subordinate classes—workers (labor) and employers (capital), or the Caribbean masses and state authorities—is interpreted as basically flexible and nonantagonistic. For Jagan, on the other hand, strategies toward working-class empowerment were for the greater part of his political career viewed primarily in classical Marxist terms, that is, in terms of a much more combative interaction between mutually opposed classes or class interests within the particular social system. Jagan also advocated a stronger internationalism with closer ties to the then Soviet Union and Eastern bloc communist countries. However, with respect to relations with Cuba and solidarity with liberation struggles abroad, both Jagan and Manley were almost at par.

The domestic and historical derivation of the idea of the working-class project emanated from a series of episodes of major labor unrest, which included spontaneous strikes and extensive political and state violence, that swept the entire English-speaking Caribbean during the late 1930s (Lewis 1939, Chase 1964, Henry 1972), and continued intermittently up to the time of the birth of the PPP in 1950. The PNP was born out of West Indian solidarity meetings in Harlem in support of the embattled strikers in the region at the end of the 1930s, while Jagan swore by the blood of the martyred Enmore sugar workers who were slain by the colonial police during a strike in 1948 that he would thenceforward dedicate his life to the struggle for workers' economic and political rights (Jagan 1972).

Both Jagan and Manley concretized their working-class theoretical or ideological commitments through leadership and organization of trade unions that had close associations with the political parties they led. The PNP-affiliated union led by Michael Manley was the National Workers Union (NWU), which between 1956 and 1974 surpassed in terms of paid membership the older Bustamante Industrial Trade Union (BITU) (Gonzalves 1977). In Guyana, Cheddi Jagan led first the Sawmill and Forest Workers Union (SFWU) until the 1970s when that union folded and subsequently the Guyana Agricultural and General Workers' Union (GAWU) up to the time of his death in 1997. As an indication of the militancy of trade union leadership on behalf of the workers' cause, various confrontations took place against employers, for better wages and working conditions; rival unions, in competition for membership; and the state, to ensure more liberal worker-oriented laws or greater industrial democracy. In addition, overt political strikes such as those in support of adult suffrage and political independence during colonial times, or against political dictatorship as in the case of Guyana during the Burnham era (1964–85), demonstrated the high degree of labor militancy among the more politically conscious workers in the Caribbean (Mars 1998).

It was in the conduct of militant labor-political struggles for working-class empowerment that the most critical contradictions of Caribbean politics, particularly at the leadership levels, were revealed. The results, paradoxically enough, were often setbacks for the working-class project in both Guyana and Jamaica, as elsewhere throughout the Caribbean. For Manley and Jagan these contradictions manifested themselves principally at two critical levels: (1) at the domestic social-structural level, demonstrating significant fragmentation of the labor movement along both class (or occupational) and ethnic (or color-conscious) lines, and (2) at the international level, in which case the initial opposition by the PPP in the 1960s and by the PNP in the 1970s to international capital eventually succumbed to relentless international pressures toward conformity to global capitalist forces. Thus, from an early commitment to a pro-labor and pro-working-class ideological position, both Jagan and Manley, and indeed, most of the Caribbean labor and leftist political movements, capitulated wholly to a pro-international capitalist, or neoliberalist, position during the 1980s and '90s (Mars 1998). In the process, the gap between the typically middle-class leadership of Caribbean workers and political movements and the Caribbean masses and working classes themselves became increasingly widened. To understand the critical issues that the Jagan and Manley political leadership faced and their responses to these issues, it is necessary to examine more closely the nature of what is here termed the ethno-political dilemma.

The Ethno-Political Dilemma

Ethno-politics in the Caribbean refers to the efforts by political leaders to politicize ethnic or localized communal groups as a strategy toward the attainment of political or state power. Such ethnic or communal groupings in the Guyana and Jamaican contexts relate to the variety of racially, ethnically, or communal and neighborhood-dominated constituencies that have over the years developed into electoral strongholds of particular political parties. Observed racial and ethnic ties to parties such as the PPP and People's National Congress (PNC) in Guyana, or neighborhood communal as well as color-class ties to both the PNP and the Jamaica Labor Party (JLP) in Jamaica, are almost legendary as ethno-political conflict zones in these Caribbean countries. In Guyana the working-class East Indians support the PPP, while the working and middle-class Afro-Guyanese support the PNC; in Jamaica lumpenproletarian elements, Rastafarians, and brown-skinned Jamaicans clamor for the PNP, in contrast to the darker-skinned working classes and white or very light-skinned upper-class Jamaicans who support the JLP. Trade unions too become affected by this type of ethno-political divisiveness reflected, for example, in what Ralph Gonzalves called the "tribalization of unionism" in Jamaica (see Gonzalves 1977, 99).

However, ethno-political divisiveness goes beyond the simple clientelistic types of commitments that Carl Stone regarded as the pivotal characteristic of political life and relationships in Jamaica (Stone 1980). The clientelistic commitment presupposes the expectation by the subordinate supporters or "clients" of some kind of tangible reward from the party for their support, particularly if that party gains political power. In ethno-political linkages, however, rewards accrue mainly to the political party leaders in the form of secured votes and a reliable catchment of agitators, protesters, and demonstrators on the party's behalf. Any expectation of rewards on the part of supporters is largely incidental to the main objective of ethno-political affiliations, which buttresses the political leadership. Nor is it simply a case of the legitimation of political leadership through cultivating links with particular communal constituencies or grassroots supports (Hintzen 1989). Ethno-political associations are usually not acknowledged or represented as such by the political leadership but are invariably couched in terms of some universalistic ideology like appeals to nationalist, mass, or "people" consciousness on the part of the national population. It is these univeralistic appeals that are usually offered as the basis of the legitimization of partisan or ethno-political leadership. In short, fundamentalist appeals to ethnic, tribalistic, or communal loyalties are transposed into notions of justice, equality, or socialistic idealism.

Ethno-political divisiveness is rooted in the structure of the colonial-imposed division of labor in Caribbean economies. This ethnicized division of labor is manifested in the occupationally differentiated hierarchy in which the darker-skinned groups such as blacks and East Indians occupy the lowest rungs of the labor hierarchy and do most of the menial work while the lighter-skinned groups such as Chinese, Portuguese, and "mixed races" are predominant in the commercial and business sectors of the economy. And even among the lower paying occupations, there are divisions along ethnic lines as is the case in Guyana where East Indians on sugar plantations do mostly field work while Afro-Guyanese are more represented in factory and technical work. Also East Indians in Guyana work predominantly in a rural setting while Afro-Guyanese tend to be more urban based and predominate particularly in the mining industry. As a result of this kind of ethnicized division of labor, the organized labor movement tends also to be affected by patterns of ethnic differentiation.

The central issues for ethno-politics are conflict and conflict management. The very politicization of ethnicity, that is, mobilization of ethnic or communal groups for political purposes, can transform relatively benign and complementary groupings into lethally contentious units. Within the Caribbean context, a colonial-imposed Westminster electoral system, the inadequate "polyarchic democracy" as Robinson termed it (1996), itself becomes part of the problem in that the quest for political power is a zero-sum game: it requires what is called a winner-take-all competition among parties for control of political power. Ethno-political conflicts and violence seem endemic in such limited polyarchic systems as exemplified in the English-speaking Caribbean. Both Jagan and Manley inherited this conflict-prone political system within which they had only limited room to implement the far reaching political changes toward the realization of the working-class project.

The cataclysmic impact of ethno-political conflicts on the relationship between the Caribbean working classes and political movements can be viewed from both the national societal level and within political parties and trade unions in the region, particularly in Guyana and Jamaica. Among the most devastating ethno-political conflicts in Guyana are the persistent spates of African–East Indian hostilities that began in 1962–64, and were spearheaded by both the Forbes Burnham-led PNC and the Cheddi Jagan-led PPP. Particularly during the 1960s, ethno-political violence reached the intensity whereby ethnic minorities in rival political strongholds, and even in simply ethnically mixed communities, had to flee for their lives or safety to more ethnically compatible communities. In Jamaica, this level of conflict is observed in the repeated violent confrontations between politicized neighborhood communities, spearheaded by both the Edward Seaga-led JLP, and Michael Manley-led PNP. In these events, hostilities reached such heights that dead PNP supporters in May Pen could not be buried in Calvery cemetery, since the funeral procession had to pass through the neighboring JLP stronghold of Tivoli Gardens where residents threatened more violence against PNP "socialists" (Ray and Schapp, *CAIB* 1983, 12). In short, ethno-political violence in Guyana and Jamaica resulted in the serious polarization of the working classes and their communities along both ethnic and geographic lines.

Caribbean political parties contribute to the self-reinforcement of this ethnicized polarization of the working classes by their tendency to bypass what are viewed as "die-hard" rival constituencies in their electoral mobilizing appeals, not only because of fear of reprisals but because lobbying these constituencies is considered a waste of time for the ultimate sake of obtaining votes in the centralized polyarchic system. But neglect of the difficult rival constituencies is tantamount to a neglected opportunity to bridge ethnic or tribalistic gaps affecting working-class unity. This observation applies equally to both the PPP, which in many instances sought to avoid campaigning in PNC electoral strongholds in Guyana, particularly in the remotest regions of the country that demand a great deal of the party's resources, and vice versa, and the PNP in Jamaica, which sought to avoid JLP electoral strongholds (and vice versa) for similar reasons (see Robertson 1967).

Conflicts within the party have also taken their toll on the ability of the leadership to successfully mobilize a unified working-class support. The most significant dimensions of such internal conflicts manifest themselves in terms of splits and purges that tend to eliminate either the left wing of the party—which is usually more dedicated, consistent, and skillful in relating to the masses and subordinate classes—or critical sections of ethnic support allied to the left. The combination of these exclusivist strategies usually ends up reinforcing ethnic divisiveness among the working classes in the society as a whole. From its inception, the PNP had engaged in purges of leftists members such as Ken Hill and Richard Hart who had established deep roots in the Jamaican labor and working-class movement—actions that brought about the disarray and defeat experienced by the Jamaican TUC during the 1950s. Ironically enough, the young Michael Manley was brought into the party by his father Norman to accomplish just such a purge (Gonzalves 1977, Hart 1989). Manley's later ostracism of the more modern left within his party, including D. K. Duncan and others during the 1980s, might have accomplished the same distancing of the party from significant sections of the Jamaican working classes.

Within the PPP in Guyana, splits and purges had similar disruptive effects upon working-class unity. The first split in 1955 between so-called moderates and extremists on the leftist ideological spectrum served to divide the Guyanese working classes along racial and ethnic lines, with blacks polarized around the moderate (socialist) Burnhamist faction on the one hand and East Indians holding fast to the extremist (Marxist) Jaganite faction on the other. The second split (or most probably purge) in 1956 targeted and ostracized the left of the party including the cream of the black leadership within the PPP hierarchy. At the root of this split was Jagan's address to the 1956 PPP Congress that sought to attract more middle-class support (mainly from East Indian businessmen) for the party (Despres 1967). The effect was to further alienate blacks within the party, and black working-class support nationally, despite Jagan's subsequent argument that the 1956 statement was meant to be simply tactical. The third split in the early 1960s amounted to a black left rebellion within the party hierarchy involving Brindley Benn and others, and supported by the youth arm of the party, the Progressive Youth Organization (PYO), over the issues of (1) the party's neglect of the black predicament within an organization that was becoming increasingly East Indian dominated, and (2) apparent refusal of key members both within the leadership and rank and file of the party to accept political independence from colonial rule under Burnham and a black-dominated PNC government (see New World [Guyana] 1965, 1–3).

Ethno-political conflicts within the party carry over into the labor movement with equally divisive impact on the working-class project. This impact is particularly noted in cases of the general strike, which has become the modal weapon of struggle embraced by left-wing parties in the interest of advancing working-class causes. Difficulties of organizing general strikes across ethnic boundaries became apparent during the postcolonial struggles in the region, whether against the Burnhamite dictatorship in Guyana, Edward Seaga's procapitalist rule in Jamaica, or Eric Williams's political domination in Trinidad and Tobago. Examples of this process include the lengthy sugar workers' strike in Guyana in 1977 and the anti-IMF strikes and riots in Jamaica (1985), Guyana (1989), and Trinidad and Tobago (the 1980s). Both Jagan and Manley were in the forefront of the respective general strikes in Guyana and Jamaica. Many of the difficulties of the class-unified general strike inhere in the occupational division of labor along ethnic lines. The divisions give managers an additional divide-and-rule weapon, in that members of rival ethnic groups can be used to break strikes, which has the side effect of furthering the degeneration of ethnic group relations in these Caribbean societies.

Foreign Destabilization

Behind the domestic sources that tend to be destructive of the Caribbean working-class project are foreign interests that are aimed at protecting the international hegemonic position of foreign capital and a neoliberal ideological regime. Such a neoliberal regime, as William Robinson points out, involves foreign imposition of what he termed "polyarchic" democratic systems that are designed to serve the interests of global capital (1996). Pressures toward conformity to this hegemonic system of global neoliberalism stemmed from the cold war context in which hegemonic capitalist states like the United States, and Britain before it, sought to prevent the emergence and development in peripheral capitalist countries like in the Caribbean of forces that challenge international capitalist interests. Any such counterhegemonic challenges from within the periphery were regarded as supportive of rival international regimes such as the Soviet Union and the People's Republic of China. Within this context, therefore, the idea of the working-class project pursued by Caribbean leftist movements were regarded by these globally hegemonic states as too Marxist or communist, and consequently destined for containment, destabilization, or even eradication (see Watson, this volume). For this reason, foreign governments used destabilization methods liberally against leftist-oriented working-class movements in the region. In the process, even the labor movements in internationally hegemonic capitalist states, particularly the United States, played a significant vanguard role in the destabilization of Caribbean working-class activism (see Jagan 1972, Mars 1998, Watson, this volume).

A critical role in the entire destabilization process was reserved for the American labor movement and to some extent the British TUC. The AFL-CIO's mission seemed to have been synonymous with the anticommunist cold war foreign program of the U.S. state department. For the Caribbean region, the foreign policy arm of the AFL-CIO, the American Institute for Free Labor Development (AIFLD), was assigned the specific task of infiltrating and converting the major Caribbean labor organizations to a more pro-U.S. orientation. Jagan has documented his experience with the destabilizing involvement of the AIFLD, assisted by the CIA, in the massive TUC general strike of 1963–64 and the resulting rebellious upheaval over the issue of the Labor Relations Bill (LRB) that his government had introduced in 1963 in order to democratize the feudalistic Guyana TUC and labor movement (see Jagan 1972). The result was the highest levels of ethnic violence, death, and destruction the country had ever experienced in modern times and the entrenched ethnic polarization of the Guyanese working classes.

Michael Manley experienced similar CIA and other foreign destabilization of his democratic socialist government between 1976 and 1980. CIA strategy, as Maurice Bishop discovered in his experience as head of Grenada's revolutionary government between 1979 and 1983, involved sequential levels of application, notably (1) propaganda destabilization, which includes negative and damaging press releases about the target country and government; (2) economic destabilization, involving the withholding of loans and other forms of economic assistance; (3) political destabilization, involving financial and other material support to strengthen rival, usually right-wing, political parties; and finally (4) violent destabilization, involving the use of armed groups against the state and supporters of leftist movements in the system (Bishop 1979, Searle 1983). In Jamaica all levels of destabilization were applied to defeat Manley's efforts to develop a closer party–working-class alliance and friendly diplomatic links with Cuba and other socialist bloc countries in the world. In addition to CIA subversion, private foreign financing went into creating private armies, such as Charles Johnson's armed group, as well as supplying arms and sophisticated military equipment to the rival JLP to topple the Manley regime (Ray and Schapp, *CAIB* 1980, 9). And as in Guyana, hundreds of Jamaicans were killed, and the working classes became significantly alienated from party politics (see Carl Stone 1983).

Ultimately, legitimation of the gap between trade unionism and working-class politics today is fostered by the unavoidable structural adjustment arrangements between the IMF (or World Bank) and Caribbean states, including Guyana and Jamaica, which have become entrapped in a serious international debt crisis (see McAffee 1991). A crucial aspect of IMF conditionalities that these indebted countries are obliged to follow if they are to retain their international credit worthiness is to curtail labor activism and demands for better wages and working conditions, since these labor demands could be interpreted by prospective foreign investors as precipitating an unstable and, therefore, unwelcoming industrial environment. In anticipation of the economic hardships that are known to accrue from imposition of IMF conditionalities, in the 1980s the Caribbean working classes and many of their labor unions unleashed a series of strikes and demonstrations that often resulted in full-scale political violence, not only in Jamaica, Guyana, and Trinidad and Tobago but in the Dominican Republic, Haiti, Venezuela, and Colombia.

Through the policies, therefore, of international economic institutions, foreign destabilization has come full circle, from the use, by internationally hegemonic states, of trade unions to decimate leftist political parties to the use of the IMF to decimate progressive trade unions. By the end of the 1980s, therefore, Caribbean states and political movements did not have to wait for the collapse of the Soviet Union and international communism to dismantle their own struggle toward the realization of socialism and the working-class project. Much of the momentum toward an embrace of the capitalist realities, and retreat from class politics in the region, had already been accomplished through the increasing rightward shift of the Caribbean left, occasioned by the twin perils of entrenched ethno-politics and deadly foreign destabilization (see Mars 1998).

Toward Conflict Resolution?

Both Jagan and Manley attempted to deal forthrightly with the contradictions emanating from the twin perils of ethno-political conflicts and international destabilizing processes. In the process they themselves often contributed, perhaps unwittingly, to these very contradictions that ultimately undermined or defeated their prospective working-class projects. In this section we are interested in evaluating the nature of their varied efforts toward these ends, their possible levels of success or failure, and the lessons of these experiences for understanding the future of working-class struggles in the Caribbean region as a whole. Here we are dealing with the theoretical, and practical, issue of the extent to which political leadership could indeed be autonomous or independent of the apparently deterministic forces of both inherited history and inexorable external pressures. The experiences of Jagan and Manley in this respect will undoubtedly shed light on the traditional leftist debate on the relationship between race and class under capitalism.

The relatively autonomous efforts of Jagan and Manley to deal with these critical issues involve programmatic and policy initiatives at basically three levels of operation: the party, the national, and the international. Within the party, the leadership of Jagan of the PPP and Manley of the PNP tended to be largely status quo oriented and hardly proceeded to change the structures within the party to address issues of ethno-political conflict resolution. In fact it is at this level that much of the leadership contradictions became apparent. The preservation of the typically middle-class leadership hierarchy, the ostracism or purge of the left wing, and neglect of issues of ethno-political divisiveness within both parties are cases in point. Within their respective parties, leadership initiatives on the part of both Jagan and Manley tended, at critical moments, to exacerbate the ethno-political contradictions throughout their respective societies. This is evidenced in the cases of the proposed creation by the PNP of a private thug army to combat similar thug forces of the rival JLP in the late 1970s, or the fostering of the "die hard" mentality of PNP support groups against admission of former JLP supporters (see Robertson 1967). Similarly, in the Guyana case the PPP youth arm (the PYO) created what they regarded as a self defensive force to counteract similar violent confrontations with well-armed PNC and UF supporters during the politically violent period of the early 1960s, while, also, the party, notwithstanding Jagan's isolated interventions to counteract these trends, largely ignored the concerns of black party members about the rise of East Indian chauvinism within the party since that time.

The more positive initiatives, however, were witnessed at the interparty levels, that is, in overtures from both Jagan and Manley to rival parties, the PNC and JLP respectively, toward the deflation of the long-standing tensions and hostilities between these groups. In this respect Jagan had a longer and more consistent record than Manley. Since the violent crisis days of the 1960s, Jagan offered a series of peace compromises to opposition political and trade union forces, including the signing of peace pacts, withdrawal of the contentious Labor Relations Bill, and equal sharing of cabinet posts in his government with the major opposition PNC party. Although the PNC, under Burnham, signed the peace accords, the opposition forces on the whole (PNC and UF in particular), championed by the more resource-rich foreign interests, rejected Jagan's peace packages. A peace pact was also signed between Manley and Seaga in the wake of the massive political vio-

Michael Manley shaking hands with the people of Kingston. © The Gleaner Co. Ltd.

lence between their two respective parties in 1988 to ensure freedom of movement of their respective supporters across party territorial strongholds.

In the interests not only of peace but more importantly of reconciliation of the largely polarized Guyanese working classes, Jagan during the 1980s went beyond the earlier offers of peace pacts and official compromises, toward the development of more far-reaching, comprehensive initiatives embracing all the major parties in the political process. These new initiatives took a variety of forms including (1) proposals for a national-front government involving the three major political parties at the time, the PPP, PNC, and WPA (PPP, 1977), (2) the unilateral offer of "critical support" to the ruling party, the PNC (PPP, 1985), (3) involvement in private talks toward reconciliation with the

PNC, and (4) alliance formations with a variety of political and social organizations that were then in opposition to the PNC regime.

These initiatives, although backed by popular demand, failed mainly because of the intransigence of the ruling PNC party, and secondarily, because of the reluctance of the PPP to compromise on its ideological position of anti-imperialism and socialism. The PNC's argument was that the PPP's "national front" and "dialogue initiatives" represented collaboration only from the top, rather than from the grassroots where it matters most. This argument neglected the fact that the source of the ethno-political divisiveness in Guyanese society was the instability inherent in the middle-class leadership (that is, at the top) of both parties. But more fundamentally, the PNC's intransigence was buttressed by the security it enjoyed from the foreign support gained by being readily identified as the noncommunist party. Jagan's overtures to the other opposition political forces were also rebuffed primarily because, as the WPA contended, of the PPP's insistence on including anti-imperialism and socialism on any agenda toward political alliance formation (WPA 1983). The bottom line, however, was that most of the smaller opposition parties were still suspicious of the PPP for being much like the PNC in harboring entrenched ethno-political interests within its ranks.

At the national level, both the PPP under Cheddi Jagan in Guyana and the PNP under Michael Manley in Jamaica initiated policies aimed at improving the level of democratic participation among the working classes in these two countries. Both the Labor Relations Bill introduced by Jagan in the 1960s and the Labor Relations and Industrial Disputes Act (LRIDA) introduced by Manley in the 1970s intended to legislate an atmosphere of democratic choice within the labor movement such that workers rather than employers could determine which union should represent them, along with other considerations such as prevention of dismissal of workers for union activities or of lockouts without just cause. Controversy soon followed these pieces of labor legislation both within the labor movement itself and among overly sensitive political opposition in both societies. We already noted the foreign-inspired destabilization of the Jagan government over the LRB. On the Jamaican LRIDA, the PNP was roundly criticized from both the left and the right for passing what was seen as an essentially anti-working-class legislation since it conjured images of the notorious Industrial Stabilization Act (ISA) in Trinidad under Eric Williams, which effectively banned strikes and fettered the independent maneuverability of the working classes of Trinidad and Tobago (*Caribbean Dialogue* 1976, 2:20).

It was at the international level that the bold diplomatic genius and political credibility of both Jagan and Manley revealed themselves. Manley's leadership, for example, in sponsoring the radical international proposal for a new international economic order (NIEO), was masterful—a proposal aimed at transforming the structure of international economic relations in such a way that economically disadvantaged states get a fairer deal in the international system. The NIEO proposal represented the expansion to the international level of Manley's long-standing efforts to bring greater social and economic justice to the disadvantaged working classes. Although widely acclaimed and supported by the overwhelming majority of international states, particularly the Third World countries in the United Nations, the NIEO project crashed, principally because of objections and lack of support from the hegemonic capitalist powers in the international system.

Severe challenges to the leadership of both Manley and Jagan resulted from their dealings with the IMF and World Bank. These two international lending institutions often pose serious dilemmas to Third World leaders interested in improving the lot of the disadvantaged classes, since IMF conditionalities, through a regime of structural adjustment, advocate curtailment of working-class demands for better wages and working conditions. Equally troubling to most leftist leaders of varying persuasion, from the pro-Marxist Jagan to the reformist Manley, is the IMF insistence on dismantling public enterprises in favor of exclusive emphasis on privatization, much to the disadvantage of workers who see this shift as a potential loss of benefits. On the issue of whether to borrow money and accept the stringent IMF conditionalities Manley vacillated during the 1970s, and left much of the implementation of the conditionalities to the succeeding Seaga JLP government in the 1980s. Jagan inherited an IMF austerity plan that the previous PNC regime had already imposed on the Guyanese working people, but he promised to maintain the agreement including the fulfillment of the controversial privatization program (Ministry of Finance, 1993). However, Jagan was rumored to have said privately that he was not entirely happy with the IMF package, particularly the privatization aspect (Jagan confirmed this rumor in a private conversation with the author in Georgetown in the summer of 1993). In any case, much of the privatization implementation is moot, since private buyers of unprofitable government-run enterprises are hard to find.

Jagan's master stroke at the international level relates to his relentless private diplomatic moves to discredit the illegitimate PNC regime, and so shift international support toward his campaign for democratizing Guyanese politics through a return to free and fair elections. Through his diplomatic efforts, Jagan eventually overcame the major obstacle of the cold war years, that is, foreign opposition to his leadership role. But several factors combined to work in his favor by 1992. First, Burnham died suddenly in 1985. Second, Burnham himself had contributed to the alienation of international interests with a series of noncapitalist policies, including the nationalization of foreign-owned industries. Third, by 1989 the cold war ended with the collapse of the Soviet Union and the fall of the Berlin Wall. But most of all, Jagan's persistence and persuasiveness had managed to eke out a public confession and apology from Arthur Schlesinger, Jr. about his role in the White House and British conspiracy to unjustly discredit and topple his PPP government in the 1960s. Further, Jagan's diplomacy succeeded in obtaining significant backing for his cause from the Congressional Black Caucus, Senator Edward Kennedy, and former U.S. president Jimmy Carter, among others. International mediation in 1992, spearheaded by the Carter Center in Atlanta, helped ensure the freedom of the Guyana elections, and Jagan and the PPP returned to power (under the new appellation PPP/Civic).

No sooner, however, had Jagan won this international diplomatic victory than he again became confounded by the ethno-political reality at the domestic level, and within his party in particular. The PPP victory at the polls in 1992 seemed to have accentuated, rather than reduced, ethnic chauvinism within the ruling party, even to the isolation of Jagan and his working-class project. In particular Jagan's failure to implement a promised Race Relations Commission, the idea of which was very popular among a wide cross section of Guyanese people, tended to further legitimize entrenched ethnic divisions in Guyanese society. The ethno-political violence following both the 1992 and the 1997 elections, despite a free and fair process observed by regional and international mediators, is an indication of the tenacity of ethnic suspicions throughout Guyanese society. Similarly, Jagan promised before the election to support a more militant trade unionism in the form of the late 1980s creation of the Federation of Independent Trades Unions of Guyana (FITUG) as an alternative to the pro-PNC and relatively conservative TUC. After the election, he acquiesced to IMF expectations of support for the more status quo oriented TUC.

It would seem, therefore, that both Jagan and Manley, despite their boldest independent efforts, fell prey to the relatively more powerful historical and international deterministic forces. Their room for independent maneuver was severely limited by both class and racial configurations at the domestic level, and ideological and political considerations at the international level. They were unable to transcend the entrapment of middle-class leadership within their own parties, the strategic significance of ethno-political mobilization toward political power, and, until late in their careers, their largely nonaligned nationalistic loyalties in the face of an increasing internationalization and globalization of political and economic processes.

The Guyana and Jamaica experiences also suggest that, unlike the assumptions of orthodox leftist theories, the relationship between race and class is not necessarily fixed or linear, in the sense that class is invariably prior to race in the determination of significant outcomes in the political process. Rather, the relationship is a flexible, often interchangeable one, such that racial or ethno-political configurations can become relatively autonomous of class. The bottom line though is that in most working-class struggles in the postcolonial period, it is difficult to absolutely separate class from ethno-political considerations, particularly in the context of the pursuit of power in the competitive, polyarchic political system characteristic of Guyana, Jamaica, and the other English-speaking Caribbean countries. This observation, however, does not take away from the argument that ultimately it is global or international class and power relations that govern the dynamics within Caribbean and Third World political and economic processes.

Conclusion

In retrospect, several important insights into the future development of Caribbean working-class projects are discernible from the experiences, perspectives, and political practices of Cheddi Jagan and Michael Manley. The first important lesson from their difficult struggles to uplift the status of the working classes in their respective societies is that it becomes perilous to ignore the significance of global and international influences on domestic political realities. Such international realities as the cold war paranoia of hegemonic powers, or IMF structural adjustment conditionalities, must be considered in estimating the potential for success of working-class struggles against capital in the domestic political arena. For this reason, political struggles within Guyana and Jamaica become successful to the extent they involve the simultaneous waging of struggles at the levels of, say, the U.S. Congress, the British House of Commons, or the U.N. General Assembly or Security Council, or other such forums of international support. Political leaders in the capitalist periphery like the Caribbean, therefore, should conceptualize their domestic struggles or strategies toward political and economic transformation within an international or global perspective, if genuine and lasting successes are to be attained.

The second important lesson from these experiences is that waging working-class struggles within the context of the polyarchic contest for political power, particularly in societies divided strictly along ethno-political lines like Guyana and Jamaica, almost invariably degenerates into a zero-sum mutual elimination contest, with negative implications for the prospects of realizing the unified working-class project. Conceptualization of ethno-political or communal conflicts within the working-class project had always attracted at best an ambivalent commitment on the part of most leftist Caribbean leaders, including Jagan and Manley. At worst ethno-political and communal divisions were used as an opportunity to maximize chances of success at the polls in pursuit of centralized political power. Ultimately such ambivalent commitments result in the fragmentation of the working classes themselves.

Third, among the lessons of the Caribbean working-class struggle is comprehending the tremendous difficulties of realizing a totally independent trade union movement. Indeed, trade unions might declare their nonalignment vis-à-vis existing political parties, but they can hardly escape ideological commitment to issues relating to support for class interests, whether in the cause of working-class struggle, or of capital in its spurious claim that it advances the interests of everyone including the working classes. The very notion of an apolitical unionism situated midway between the harsh economic pressures from IMF conditionalities and a continually battered working class struggling for its very survival, both as a class and in terms of the welfare of its individual members, is largely unthinkable in the Caribbean and Third World contexts. However, in their eventual submission to the imperatives of IMF/World Bank structural adjustment conditionalities, both Jagan and Manley might themselves have contributed to the prevailing ambiguity about the necessity of a politicized labor movement.

At the same time, however, what is more appropriately called the autonomy of the labor movement in the Caribbean is a critical issue. Indeed, such autonomy does not necessarily imply maintaining political apathy or ideological neutrality. It should imply that the trade union organization or movement is able to control its own leadership, rather than become subordinate to traditional middle-class politicians who often represent interests (including foreign interests) that undermine working-class pursuits. Trade union autonomy in this sense means the development of a political agenda of its own, that is, strengthening its own political/ideological awareness and capability to engage the political powers on its own terms. Realization of this ideal will be helped greatly by more fully democratizing the trade union movement, a prospect that both Jagan and Manley consistently fought to implement during their careers.

A fourth lesson, therefore, from the Jagan-Manley experience is the need for persistent efforts toward greater democracy within the labor and working-class movement itself. Such a democratization process will not only help bridge the apparently increasing gap between middle-class politicized leadership and working-class supports as a whole. It is also a process that legitimizes the trade union and political leadership in the eyes of the population as a whole, and so enables a more successful hegemonic struggle that gives priority to a working-class agenda in the political policy process. It is only within this more democratic labor-political process that a program of worker participation advocated by Jagan and Manley becomes meaningful.

Finally, what we learn from the experiences of Jagan and Manley is, contrary to the more orthodox argument about the absolute priority of class over race and ethnicity, that without simultaneously confronting the ethno-political issues, such as making deliberate efforts at bridge building across the ethno-political or communal divide in complex pluralistic societies like Guyana and Jamaica, the more fundamental objective of realizing the unified working-class project is doomed. For this reason, the failure of Caribbean political leaders like Cheddi Jagan and Michael Manley to put in place institutionalized arrangements toward ethno-political conflict resolution, as for instance the Race Relations Commission promised by Jagan in Guyana, is unfortunate if not tragic as far as harmonious working-class and indeed social development in the region is concerned. Nevertheless, by their sheer energy, dedication, and commitment to working-class struggle and development, both Cheddi Jagan and Michael Manley have indeed laid the foundations for the inspiration and creative efforts of future generations of Caribbean political and social leaders.

References

Beckford, George, and Michael Witter. 1980. *Small Garden . . . Bitter Weed: Struggle and Change in Jamaica*. London: Zed Press.

Bishop, Maurice. 1979. "Organize to Fight Destabilization," St. Georges: People's Revolutionary Government (pamphlet), May 8.

Caribbean Dialogue. 1976. "Facism on the Rise," March, 12–16.

Caribbean Dialogue. 1976. "State of Emergency," June–July, 2–4.

Caribbean Dialogue. 1976. "Manley Reveals Rightist Plot," June–July, 5–6, 14.

Chase, Ashton. 1964. *A History of Trade Unionism in Guyana.* Georgetown: New Guyana Co. Ltd.

Despres, Leo. 1967. *Cultural Pluralism and Nationalist Politics in British Guyana.* Chicago: Rand McNally.

Gonzalves, Ralph. 1977. "The Trade Union Movement in Jamaica: Its Growth and Some Resultant Problems." In *Essays on Power and Change in Jamaica,* ed. Carl Stone and Aggrey Brown. Kingston: Jamaica Publishing House.

Gray, Obika. 1991. *Radicalism and Social Change in Jamaica.* Knoxville: University of Tennessee Press.

Hart, Richard. 1989. *Rise and Organise: The Birth of the Workers and National Movements in Jamaica (1936–1939).* London: Karia Press.

Henry, Zin. 1972. *Labor Relations and Industrial Conflict in Commonwealth Caribbean Countries.* Port-of-Spain, Trinidad: Columbus Publishers.

Hintzen, Percy. 1987. *The Cost of Regime Survival.* Cambridge: Cambridge University Press.

HMSO. 1954. *Report of the British Guiana Constitutional Commission* (Robertson Commission). London: Colonial Office.

Jagan, Cheddi. 1972. *The West on Trial.* Berlin: Seven Seas.

Knowles, William H. 1959. *Trade Union Development and Industrial Relations in the British West Indies.* Berkeley: University of California Press.

Lewis, Rupert. 1998. *Walter Rodney's Intellectual and Political Thought.* Detroit: Wayne State University Press; Mona: University of the West Indies Press.

Lewis, W. Arthur. 1939. *Labor in the West Indies: The Birth of a Workers' Movement.* London: Fabian Society.

Manley, Michael. 1982. *Jamaica: Struggle in the Periphery.* London: Writers and Readers.

McAffee, Cathy. 1991. *Storm Signals: Structural Adjustment and Development Alternatives in the Caribbean.* Cambridge: South End Press.

Ministry of Finance (Government of Guyana). 1993. "Privatization Policy Framework Paper." Georgetown: mimeo.

Munroe, Trevor. 1990. *Jamaican Politics: A Marxist Perspective in Transition.* Kingston: Heinemann/Lynn Reinner.

New World (Guyana). 1965. April 30.

People's Progressive Party (PPP). 1982. *Strengthen the Party! Defend the Masses! Liberate Guyana! Report to the Twenty-first Congress.* July 30–August 2.

———. 1985. *Report of the Central Committee to the Twenty-Second Congress of the People's Progressive Party*. Annandale, Guyana. August, 3–5.
Ray, Ellen, and Bill Schapp. 1980. "Massive Destabilization in Jamaica." *Covert Action Information Bulletin (CAIB)* 10 (spring–summer): 7–17.
Robertson, Paul D. 1967. "'Grass Roots' Organization and the P.N.P: A Study Based on Central Tower P.N.P. Group, Central Kingston, Jamaica," Mona: Department of Government, University of the West Indies (mimeo).
Robinson, William I. 1996. *Promoting Polyarchy*. Cambridge: Cambridge University Press.
Rodney, Walter. 1981. *A History of the Guyanese Working People*. Baltimore: Johns Hopkins University Press.
Searle, Chris. 1983. *Grenada: The Struggle against Destabilization*. London: Writers and Readers.
Smith, M. G. 1964. "Social and Cultural Pluralism," in *Social and Cultural Pluralism in the Caribbean*, ed. Vera Rubin. New York: Annals of the American Academy.
———. 1965. *The Plural Society in the West Indies*. Berkeley: University of California Press.
Stone, Carl. 1980. *Democracy and Clientelism in Jamaica*. New Brunswick, N.J.: Transaction Books.
Thomas, Clive Y. 1988. *The Poor and the Powerless: Economic Policy and Change in the Caribbean*. New York: Monthly Review Press.
Wallerstein, Immanuel. 1998. *Utopistics*. New York: New Press.
Waters, Malcolm. 1995. *Globalization*. London: Routledge.
Working People's Alliance (WPA). 1983. *Argument for Unity against Dictatorship*. Georgetown: WPA.

9

Women Trade Union Leaders in the Anglophone Caribbean

A. LYNN BOLLES

In the host of volumes written concerning change—political, economic, and social—in the Caribbean, there are few that remember women as subjects worthy of consideration or inclusion in the discussion. Despite the fact that women have been the "backbone" of most Caribbean societies, tend to be just as active in the political systems, and have generally superior academic performance records, they are nonexistent at worst, and rendered invisible or devalued at best in histories, treatises, and other mechanisms of recording events. This omission however is ceasing to be the norm. Since the rise of Caribbean feminist scholarship in the 1970s, the contributions in theoretical, methodological, and corrective research have taken on the tremendous job of inclusion (Barrow 1998). Gendered scholarship is an ongoing process in heretofore male-dominated social, political, and economic analyses.

Nonetheless, consider this statement: "The disabilities from which they [women] suffer in adult life are the products of systematic discriminations reflecting deep-seated prejudices in the society. . . . It is an intolerable invasion of the principle of equality." Michael Manley wrote those words in 1975 in his political treatise *The Politics of Change* (214). Here are absolutely revolutionary challenges to the status quo regarding the equality of opportunity for women in Jamaica. Gender equality made sense in terms of human resource development: the tapping of reservoirs of energy and talent. With women taking their full and equal place in society, the dynamics would include their participation in decision-making processes on all levels of society. In sum, Michael Manley notes, "Each sex views reality from the perspective of its particular role in the family relationship. Each ... complements the other and policy proceeds most wisely where it represents a resolution of forces as between the male and the female perspectives" (1975, 215).

This declaration, no more than two paragraphs long, represents a great departure for any leader from Jamaica or elsewhere in the Caribbean. It is most insightful when one considers when Manley wrote these words, circa 1972–73. Clearly Manley was influenced by the company he was keeping: Beverly Anderson (who later married Manley) and the tremendous outpouring of women voters for the People's National Party (PNP) in the 1972 election. Manley was beholden to both. When he acknowledged gender inequality alongside race and class, this was indeed in the vanguard. Between 1972 and 1980, Manley's public policy went on to rectify certain elements of gender inequality in Jamaican society, including some of the most profound legislation of the day concerning citizen's rights, equal opportunity, minimum wage, the establishing of maternity leave with pay, supporting the Women's Bureau and moving it into the Office of the Prime Minister, and more.

However, Manley's other source of political power, the trade union movement, did not seize this moment for social change with regards to gender inequality. Further, Manley himself never connected the two in any of his writings or in his role as trade union leader, which ended in 1969 when he focused on electoral politics. The labor movement had its own set of problems and issues, and inherent sexism was high on the list, but it was barely visible except to those who were most affected by it—women trade unionists.

How did women in the labor movement, especially those in leadership positions, take up the challenge of equality within the movement itself? How was it possible that an institution built on workers' rights, and a strategy for change in the power structure, was itself a site of blatant sexism and gendered inequalities?

Over the past two decades, much attention has focused on women in organized labor in the Caribbean (see Bolles 1996; Reddock 1988, 1994). In all the literature on the labor movement, there were only a handful of women who were identified as trade union leaders, or who had led a special role in the history of organized labor in the region (see Haniff 1988, Ford-Smith 1986). Some of the names are familiar ones, for example, Aggie Bernard was a well-known figure in Jamaica's 1938 riots. But there had to be others considering the critical role trade unions played in Commonwealth Caribbean societies. Where were the women? Who were the women? And why are they invisible and unrecognized?

To address these questions, and to move beyond the position that Manley articulated twenty-five years ago, the analysis must focus on the social construction of gender in the organizational structures of Caribbean labor unions. It must also underscore the inventiveness of women leaders who skirted, as it were, outflanked and outmaneuvered male trade union leaders as they did their jobs and kept these groups financially afloat. Besides the theoretical discussion, it is essential to hear the women speak for themselves, telling the story and thereby completing the history of the trade union movement in the English-speaking Caribbean for a moment in time.

Social Construction of Gender and Trade Unionism

In societies like those in the English-speaking Caribbean, all classes of women are taught two kinds of histories and aspirations to guide them in their walks of life. One is the traditional African heritage rooted in the experiences of slavery. From it comes the struggle, activism, collectivity, and community spirit, which are the elements that support women, men, and children in their survival. In addition, both women and men engage in the social, cultural, and economic activities that value the contributions of people regardless of their gender. Due to the variation in mating relationships and the constraints of the division of labor, the majority of women in the region find themselves, for better or for worse, at the center of many social and cultural arenas.

The second type of history and culture learned is based on a Eurocentric model, which is part of the legacy of British colonialism and of the division of labor on which capitalism is founded. Simply, in this patriarchal view, men are the breadwinners and women are the housewives. Women deal with the world of biological reproduction, family, domestic labor, and are subordinate to men. Through the constructs of the capitalist system, men's labor is valued, and women's labor is devalued. The wage labor of people is encoded by gender whereby jobs that women perform are based on their "natural" suitability, such as sewing, cleaning, tending to the sick, and housekeeping. Needless to say, since men are the "biological" family breadwinners—whether engaged in work demanding physical strength or mental aptitude—they receive greater compensation for their work than women do. Even though the slave system had men and women working side by side, in the modes of production that directly followed emancipation until modern times, men's and women's labor is usually divided, inequitably valued, and differentially compensated. These gender identities reveal the distribution of political, economic and social power, and material resources (Barriteau 1998, 439).

In the region today, women deal with male domination, female subordination, and the sexual division of labor in their productive lives and incorporate this ideology into their perceptions of the way things ought to be (Anderson 1988, 320). Men, as the dominating gender, are seen as "born leaders," regardless of their class origin. Of course, ruling-class membership is an additional attribute for doing what is considered a male inclination. In the societies of the Americas, the nature of social and economic inequality was and still is measured by the status of one's birth and, in some regions, the color of skin and/or race. For the majority of women of African descent, there is the added dimension brought about by both racism and sexism.

Even in the Caribbean today, there are some instances in which to be black and poor places one in a situation not much changed from the days of slavery. The economic agents of wealth and power have maintained in contemporary times the social hierarchy that was so critical to the success of European colonialism. To be middle-class implies the continuation of the privileging of color and class. National independence did improve access to education and employment for blacks and East Indians who took advantage of those opportunities. And, although the current economic crisis has dealt a blow to the Caribbean middle class, they have more options to explore for their survival in hard times than do those of the lower classes.

Class, as an economic relationship expressing productive and social reproductive relations, is embedded not only with race but also gender. Black feminists (Collins 1990, Brewer 1993) refer to this set of relations as "the matrix of domination." The matrix is the multiplicative nature of race, class, and gender relationships that require theorizing that is both historical and contextual, as Patricia Mohammed reminds us (1994). In Caribbean societies, the matrix of domination can be a useful concept because of women's divergent economic, racial, and ethnic situations. The matrix is also helpful when examining power relations and women's access to various domains of society.

Patricia Anderson argues that in the Caribbean, female power seems to exist at a subterranean level, especially in regard to kinship and the family (1986, 320). However, she says, women's power is severely curtailed in terms of sex-segregated activities, for example, duties and occupations with their inferred low status. In a study of Trinidadian women factory workers, power is defined as a determined causal property achieved through means of resources that are hierarchically distributed (Yelvington 1995, 15–16). Power is derived from scarce resources, for example, time, money, or commodities, where the control over these resources by a social entity (an individual, a group, a class) is based on relations between the social entity and the resources. When using the matrix of domination, subterranean familial power, and relational definitions of power as guides, women's power is clearly constrained by all of the limiting forces in a particular society. Women also critically exercise power available to them under those social conditions, too. For middle-class women and men, there is more of a striking discord than seen in the literature on the poor and working classes.

Peggy Reeves Sanday observes that antagonism between the sexes may exist in societies where female power exists in contradiction to the dominant ideology (1981). Preliminary findings on research on Jamaican middle-class women support this concept (Rawlins 1987). In this case, the upper classes are advocates of the tenets of a patriarchal ideology even though women exert familial power. The key to understanding the matrix of domination here is to determine in what domain women have power and the ideological web of relations used at home, at the office, and in organizations.

Middle-class women have the responsibility of maintaining a sense of propriety and socializing children in that mode. Women are to be keepers and managers of the home. They are never to permit wage employment to interfere with child bearing and rearing. These unwritten rules resulted partly from the division of labor derived from the legacy of slavery and partly from the availability of domestic workers. They have been socialized to carry on the tradition of propriety, civility, and "teatime" in various forms. Moreover, many members of the middle class maintain the colonial privileged ideology of the class/color system in regards to their perceptions of women of poor and working-class backgrounds.

Here are the apparent contradictions of Caribbean middle-class women's lives. The dominant prescription of patriarchy moves back and forth between the cultural meanings of middle-class women's familial power, and other arenas of women's activities, especially in other settings such as the workforce. Since the jobs that middle-class women occupy are class based, the matrix of domination of race, class, and gender takes on other nuanced features of inequality. When middle-class women become conscious of the multiplicative nature of the relationships, they come to realize how these structures influence them and other women as well. Subsequently, from the ranks of the middle class have come some of the region's most committed women activists for social change. Likewise, some of the vital forces of female leadership in the organized labor movement have middle-class origins. This occurs in the context of an ideology that does not accommodate women's participation in the public arena (Barriteau 1998, 445).

Women trade union leaders, conscious of the constructs of their society, recognize these forces within the organized labor movement. They face situations whereby they seek to reconstruct their organizations so that they will be more democratic, less hierarchical, nonsexist, and politically and economically meaningful in this changing world. What is required in this reconstruction, or upending the matrix of domination, is to perceive alternative methods of exercising power.

Theories on women who achieve and exercise power in organizational settings first look at what constitutes a powerful person. Basically, a powerful person may directly, as well as indirectly, influence others through structural avenues, such as decision channels or resource control. In the end, the structural context of the organization will shape and be shaped by the behavior of the women themselves, and that *structure and behavior together* determine power (Smith and Grenier 1982). There are three overlapping sources of power: (1) participation in central and essential activities of the organization, (2) participation in activities that set the future agenda, and (3) access to and control over resources. Coping with uncertainty is a critical structural category because it is often used against women in their upward mobility within organizations. Women must "prove" their ability, while it is assumed that men are competent until proven otherwise. Controlling resources includes not only a person's ability to channel funds and resources but the degree of access a person has to future information and assets.

Depending on the setting and situation, then, both structural and behavior strategies are necessary for women to gain, exercise, and maintain positions of power. However, as the overarching discourse of the matrix of domination is in operation, women still face sex stereotyping, old-boy rules of entry and conduct, and other impediments that restrict and contain their access to organizational power. Multiple theories must be used to best understand the lives and experiences of Caribbean women. As one theory after another has shown, the multiplicative nature of race/ethnicity, class, and gender demands such an approach. With this collective body of theories, we can start to examine the general culture meanings of power embedded in structures of Commonwealth Caribbean trade unions, and how they are expressed by the behavior of men and women involved. The clash of the Eurocentric ideal and Caribbean reality becomes more than a binary to-and-fro movement. Women and men negotiate gender, race, and class in a particular context. Consequently, the social construction of the matrix of domination is embedded in institutions, such as in the labor movement.

Trade unionism, as it found its way as an institutional structure in the region, was based on a British model. And like many other models that were replicated in the colonies, the inherent gender bias remained unchallenged, even in situations where human resources were scarce. Moreover, the class identification of the early trade union leaders was in keeping with the Eurocentric notions of male domains of work and politics. Women leaders, representing every class, whose socialization made them ideal trade unionists, were locked into a system that rendered them invisible. Thus the trade union movement reflected the gendered stratification found throughout the West Indies. This stratification was based on class, race, and ethnicity and determined who assumed leadership positions.

What have women trade union leaders done to challenge their specific circumstances in the organized labor movement, while they still fight, as women and as members of their societies, for the elimination of the broader social conditions that keep them oppressed, exploited, and powerless? The complexity and varied experiences of these women leaders in organized labor figure significantly in positions they hold in key institutions found at every level of society. Furthermore, the extent of women's contributions—those deemed "indispensable" as well as those that are stereotyped and marginalized—contribute to the lack of recognition and esteem accorded them by their peers, scholars, politicians, and those who record events. And finally, there are the issues of a personal nature: what role has trade union work played in these women's personal lives as citizens, mothers, mates, and kinspeople.

Trade Unions and Women Leaders

The trade union movement in the English-speaking Caribbean relied on the twofold premise of meeting the worker's needs and of practicing electoral politics (see Bogues, this volume). Managed for the most part by middle-class male leadership, the organizing principles follow the prescribed notions of gender relations, that is, the dominant ideology of female subordination.

The gender inequality in labor unions/political parties was inherited/modeled after the labor groups in Britain and the United States. Such inequitable relations between the genders devalue, oppress, subordinate, and restrict women's activities. According to a 1979 International Labor Organization (ILO) report, men held executive positions at a ratio of three to one in the Commonwealth Caribbean. Over the more than twenty years since that report was written, things have changed in a positive direction, but the number of women executives is less than a handful in the entire region. Since middle-class men direct this movement, they operate with the dominant ideology that places women's labor of any class background second and that overtly devalues the contribution of women (whether or not it is in their best interest to do so), in order to maintain a sense of control.

The roles that women played in the early days of the labor movement, and continue to play in contemporary times as movement leaders, reflect the reality of the situation. That reality is that women with skills and leadership abilities are desperately needed in trade unions because they are vital to the survival of these organizations. But another part of women trade unionist reality is the impediments to their receiving proper recognition and advancement within their organizations. For some of the elderly women leaders, social location also tempered their activities. Consider these examples that come from interviews and research conducted in the late 1980s.

At the time of the interview, Mrs. Maggie Peters was a ninety-three-year-old politician/labor leader from Montserrat. Only during World War II and when she was having babies was she not on the movement's front lines. She was never elected an officer of the trade union she helped to found, nor did she hold a political position. Peters did not see that as her role. However, events would not have materialized as they did if she had not been there.

Another woman who was on the front lines in the late 1930s was Lady Gladys Bustamante, widow of the national hero of Jamaica, Sir Alexander Bustamante. Not promoting her own position, she says, "I was secretary to Sir Alexander Bustamante for three years before the start of the BITU." The BITU (Bustamante Industrial Trades Union) was formed in 1939. So for fifty years and more she had been a member of that organization. When asked if Caribbean trade unionism would be different if more women were in leadership positions, Lady Bustamante replied, "Yes, because women can manage very well since women put their minds to what is needed."

Another elderly trade unionist is Miss Halcyone Idelia Glasspole, former office manager of the National Workers Union in Jamaica. Her brother was a trade union man and one of the founders of the modern labor movement in Jamaica. In 1988, when Glasspole was interviewed, her brother Florizel Glasspole was the governor general, the queen of England's representative in Jamaica. Miss Glasspole entered union work in 1938 because of her brother's involvement. She stated:

> Everybody decided that we were going to form this big organization, the TUC (Trade Union Congress). And so it was formed and we carried along. We only had a few female workers who did just the clerical work. We weren't interested in the organizing part of it, because it was terrible uphill work, and the men did that part of it, and we stayed inside and did the clerical work. And we struggled along, as I told you, it was a terrible fight, fighting the employers and we went right along until around 1945 when we decided to call a strike at the Mental Hospital . . . the Bellevue Hospital now, and that was when you had the terrific upheaval. That struggle goes on, and we were threatened to be sent to jail and that was hard, particularly for my brother because he was the general secretary so he was the mainstream of the struggle.

When asked if this is how she got involved, she replied, "Yes, this is how I became involved."

Glasspole was not free with information because she still saw herself as one of the few confidential and competent persons to have served in the early Trade Union Congress and the National Worker's Union. She was still very willing to give service and remains loyal and faithful to the labor movement.

The organizational structure of most Commonwealth trade unions continues to be exceedingly hierarchical in nature. This formation has worked against women in their attempts to assume positions of primary influence and control, and in their moves to establish future directives for their organizations. It is true that, even within this rigid structure, women have played critical roles, and exceptional women have attained prominent status within the labor movement and society at large. Yet, except for the major strides taken by the Project for the Development of Caribbean Women in Trade Unions (1982–84) and other efforts by and for women, there have been few attempts to alter long-standing views.

The following is a sample of the statements of other women who participated in the work that is the basis of the book *We Paid Our Dues* (Bolles

1996). Here the women leaders (pseudonyms are used) talk about the organizational structure of their trade unions. They also assess the overall effectiveness of their organizations in improving the working conditions of members and in influencing broader societal issues within their countries and the region.

I asked them if the structure of their unions impeded their development or other trade union activities. According to Alexandria McDonald from Guyana: "It impedes, because of the fact the organization is not made up only by males . . . it has males and females. I feel that [because of] the fact that the senior positions are held by males, the women are kind of left [out]. And I don't think we have a fair chance of voicing opinions." Retired leader septuagenarian Enid Green of Barbados, a woman with a third-grade education, recalled an incident that occurred sometime in the late 1950s at a trade union council meeting:

> At the meeting one of the labor leaders—one of the highest secretaries in there said, "well, it cannot have a chart" [referring to a proposal Green had made]. Since I could not talk to him inside the union hall I had to wait until we had a break and were standing outside. I wasn't frightened of him. When I come outside, I told him, you are dogmatical, [as] some of them were big mouth and talk [a lot]. And some were like me, keep their mouth shut [at certain times] and get the job done despite them. You understand?

The people of the Commonwealth Caribbean do understand the link between trade unions and electoral politics. At issue here is the degree to which trade unions, as institutions with a well-defined identity in Caribbean societies, will work on behalf of women trade union leaders entering the political arena. Can trade union activity be considered a stepping stone for politically ambitious women, as it has been for their male counterparts?

A couple of women could not express themselves as they would have liked on the issue of politics in part because they had not considered women entering politics. The responses were monosyllabic at best. Other women leaders had definite opinions on the question. Some of their responses are indicative of the sociopolitical reality of their individual countries. Region-wide, only a dozen women have sat at any given moment in the elected seats of national parliaments. There have been only two women prime ministers.

Sandra Merriweather of Barbados had thought a lot about this:

Stepping stone in terms of being the politicians, being elected as a politician: women have not had that glory. The women, if they have done anything in that light, let's say it has been behind the scenes or assistant [to] the men. I cannot, in Barbados, think of any political women who have come out of the trade union movement that I can refer to right now in terms of being elected as a politician. Maybe you can. Somebody who might have attached in some way to a senator or something like that, but not being elected that I can think of, offhand at least. There haven't been many women politicians anyhow. So there is only one woman in parliament. Last count there was only one woman, [she was] not attached to the trade union movement as such.

I don't see [trade union affiliation] as helping the women to be elected or go into politics. I think the problem with women in politics in Barbados and maybe in the Caribbean, or maybe in the world, is wider than even the trade union movement. Never mind how you boast within the trade union movement or how much the opportunities they have: the other problems are stronger and keep them down more, surface more for women. They tend to be looked at and be criticized—even to the point [when allegations become] being nasty. I mean more people would question a woman than they would a man. If whoever you've gone out with when you were sixteen, seventeen, [becomes] of great importance. It becomes very nasty, and women are not ready to face up to that type of behavior, and men are not ready to take the chance with them. The men who are in charge of politics will say, "Look, if you have a nasty record, we are not ready for you." In terms of how people look at the record, they are [not] ready to lose their seat for you. So you know, women have not yet come of age when you're going to look at that in a different light. And I think that this in itself has stopped a lot of women even putting themselves into the forefront of running for politics. That is a key area. I don't think sometimes it has anything to do with even self-confidence. I think there are a number of women who are confident and who have self-confidence enough that they can do it. But there is this whole question of the moral thing that is being pointed at you. The men are not ready to take that chance.

In contrast, two Guyanese trade union leaders had this to say: "Trade union activity has, in fact, served as a political springboard for a few, though most of the posts women have filled have been appointed rather than elected ones. The hope is that, in time, these women and those who follow them in office will make up for exclusion in the past."

The late Jane Phillips Gay, who passed away before publication of *We Paid Our Dues*, said about her affiliation with the union, "It has been very helpful to me. Because of my activity in the Guyana Industrial Workers' Union, I was able to defeat all the other candidates who contested the 1983 elections in my area."

Another Barbadian woman had the last say on the topic:

Well, like I said, if you look through the region you will see that those persons that are in politics, most of them have first been involved in the trade union movement; and I feel that being in the trade union movement, it gives you the sort of facility to make yourself known to people, if nothing else. Because here you have membership as a base; and when you deal with the membership whether it be negotiation, grievance handling or anything like that, you become some person that workers know. And from that aspect, if nothing else, it can give you the exposure needed that can help you in any political endeavor.

Conclusion

Without a doubt, these women leaders are tremendous supporters of their individual organizations and of trade unionism in general. As workers, they have benefited both materially and socially from their affiliation. They have also, in some cases, spent many years in the movement, preserving labor's gains and moving toward the social uplift of both themselves and the people they represent. Since the 1990s, women made the transition from trade unionism to local and national politics, or entered politics via other avenues than organized labor. The work ahead then is to increase women's representation in political office and at the same time to eliminate the link to sexual discrimination that, according to one woman trade unionist, exists at various levels of the political process.

To paraphrase one leader, it does not matter if you are a true trade unionist or not. If you are a very dynamic person, nothing prevents you from advancing in the field. That kind of optimism is what keeps women pushing against the odds, and what makes this group of women unique.

When Michael Manley called for massive reeducation of trade union leadership to be able to better perceive a new vision of fundamental relationships, the vision did not include women leaders. Today, when the labor movement is in a greater crisis than experienced two decades ago, reeducation, democratization, and gender equality are at center stage. Can women trade union leaders, with newly acquired skills, training, and democratic principles deal with labor negotiations in the twenty-first century? Perhaps. At this point, it is worth a try.

Notes

A slightly revised version of this chapter was published in *Caribbean Quarterly* 48, no. 1 (2002).

References

Anderson, Patricia Y. 1986. "Conclusion: Women in the Caribbean—Afterview." *Social and Economic Studies* 35, no. 21: 291–324.

Barriteau, Eudine V. 1998. "Liberal Ideology and Contradictions in Caribbean Gender Systems." In *Caribbean Portraits*, ed. Christine Barrow. Kingston: Ian Randle.

Barrow, Christine, ed. 1998. *Caribbean Portraits*. Kingston: Ian Randle.

Bolles, A. Lynn. 1996. *We Paid Our Dues*. Washington, D.C.: Howard University Press.

———. 1998. "Working on Equality: Commonwealth Caribbean Women Trade Union Leaders." In *Caribbean Portraits*, ed. Christian Barrow. Kingston: Ian Randle.

Brewer, Rose. 1993. "Theorizing Race, Class, and Gender: The New Scholarship of Black Feminist Intellectuals and Black Women's Labor." In *Theorizing Black Feminisms*, ed. Stanlie James and A. Busia. New York: Routledge Press.

Collins, Patricia Hill. 1990. *Black Feminist Thought*. Boston: Unwin and Allen.

Ford-Smith, Honor. 1986. "Women's Place in Caribbean Social Change." In *A Caribbean Reader on Development*, ed. Judith Wedderburn. Kingston: FES.

Haniff, Nesha. 1988. *Blaze of Fire*. Toronto: Sister Vision Press.

Manley, Michael. 1975. *Politics of Change*. Washington, D.C.: Howard University Press.

Mohammed, Patricia. 1994. "Nuancing the Feminist Discourse in the Caribbean." *Social and Economic Studies* 43: 135–67.

Rawlins, Joan. 1988. "Preliminary Findings: Study of Jamaican Middle-Class Women." Paper presented at the Caribbean Studies Association, Pointe à Pitre, Guadeloupe.

Reddock, R. 1988. *Elma Francois: The NWCSA and the Workers Struggle for Change in the Caribbean in the 1930s*. London: New Beacon Books.

———. 1994. *Women, Labor, and Politics in Trinidad and Tobago: A History*. Kingston: Ian Randle.

Sanday, Peggy Reeves. 1981. *Female Power, Male Dominance*. New York: Cambridge University Press.

Smith, Howard L., and Mary Grenier. 1982. "Sources of Organizational Power for Women." *Sex Roles* 8, no. 7: 733–46.

Yelvington, Kevin A. 1995. *Producing Power*. Philadelphia: Temple University Press.

PART III
Critical Current Challenges

10

Global Economic Crisis and Caribbean Women's Survival Strategies

ALMA H. YOUNG AND KRISTINE B. MIRANNE

During the years that Cheddi Jagan and Michael Manley struggled to put in place their visions for social and economic justice, women were never in the forefront of their agendas although they gained some benefits in their roles as workers and mothers. Today in the Caribbean, even some of these hard-earned benefits that accrued to women are slipping away as governments restructure to meet the global economic crisis. Poor women in the Caribbean, especially those who head their own households, face an ongoing struggle to provide for themselves and their families at a time when global, national, and local economies are continually in flux. For the past three decades, Caribbean women have had to survive within a substantially reduced system of social welfare, as national governments cut services to respond to the global economic crisis.

This chapter investigates strategies employed by women heads of household in the Caribbean in response to the shrinking welfare state. They have had to respond for almost thirty years to structural adjustment policies that, among other things, limit the state's provisioning of social welfare. The critical question asked in this essay is how do women create and implement survival strategies for themselves and their families under challenging conditions of economic and social change? We argue that the focus should not be on how the state thinks women should adapt to changes in their life circumstances but rather on how women actually respond as they carry out the multiplicities of their roles. It becomes readily apparent that women are not merely reacting to a set of circumstances imposed on them by the local state and the global market but are active participants in fashioning a life for themselves and their families. Thus women find ways to resist the state's limited construction of gender, which sees women as either workers or as mothers.

The Concept of Gender

The concept of gender cannot be considered as only a descriptive term. A gendered perspective such as we have undertaken here must reveal the many forms of inequality that women experience in their daily lives. Thus, we adopt Barriteau's definition of gender as it refers to the "complex systems of personal and social relations through which women and men are socially created and maintained and through which they gain access to, or are allocated, status, power and material resources within society" (1998, 188).

An analysis of the broad contours of gender systems, as defined by ideological and material dimensions, would expose the underlying network of power relations (Barriteau, 1998: 188–90). The ideological dimension reveals the ways in which masculinity and femininity are constructed: the woman as mother, for instance; the man as breadwinner. Or, the man as citizen; the woman as dependent (Safa 1996, Abramovitz 1988, Mink, 1990). The material dimension reveals the ways in which resources are allocated: for instance, whether the state removes discriminatory wage differentials between men and women workers, whether women have gained a voice in political decision making, or whether women and men have equal opportunities for higher education. Gender must be understood within the context of its interactions with other social relations. In other words, women are defined by a social construction of gender that is based on the complex ways in which society interacts with them—as mothers, workers, citizens, and women within society.

Gender relations often obscure the power differential between women and men and between women and the state. An investigation of women's survival strategies makes visible the distribution of economic, material, and social resources available to them. Furthermore, the state's response to economic restructuring shows how the ideological dimension has been used to construct women as workers as well as mothers. Although states may intend to act in the best interests of all their citizens, implemented state policies often intensify, decrease, or subvert gender systems. In this manner, state policies are not gender neutral.

Barriteau asserts that states must be held accountable for the inequitable gendered nature of civic and political life that is continued and sustained (1998, 194). In Jamaica, just as women became the preferred workers within the newly developing export enclaves of the 1960s and 1970s, the government passed legislation that promoted the role of the father and eroded the mother's position vis-à-vis her children (LaFont and Pruitt 1997, 221). In this instance, the state forced the construction of women as workers and downplayed their role as mothers. Another example can be seen in Barbados, a country that introduced policies including salary cuts for all government workers, increases in mortgage interest rates, health taxes, and transportation levies while also moving to privatize public transit companies. These policies increase the burden on women to make ends meet. The shrunken public sector resulted in many private companies going bankrupt, further reducing the workforce. In Barbados, as in other Caribbean countries undergoing structural adjustment, the quality of life for women and their families was substantially reduced as former "people-oriented goals" and previous gains were halted (Barriteau 1996, 146–47).

Caribbean governments that focus on the market miss the impact of household economic decisions. Widespread unemployment results in less disposable income even though families still must meet their basic needs of food and shelter. As stated by Barriteau, "Two factors are pertinent. In the Caribbean at least 37 percent of households are headed by women . . . in some countries the figure is as high as 45 percent . . . even when a male partner is present, research has shown that when disposable income is reduced, men decrease the amount of money they allocate to households, while women decrease what they allocate to themselves in order to maintain household consumption patterns" (1996, 150). States have choices; they often choose to maintain unjust gender systems primarily because the system meets specifically defined political, economic, and ideological objectives.

Gender and the Global Economy

The social and economic underpinnings sustaining the discourse on women as specialized homemakers and men as providers for the family is being replaced by a discourse that obligates individuals to participate in the labor market regardless of gender and/or domestic responsibilities (Cope 1997, also see Safa 1996). What is new is not the extent to which women have been, and continue to be, economic actors but, rather, the recognition by society of them as workers, a recognition concealed by earlier ideologies that defined them solely as domestic beings (Abramovitz 1988, Mink 1998).

This new discourse is the direct result of global economic restructuring: women throughout the world are now a central element in a workforce that has increased with the shifting production patterns of manufacturing, finance, and business services (Acevado 1995, Safa 1996). In those countries that gained manufacturing jobs, often due to manufacturers relocating from industrial countries to developing ones, women constitute approximately 80 percent of the total export-industry workforce (Christopherson 1995, 198). In countries and cities where headquarter functions and business services have expanded dramatically, there has been a substantial demand in those economic sectors, such as banking, that have historically employed large numbers of women. There has also been a large increase in the number of women involved in personal services, including child care, housekeeping, and tourist-oriented activities (Christopherson 1995, 198–99).

The labor market today is even more segregated by gender than before the economic crisis, as export manufacturers in developing countries have shown a distinct preference for women workers: they cost less, are less likely to unionize, and have greater patience for the work involved. As stated by Deere et al., "in a departure from the global pattern of [hiring] young, single, women, there is a preference [in the Caribbean] for women with children because they feel their need to work ensures greater job commitment" (Deere et al. 1990, 66). Governments, in turn, encourage these market preferences in a number of ways: by limiting alternative income sources from transfer payments, migration, and self-employment; and by restricting union activity, facilitating "the doing of business," and reducing social provisioning.

Yet, even as some women gain jobs in the new global economy, others are made redundant as governments cut back on social provisioning. In particular, there is less need for government employees in areas where women tend to be predominant, such as teaching, health care, and transportation (Deere et al. 1990, 59). In response, many women seek employment in the informal sector where they are likely to find growing amounts of work, due in part to the increase in the systems of subcontracting and home outwork used by manufacturing and export processing zones (Christopherson 1995).

Thus, when we look at women's employment in particular, we see that the industrial and family-based economies have grown side by side.

Whether employed in the formal or informal economy, women still find their household incomes meager. Several factors have contributed to this situation. First, women's wages tend to be low, and in some cases have decreased in recent years. Second, men, a traditional source of support, are also finding it more difficult to provide steady assistance to the household due to lessening wages and jobs for them becoming scarcer. Third, the state provides fewer benefits to the household as governments continue to trim their social welfare budgets. Thus, women find themselves having to be more creative in generating resources, both financial and supportive, as we will see below.

One of the reasons for the state's provision of fewer benefits is the switching of resources from the production of goods and services for domestic consumption to the production of goods and services for export. The state then has fewer resources to expend on basic domestic goods and services such as education, health care, food subsidies, and transportation. Responsibility for daily survival is shifted from the state to the household, forcing families to absorb a greater share of the cost of living. For poor families, the burden is greatest on women, who often must take up the slack for the provision of social goods and services. However, because this provisioning done by women is often invisible to outsiders, the costs of resource allocation absorbed by the household are seen as negligible by policy makers. Changing household costs have virtually no repercussions for government's main concern—the monetary economy (Pitikin and Bedoya 1997, Deere et al. 1990).

In fact, government's policies of switching resources from the household economy to the monetary economy are actually grounded in a set of assumptions, a gender ideology, that assigns certain roles and characteristics to women. As Peggy Antrobus has pointed out, whether these policies are directed at reducing consumption (austerity measures that, for instance, result in cuts in social services) or focused on increasing export-oriented production (economic activities, for instance, that make women preferred workers), they are based upon assumptions about the roles that women are expected to play in society and within the household (Antrobus 1997). That is, it is assumed that women will subordinate themselves to men in terms of power and resources (see Bolles, this volume). It is assumed they will do whatever is necessary to provide for their children and families, including undertaking arduous work outside the home. Further, it is assumed that there is an unlimited supply of female labor and that this labor will adjust and compensate for any changes brought about by governmental adjustment strategies (Sadasivam 1997). These assumptions, and the important roles that women play in society, are used to justify cuts in government expenditures on basic social services.

In living with these policies, women pay a heavy cost in time, energy, and lost opportunities (see Elson 1989). Through a multiplicity of activities that combine paid work and home duties, women assume responsibilities that government has shirked: to manage household resources so as to feed, clothe, house, and educate the members of the household. It is apparent that decisions concerning household labor allocations tend to be based as much on shifting work opportunities as on gender roles (Deere et al 1990).

Caribbean Women and the Global Economic Crisis

Looking at women in the English-speaking Caribbean, specifically women of African descent, provides a good case to examine the issues of women's response to the global economic crisis. First, for more than the past two decades, Caribbean women have had to cope with the impacts of their governments' response to the global economy. This crisis has been evidenced by growing debt, fiscal and balance of payments problems, and deepening poverty (see Girvan 1997). The price governments have had to pay for being bailed out of the crisis has been adoption of structural adjustment policies demanded by international organizations such as the International Monetary Fund and the World Bank. These adjustment policies have resulted in diminished social services, lowered wages, and fewer jobs in traditional sectors.

Government-sponsored welfare programs of the 1960s and '70s have been scaled back dramatically. As an example, for the past two decades, social investment in Jamaica has fallen as a percentage of total budget, with the country's resources increasingly drained by the servicing of its external debt. One consequence is seen in the health care arena in Jamaica: while there was one physician in the public sector to every 2,678 persons in 1971, that ratio had increased to one to 5,240 by 1988 (Girvan 1997, 66). Thus Caribbean women have had to deal with policies that shift responsibility for social welfare provisioning from the state to the household.

Second, women in the English-speaking Caribbean historically have been involved in labor outside the home (Osirim 1997). During slavery, Afro-Caribbean women worked in the fields next to men, performing the same arduous tasks. Even in the immediate postemancipation period, 80 percent of the female population was employed as wage laborers on plantations (Osirim 1997, 47). Many women worked in domestic service until the mid-twentieth century. Today, the job opportunities may be slightly more varied, but growing numbers of women continue to work outside the home.

Third, women's work in the Caribbean is often critical to the processes structuring a global economy. In fact, in many of the fastest growing segments of the global economy, women are the preferred employees (Christopherson 1995). Throughout much of the Caribbean, for instance, there has been a conscious decision to promote tourism as a mainstay of the economy. Sex workers, most of whom are female, form an integral part of the tourist industry (see Kempadoo 1999). However, these jobs in the global economy, ranging from export-processing to tourism, tend to be poorly paid, seasonal, and provide little if any benefits. In fact, the demand for cheap female labor to perform repetitive tasks in dead-end jobs within the export industry is an indicator of economic distress—increasing male unemployment and lessening women's opportunities in the public sector or among traditional industries (Sadasivan 1997).

Through their individual and collective efforts, Caribbean women develop resources both inside the home and in the labor market that allow them to satisfy the basic needs of their families and their communities.

Strategies of Livelihood

Women in the English-speaking Caribbean see work as broadly defined (see Massiah 1986). The ability to earn an income is still considered important to them, and few seem to be content to be entirely supported by others (Barrow 1986, Senior 1991). Yet the status of even the employed is perceived by working-class women as marginal and insecure, since their jobs in garment factories, hotels, or assembly plants are often subject to layoffs, low wages, and inflexible working hours. Women also know that the likelihood of their finding a job in the first place is low; that lack of education, skills, and occupational training limit their options; and that household instability might prevent them from keeping a job for any length of time. Moreover, women are also conscious of class and racial exploitation in the workplace. Thus, if conditions for wage labor are perceived as unattractive, then women will concentrate on other strategies of livelihood (Senior 1991).

Because an overwhelming majority of women in the English-speaking Caribbean are responsible for meeting the daily needs of their families, and because resources are so scarce, many women are involved in "making do"; that is, taking whatever is available and maximizing its utility to oneself and family (Senior 1991). A fundamental strategy for these women is to make do with what they have or, better still, "make something from nothing" in order to maintain their families. Women who do not have regular employment will contribute to the total family welfare by turning to innovative, if marginal, ways to earn or supplement income. These activities might involve selling sweets, preserves, cakes, coconut oil, or fruit and vegetables from the family backyard, occasional baby-sitting, sewing, providing laundry or other services, or making handicrafts. Payment may not necessarily involve cash exchanges but other forms of reimbursement, including reciprocal exchanges of labor or goods.

Another strategy is higglering. Although higglering is a very old practice, its numbers have grown in recent years as a result of the economic crisis. Higglers trade through extensive distribution networks throughout the Caribbean. These women supply local markets with inexpensive food, clothing, footwear, and other goods, thus meeting consumers' needs and providing income for themselves and others. Higglers contribute substantially to their country's economy by often dominating the informal sector of the domestic economy (Vickers 1991). Women engaged in this activity travel throughout the Caribbean region, circumvent language barriers, negotiate in a variety of foreign currencies, and battle import regulations that vary from place to place. By absorbing many of the costs of transporting goods, they free larger businesses that, in turn, can employ their own labor elsewhere (Barriteau 1996, 148).

Higglering remains an important option for Caribbean women with low levels of educational attainment while also constituting an alternative for women in dead-end, white-collar occupations. In fact, many of these informal commercial importers were previously employed as secretaries and teachers in government service, increasing numbers of whom have been laid off as a result of the economic crisis (see LeFranc 1988). The flexibility of higglering allows women to be in control of their own operations, enabling them to meet their changing household demands. The traveling and socializing that are part of this occupation also assist women in building stronger networks of shared knowledge and support (French 1994).

In fact, Caribbean women spend much time building and maintaining kinship and friendship networks that provide both a mode of survival and a source of affirmation for these women (Deere et al. 1990, see also Pitkin and Bedoya 1997). It is through networking that poor women assist each other in coping with their multiple roles and in supplementing their income. The reciprocal nature of these exchanges is demonstrated through the saying, "han[d] wash han[d]." These exchanges might not involve cash but an exchange of goods and services such as help with child care and household duties. In response to the economic crisis, these networks have been strengthened by including more members, encompassing those who are abroad and sending home remittances, as well as those who are linked by communities of interest, such as savings groups and sports clubs. As networks grow, they provide more opportunities for assistance, but they also require more effort to maintain, a responsibility that falls heavily on women.

Other strategies include a longer and more intense use of the family home that, traditionally, has remained a source of support for young adults, especially for young women who often stayed in the home until after a first child was born. Today, conscious efforts are made to increase the size of the household, thereby increasing the number of potential income earners (see Bolles 1986). Each person in the household is expected to do his or her share, whether it is providing cash or undertaking household chores or child care (Senior 1991). For example, a young mother may engage in income-earning activities while her mother looks after the children, or an older brother living in the house may provide for his sister's children instead of his own since they live with their mother in her family home. The home is also becoming the center of small-scale entrepreneurial activity such as making crafts, sewing clothing, or growing vegetables and/or fruit for sale (see Blumberg 1995).

International migration continues, as it has for many years, as the bottom-line survival strategy for poorer households throughout most of the Caribbean (see Gordon, this volume). The region as a whole sends out a greater percentage of its population than does any other region worldwide, and during the 1980s, the rate of female migration increased to where it surpassed that of men (Deere et al. 1990, 72–74; also see Chaney 1985). These migrating women tend to find work in the lower end of the personal services and the manufacturing sectors in the United States and Canada (Fernandez Kelly and Sassen 1995). The remittances that they send home appear to be spent mainly on household expenses and consumer goods. In some cases, remittances may be used to reduce the need to seek local sources of employment, thus reducing demands on governments for the creation of jobs while increasing dependence on this external source of income (Deere et al. 1990). Remittances from abroad, however, are unreliable: the money comes sporadically, it comes in unequal amounts, and some women receive it and others do not.

Thus, given the multiplicity of strategies that Caribbean women employ to "make do," they may be seen as domestic brokers; manipulating a variety of sources for goods, services, knowledge, and money in order to meet daily commitments (Senior 1991). Support from male partners; the switching of partners; kinship and friendship networks; remittances from dispersed relatives and adult working offspring; gifts from friends, neighbors, and employers; and handouts from the state, the party, and private institutions are all used by women to provide for their families. Regardless of how they go about it, the acquisition of what can be considered livelihood resources plays a major part in their lives and consciousness. While the brokering of resources demonstrates great creativity and flexibility, it also highlights the fact that women operate in contexts in which they are vulnerable and must spend a great deal of time in efforts that are risky and unpredictable.

Alternative Strategies

In a world of escalating living costs and eroding living standards, some women are coming to realize that their traditional weapon—their ability to "make do"—is not enough. More and more women (and men) in the informal sector in the Caribbean have been forming their own organizations to confront state policies and the economic crisis. In urban areas, women's organizations have been in the forefront of the fight for labor rights in export assembly industries and for the unionization of workers in export-processing zones. Some groups are working to develop collective solutions to needs such as child care and transportation (McAfee 1991).

Throughout the 1980s, small women's organizations formed to confront the economic crisis by doing two things simultaneously: concentrating on consciousness raising through popular education while developing income-generating projects and cultivating skills training in both traditional and nontraditional areas. Some of these groups included the Committee for the Development of Women in St. Vincent and the Grenadines (1984), the

Belize Rural Women's Association (1985), Sis No Dada of St. Kitts and Nevis (1985), Red Thread of Guyana (1987), and the Women's Forum of Barbados (1988) (Reddock 1998, 92). These groups of women have worked to develop strategies to relieve both the short-term impact of the crisis on them and their families, and to generate a longer-range consciousness of the need for social change. In so doing, they are attempting to mobilize to meet practical and strategic gender interests (Moser 1989, also see Antrobus 1997).

For example, in Grenada, the Grenfruit Women's Cooperative grew out of an attempt to produce income for its members by preserving jams and jellies and making candied fruits, and distributing them nationwide and abroad. The women received higher than average wages and hospital insurance for themselves and their children. They also contributed to a pension scheme, and they established a revolving loan fund from which they can borrow for essential things like repairing a leaking roof or buying school uniforms. Perhaps just as important, the women met each month to discuss co-op problems as well as seek solutions to the problems they are experiencing in their daily lives (see Deere et al. 1990, 109–11). Another example is the Women's Construction Collective (WCC) in Jamaica, which trains and places young, unemployed, low-income women at the trade level of the building and construction industry. WCC also provides training for the development of self-esteem and has a special component aimed at helping women deal with the realities of working in a male-dominated field. It has also established a "revolving tool fund" that ensures that all who need them can acquire new tools on a credit basis (Girvan 1997, 91–92).

Many of these women's organizations are supported by a network of national and regional nongovernmental organizations that have an explicitly feminist focus. For example, in 1976, the extramural department of the University of the West Indies in Barbados created the Women and Development Unit (WAND) in order to stimulate and support women and development programs throughout the region. In the beginning, WAND sought to integrate women into the national development process. Now they are focusing on ways to increase women's empowerment that would lead to social change (Antrobus 1997). Thus, the organization aims to build the capacity of women's programs, to increase awareness of women and development issues, and (perhaps most important) to build linkages between and among related programs in the Caribbean. WAND's success has been in its outreach programs and orchestrating the integration of women in development through the "bottom up" process (Bolles 1993, Yudelman 1987).

WAND, too, belongs to an NGO, the Caribbean People's Development Agency (CARIPEDA). CARIPEDA is a network of regional NGOs covering the eastern Caribbean, Trinidad and Tobago, Puerto Rico, and Jamaica. It sponsors development work and links international agencies with regional organizations involved in building strategies for alternative economic and political empowerment in the Caribbean. CARIPEDA is at the center of the regional debate on such issues as export-processing zones and structural adjustment polices (Bolles 1993).

Organizations such as WAND and CARIPEDA contribute more than programs and expertise. They enable women to learn from each other as they devise multiple and cohesive strategies geared toward meeting the daily economic crises in their lives. In addition, women can share with each other those alternatives and options that can assist in planning for the future. Interaction with these organizations has also resulted in Caribbean women attending international conferences, in particular, worldwide women's conferences and U.N. development-related conferences.

Thus women in the Caribbean, along with other women in the developing world, have been generating their own analyses of the economic crisis and how it affects issues of gender. Thousands of women are contributing to this understanding through practical development work and by sharing the results of their experiences in women's exchanges and publications, and in international networks such as Development Alternatives for Women in a New Era (DAWN). In mobilizing to meet both practical and strategic gender interests (see Moser 1993), organizations such as these are bridging the gap between the household and the economy. Caribbean women are beginning to transform traditional roles and relationships of nurture and support into a movement for personal, social, and political change. They have been able to move forward an agenda of social and economic empowerment started by leaders like Michael Manley and Cheddi Jagan, but they are adding to the agenda an explicit recognition of the rights and responsibilities of women.

Conclusions

The ways in which Caribbean women are responding to the global economic crisis can be instructive, for we are seeing weakened workers' bargaining power in advanced industrial as well as developing countries (Safa 1995, also see Simmons et al. 1999). Identifying these strategies can provide the basis for thoughtful consideration of their relevance elsewhere. The first strategy is that Caribbean women are calling for development policies that focus on the text of their daily lives, on local knowledge, and on the direct experiences of ordinary people and their communities. This focus is both descriptive and reconstructive, as women seek consciously to bring about social change (Antrobus 1997, 52–53).

Second, it is increasingly evident that paid work does not necessarily alleviate poverty. In fact, as more and more Caribbean women enter the paid labor force (for example, to work in the export-processing zones), they find their salaries so low that they still must engage in a variety of strategies for survival. Other women who have lost jobs in the formal sector after becoming redundant as a result of structural adjustment often turn to jobs in the informal sector, where they must struggle to make ends meet. Thus there is no magic trajectory from informal sector jobs to formal sector ones, and women slip between the two sectors as circumstances in their lives change.

Third, women are very resourceful in maximizing whatever is available in order to support themselves and their families. They have been called "domestic brokers" for the skillful way in which they manipulate a variety of resources. Yet the task of acquiring resources is never far from their consciousness, and it takes a major toll on their physical and emotional well-being. This task has become more intense as women assume more of the burden, necessitated in part by government's reducing and eliminating a wide variety of social services, from health and education to low-cost housing and water supplies.

Fourth, support networks are central in the lives of these women. The reciprocal nature of these networks enables women to assist each other in coping with their multiple roles and in supplementing their meager incomes. Yet, as these networks have grown larger and more complex as a result of the economic crisis, they are requiring more time and effort to maintain.

Finally, women are beginning to realize that even with the creative pooling of resources, the survival of their households remains precarious and the multiplicity of their roles add to their burdens. No longer being able to count on political parties and trade unions for support has resulted in more and more women forming their own organizations to confront state policies and the economic crisis (Ramphall 1994). They attempt to develop collective responses to their practical needs of survival. Increasingly, some nongovernmental organizations are able to help these women see how their practical needs might better be solved through recognition of their strategic interests. Through these efforts, women become conscious of the need for major social change.

Though it is hard to plan for the future when daily crises keep cropping up, and though women's time is limited, growing numbers of Caribbean women are seeing the need to join together to fashion an alternative vision, and then to build institutions that make it more possible for that vision to be put into place. Working within a collective is helpful not only in providing for a woman's practical needs, but also her strategic needs. Organizations like WAND and DAWN have moved away from a woman-as-victim model to one of women's empowerment. No longer are women seen simply as a subordinate population whose underpaid work continues to be exploited, but as those who have the potential to create change leading to increased autonomy or independence (see Mies et al. 1988). Perhaps most important for the long term, women in the Caribbean have taken their experiences in the household and begun to band together to ameliorate the effects of the economic crisis. These women have become engaged in collective action that moves beyond the household economy into the larger global economy.

An economic crisis is not just a turning point for capital accumulation and labor dispersal (see Cope 1997); it is also a time for restructuring, which can open new opportunities for change born out of struggle. Struggles center around reconfiguring not just production but also social relations, and around creating new institutions and organizations that can sustain change. Indeed, it is struggle that paves the way from survival strategies to alternative strategies that can be transforming (Elson 1992). Even so, we must remember that alternative visions are oppositional, and therefore are difficult to initiate and to maintain (Cope 1997). But if done successfully, women can become engaged in collective action that moves their experiences in the household into knowledge of the larger global economy and their role within it. Such knowledge is important for the region as a whole, as the project for social and economic justice is ongoing.

This kind of knowledge that is grounded in the experiences of the workers themselves, and that leads to claims for change that are oppositional in focus, is what Cheddi Jagan and Michael Manley each needed to undergird his working-class project if it was to be successful (see P. Mars, this volume). Instead of looking to established leaders, most of whom were male and middle class, Jagan and Manley might have been helped more by incorporating into their project poor women who were struggling to find ways of living within a global economic crisis. In so doing, the concept of worker would have been expanded, as would our understanding of the ways in which the hegemonic global economy affects the national and household economies.

References

Abramovitz, Mimi. 1988. *Regulating the Lives of Women: Social Policy from Colonial Times to the Present.* Cambridge: South End Press.

Acevado, Luz Del. 1995. "Feminist Inroads in the Study of Women's Work and Development." In *Women in the Latin American Development Process,* ed. Christine Bose and Edna Acosta-Belen. Philadelphia: Temple University Press.

Antrobus, Peggy. 1997. "Women and Planning: The Need for Alternative Analysis." In *Gender: A Caribbean Multidisciplinary Perspective,* ed. Elsa Leo-Rhyne, Barbara Bailey, and Christine Barrow. Kingston: Ian Randle.

Barriteau, Eudine. 1996. "Structural Adjustment Policies in the Caribbean." *NWSA Journal* 8, no. 2: 142–50.

———. 1998. "Theorizing Gender Systems and the Project Modernity in the Twentieth-Century Caribbean." *Feminist Review* 59: 186–210.

Barrow, C. 1986. "Finding the Support: Strategies for Survival." *Social and Economic Studies* 35: 85–96.

Blumberg, Rae Lesser. 1995. "Gender, Microenterprise, Performance, and Power: Case Studies from the Dominican Republic, Ecuador, Guatemala, and Swaziland." In *Women in the Latin American Development Process,* ed. Christine Bose and Edna Acosta-Belen. Philadelphia: Temple University Press.

Bolles, Lynn. 1986. "Economic Crisis and Female-Headed Households in Urban Jamaica." In *Women and Change in Latin America,* ed. June Nash and Helen Safa. South Hadley, Mass.: Bergin and Garvey.

———. 1993. "Doing It for Themselves: Women's Research and Action in the Commonwealth Caribbean." In *Researching Women in Latin America and the Caribbean,* ed. Edna Acosta-Belen and Christine Bose. Boulder, Colo.: Westview Press.

———. 1996. *Sister Jamaica: A Study of Women, Work, and Households in Kingston.* Lanham, Md.: University Press of America.

Campbell, Shirley, Althea Perkins, and Patricia Mohammed. 1999. "Come to Jamaica and Feel All Right: Tourism and the Sex Trade." In *Sun, Sex, and Gold: Tourism and Sex Work in the Caribbean,* ed. Kamala Kempadoo. Lanham, Md.: Rowman and Littlefield.

Chaney, Elsa. 1985. *Migration from the Caribbean Basin: Determinants and Effects of Current Movements.* Washington, D.C.: Center for Immigration and Refugee Assistance.

Christopherson, Susan. 1995. "Changing Women's Status in a Global Economy." In *Geographies of Global Change: Remapping the World in the Late Twentieth Century,* ed. R. J. Johnston, Peter Taylor, and Michael Watts. London: Blackwell.

Cope, Meghan. 1997. "Responsibility, Regulation, and Retrenchment: The End of Welfare?" In *State Devolution in America: Implications for a Diverse Society,* ed. Lynn Staeheli, Janet Kodras, and Colin Flint. Thousand Oaks, Calif.: Sage Publications.

Deere, Carmen, et al. 1990. *In the Shadow of the Sun: Caribbean Development Alternatives and U.S. Policy.* Boulder, Colo.: Westview Press.

Edholm, Felicity, Olive Harris, and Kate Young. 1977. "Conceptualizing Women." *Critique of Anthropology* 3, no. 9–10: 101–30.

Elson, Diane. 1989. "How Is Structural Adjustment Affecting Women?" *Development* 1: 67–74.

———. 1992. "From Survival Strategies to Transformation Strategies: Women's Needs and Structural Adjustment." In *Unequal Burden: Economic Crises, Persistent Poverty, and Women's Work,* ed. Lourdes Beneria and Susan Feldman. Boulder, Colo.: Westview Press.

Fernandez Kelly, M. Patricia, and Saskia Sassen. 1995. "Recasting Women in the Global Economy." In *Women in the Latin American Development Process,* ed. Christine Bose and Edna Acosta-Belen. Philadelphia: Temple University Press.

French, Joan. 1994. "Hitting Where It Hurts Most: Jamaican Women's Livelihoods in Crisis." In *Mortgaging Women's Lives: Feminist Critiques of Structural Adjustment,* ed. Pamela Sparr. London: Zed Books.

Girvan, Norman, ed. 1997. *Poverty, Empowerment, and Social Development in the Caribbean.* Mona: Canoe Press of the University of the West Indies.

Gonzales de la Rocha, Mercedes. 1994. *The Resources of Poverty: Women and Survival in a Mexican City.* London: Blackwell.

LaFont, Suzanne, and Deborah Pruitt. 1997. "The Colonial Legacy: Gendered Laws in Jamaica." In *Daughters of Caliban: Caribbean Women in the Twentieth Century,* ed. Consuelo Lopez Springfield. Bloomington: Indiana University Press.

LeFranc, Elsa. 1988. "Higglering in Kingston: Entrepreneurs of Traditional Small-Scale Operators." *Caribbean Review* 16: 35–48.

Massiah, Joycelin. 1986. "Work in the Lives of Caribbean Women and Women in the Caribbean Project: An Overview." *Social and Economic Studies* 35, no. 2: 12–25.

———. 1988. "Researching Women's Work: 1985 and Beyond." In *Gender in Caribbean Development,* ed. Patricia Mohammed and Catherine Shepherd. Mona: University of West Indies Women and Development Studies Project.

McAffee, Kathy. 1991. *Storm Signals: Structural Adjustment and Development Alternatives in the Caribbean.* London: Zed Books.
Mies, Maria, Veronika Bennholdt-Thomsen, and Claudia Von Weflhof. 1988. *Women: The Last Colony.* London: Zed Books.
Mink, Gwendolyn. 1990. "The Lady and the Tramp: Gender, Race, and the Origins of the American Welfare State." In *Women, the State, and Welfare,* ed. Linda Gordon. Madison: University of Wisconsin Press.
——. 1998. *Welfare's End.* Ithaca: Cornell University Press.
Momsen, Janet. 1993. *Women and Change in the Caribbean: A Pan-Caribbean Perspective.* London: James Currey.
Moser, Caroline. 1989. "Gender Planning in the Third World: Meeting Practical and Strategic Gender Needs." *World Development* 17, no. 11: 1799–1825.
——. 1993. *Gender, Planning, and Development: Theory, Practice, and Training.* New York: Routledge.
Osirim, Mary Johnson. 1997. "'We Toil All the Livelong Day': Women in the English-Speaking Caribbean." In *Daughters of Caliban: Caribbean Women in the Twentieth Century,* ed. Consuela Lopez Springfield. Bloomington: Indiana University Press.
Pitkin, Kathryn, and Ritha Bedoya. 1997. "Women's Multiple Roles in Economic Crisis: Constraints and Adaptations." *Latin American Perspectives* 24: 34–49.
Ramphall, Davin. 1994. "Rethinking Poverty and Development in the Caribbean in the Age of Globalization." *Twenty-first Century Policy Review* 2: 42–61.
Reddock, Rhoda. 1998. "Women's Organizations and Movements in the Commonwealth Caribbean: The Response to Global Economic Crisis in the 1980s." *Feminist Review* 59, no. 1: 57–73.
Sadasivam, Bharati. 1997. "The Impact of Structural Adjustment on Women: A Governance and Human Rights Agenda." *Human Rights Quarterly* 19, no. 3: 630–65.
Safa, Helen. 1995. "Economic Restructuring and Gender Subordination." *Latin American Perspectives* 22, no. 2: 32–50.
——. 1996. *The Myth of the Male Breadwinner: Women and Industrialization in the Caribbean.* Boulder, Colo.: Westview Press.
Senior, Olive. 1991. *Working Miracles: Women's Lives in the English-Speaking Caribbean.* Bloomington: Indiana University Press.
Stephen, Lynn. 1991. *Zapotec Women.* Austin: University of Texas Press.
Vickers, Jeanne. 1991. *Women and the World Economic Crisis.* London: Zed Books.
Yudelman, Sally. 1987. *Hopeful Openings: A Study of Five Women's Development Organizations in Latin America and the Caribbean.* West Hartford, Conn.: Kumarian Press.

11

The Caribbean and Drugs: Challenges in Local-Global Context

IVELAW L. GRIFFITH

Michael Manley and Cheddi Jagan shared several common features as Caribbean leaders in labor and politics, two of which are germane to this discussion. One was a pursuit of political, economic, and social justice, not as ends in themselves but because of sociopolitical dilemmas that often resulted in injustice. A second feature reflected their leader-scholar approach to political dilemmas: they were predisposed to going beyond the domestic manifestations of social dilemmas to probing the broader implications and the regional and global connectivity of those dilemmas. Thus, although this volume deals primarily with Manley and Jagan and, by implication, with Jamaica and Guyana, the thrust and spirit of their leadership and activism oblige us to extend this discussion of drugs beyond their respective nations to the region as a whole, to be better able to appreciate the local-global connections and broader ramifications involved.[1]

The drug phenomenon is a dilemma that has faced Jamaica and Guyana before, during, and after the rule of Manley and Jagan. The severity of its impact has been greater in Jamaica than in Guyana, but both Manley and Jagan were conscious that drugs present threats to social justice in their nations, and the manifestations of the phenomenon in Jamaica and Guyana had ramifications reaching beyond their nation's borders. As Manley noted in his November 6, 1989, testimony to the U.S. Senate, "It is perfectly clear to us, as it is to you, that drug trafficking and all its associated problems long since ceased to be a national problem. We used to know it after it was national as regional. Now it is international" (U.S. Senate Committee Hearings 1989,

1990, 7). Yet both Manley and Jagan appreciated that the drug phenomenon was not merely international; it was and is also multidimensional and all-consuming. A four-decades-old poem by poet-activist Martin Carter, a friend and compatriot of both Manley and Jagan, captures well the essence of the drug dilemma, although Carter did not have drugs in mind when he wrote "You Are Involved":

> Like a jig
> shakes the loom;
> like a web
> is spun the pattern
> all are involved
> all are consumed! (Carter 1997)

The Drug Dilemma

The drug dilemma that affects Jamaica, Guyana, and the entire Caribbean is indeed international, multidimensional, and all-consuming. These features are captured by the concept of geonarcotics developed in 1993 to explain the nexus between drugs as a social dilemma and national security as an intellectual issue area. The concept posits several things. First, the drug phenomenon has four main problem areas: production, consumption/abuse, trafficking, and money laundering. Second, these problems give rise to actual and potential threats to the security of states, including crime, arms trafficking, and narcoterrorism. Third, the drug operations and the activities they spawn precipitate both cooperation and conflict among various state and nonstate actors in the international system.

Besides drugs, the narcotics phenomenon has developed out of and is still developing relationships among three factors; these are geography, power, and politics. Geography is a factor because of the global spatial dispersion of drug operations, and because certain physical and social geographic features of numerous countries facilitate drug operations. Power involves the ability of individuals and groups to secure compliant action. In the drug world, this power is both state and nonstate in origin, and in some cases nonstate sources exercise more power than state entities. Politics revolves around resource allocation in the sense of the ability of power brokers to determine who gets what, how, and when. Since power in this milieu is not only state power, resource allocation is, correspondingly, not exclusive to state power holders. Moreover, politics becomes perverted, and all the more so where it already was perverted.

The geonarcotics milieu involves a variety of state and nonstate actors, which vary in how they affect and are affected by the various problem areas, and in their countermeasures. Drug operations generate two basic kinds of interactions: cooperation and conflict. These are bilateral and multilateral, and do not all involve force. Some involve nonmilitary pressures, such as the application of economic and political sanctions by the United States against countries that, in its estimation, are not proactive enough in fighting drugs. Some actors are engaged simultaneously in both cooperation and conflict, perhaps the best example being the United States–Colombian relationship over the past decade, especially between the inauguration in 1994 of President Ernesto Semper and the election in June 1998 of President Andres Pastrana.

The geonarcotics approach does not view the "war on drugs" as purely a military matter (see Griffith 1993–94, Griffith 1997, 1–22). The application of military countermeasures alone is, therefore, considered impractical. International countermeasures offer the best prospect for dealing with the phenomenon, especially since all state and nonstate actors battling drugs face resource constraints. However, collaboration among states may result in conflict over sovereignty concerns, but also because of domestic factors within states, including disputes over the definition of the nature and severity of threats and, therefore, the appropriate measures to deal with them. An example of this is the controversy among the United States and Jamaica and Barbados between 1995 and 1997 over maritime and air "hot pursuit," which all parties involved agreed was vital to dealing with drug trafficking.

The controversy involved, on the one hand, the insistence by Barbados and Jamaica that hot pursuit by the United States not be extended within their twelve-mile territorial waters and, on the other hand, the push by the United States for the right to full hot pursuit to maximize the operational efficiency of maritime interdiction. The dispute developed added dimensions as Barbados and Jamaica called for linkages between shiprider agreements (see Henke 1998) and other matters, including arms trafficking, deportees, and banana market guarantees, and as the United States accused Jamaica of procrastination in fighting drugs. The matter was resolved at the May 10, 1997, summit in Barbados between President Bill Clinton and fifteen Caribbean leaders, where Barbados and Jamaica signed agreements with the United States that were slightly different than those signed earlier with most other Caribbean nations (Griffith 1997). Among the many things reinforced by the Barbados summit is the multidimensional nature of drug operations in the region.

Drug Operations in the Caribbean

Production and Consumption Abuse

The three "danger drugs" in the Caribbean are cocaine, heroin, and marijuana. However, only marijuana is produced there. Cultivation also varies from place to place. Belize, Guyana, Jamaica, St. Vincent and the Grenadines, and Trinidad and Tobago are among the countries with the highest levels of marijuana production. For decades Belize and Jamaica have had the highest levels of production and export of marijuana. In both countries, marijuana has at times been the largest cash crop.

Marijuana is cultivated mostly in the north and west of Belize in small plots of about one acre or less. By the early 1980s, Belize was the fourth largest supplier to the United States, behind Colombia, Mexico, and Jamaica. But production has plummeted since 1985, largely due to countermeasures taken by the Belize government, often under pressure from the United States. Most of the marijuana that is discovered is destroyed immediately by aerial eradication, or by hand where there is close proximity to residences or to legitimate crops. The U.S. state department reported in 1994 that "Belize, once the fourth largest producer of marijuana in the world, has reduced production to negligible levels through an aggressive aerial eradication campaign" (U.S. Department of State 1994, 137). Nevertheless, Belize halted aerial eradication in January 1995 because of environmental concerns. In 1999, the state department reported, "In 1998 the GOB [Government of Belize] eradicated 202,719 marijuana plants" (INCSR 1999, 138).

Jamaica's subtropical climate makes the entire island ideal for cannabis or marijuana cultivation. Ganja, as marijuana is popularly called there and elsewhere in the Caribbean, traditionally is harvested after two main annual seasons of five- to six-month cycles. However, the indica variety matures in three or four months, making four harvests possible. Large-scale cultivation of five-acre plots were once common, but because of eradication measures, most cultivation is now done in plots of one acre or less, with yields of about

1,485 pounds per hectare. As in Belize, the marijuana eradication agenda has been driven largely by United States efforts to deal with drug source countries, and since 1974 most of the eradication has been done under a program called "Operation Buccaneer." But unlike Belize, the results have been quite uneven. For example, only 456 hectares were destroyed in Jamaica in 1993, far short of the goal of 1,000 hectares. The eradication shortfall is partly the result of diminished resources for eradication and new strategies adopted by cultivators. On the latter issue, the national security minister reported to Parliament in 1993, "The [eradication] program has driven ganja farmers to new tactics: they now interplant ganja with other crops and grow the herb in almost inaccessible places" (Government of Jamaica 1993, 19). During 1994 about 700 hectares of marijuana were destroyed, with a slightly smaller amount eradicated the following year.

Aerial spraying of ganja in Jamaica is more controversial than in Belize because marijuana is an even larger source of income there. One estimate for the 1980s placed the number of farmers cultivating the crop at 6,000. During that same decade, ganja was once said to have contributed between U.S.$1 and $2 billion to Jamaica's foreign exchange earnings, surpassing all other exports, including bauxite, sugar, and tourism (McDonald 1988, 90). The United States complained in 1994 that "for environmental reasons and because of political opposition, the GOJ [Government of Jamaica] has failed to accept the alternative suggested by the USG [U.S. government] of eradication by aerial spraying" (INCSR 1994, 197). In commenting on that statement, one Jamaican official indicated that Jamaica will continue to spray only young plants and nurseries. Otherwise, there is a high risk of contaminating legitimate produce and the ground water supply (Edwards 1994). Since then, eradication efforts have not been stellar. For instance, in 1998 eradication operations (by two teams of four people each) resulted in the destruction of 692 hectares of cannabis, down slightly from the 1997 level of 743 hectares (INCSR 1999, 227).

Economic pressures, the lucrativeness of the drug market, the balloon effect of countermeasures in Belize, Jamaica, and Latin America, and geography are among reasons that other Caribbean countries have taken to significant marijuana production (and export). In the case of Guyana, for example, there are two features that are conducive to all sorts of clandestine activities: its physical geography and its population density of four people per square kilometer, one of the lowest in the world. It is therefore surprising that major marijuana cultivation did not begin there before the late 1980s.

Marijuana seizures have taken place mostly in the Demerara-Mahaica, Mahaica-Berbice, and East Berbice–Corentyne regions in the northeastern and eastern parts of the country. There is also cultivation in the Cuyumi-Mazaruni, Upper Demerara–Berbice, Essequibo Islands–West Demerara, and the Upper Takatu–Upper Mazaruni regions, in west-central, east-central, northern, and southwestern Guyana, respectively.

Most of the marijuana cultivation in Trinidad and Tobago is done in the forested northern and central ranges and along the coast. As in Guyana and elsewhere in the Caribbean, joint police-army operations are the center of eradication and confiscation countermeasures, destroying 783,029 marijuana plants and 2.1 metric tons of cured marijuana during 1994. Within a two-week period in 1999, from September 29 to October 10, 897 kilos of marijuana were seized in Trinidad and Tobago (U.S. Southern Command, October 15, 1999, 1–2). Elsewhere in the region, ganja is cultivated in the Dominican Republic, French Guiana, Puerto Rico, St. Kitts–Nevis, and Suriname. There is variation in the size of plots cultivated. In some places, production is primarily for domestic use, but in most, the product is also exported.

The problem of narcotics consumption and abuse in the Caribbean involves mainly marijuana and cocaine, with heroin becoming problematic in some places. Drug consumption and abuse in the Caribbean are not limited to any single social class or economic or ethnic group, although the consumption of certain drugs is higher in certain groups. Marijuana, for example, is predominantly the working-class drug of choice. Crack cocaine is widespread among lower- and middle-class people because it has the attributes of being "hard" and a "status" drug, but yet is cheap. Heroin, on the other hand, is a rich man's drug. Apart from the cost factor, the impact of heroin abuse in the region has been mitigated by a fear of using needles, but there is concern that the liquid heroin now available in parts of Latin America and the United States will spread to the Caribbean.

Like production, drug use differs from place to place. The greatest concern is in Jamaica, the Bahamas, the Dominican Republic, Guyana, Trinidad and Tobago, and in parts of the Eastern Caribbean. While marijuana is abused in many places, it has had a long history of accepted socioreligious use dating from the introduction of indentured workers from India following the abolition of slavery. Indeed, the word ganja is a Hindi word (Rubin and Comitas 1976, 16). Marijuana's socioreligious use pattern has changed over the years. This use is now associated primarily with the Rastafarians,

Afrocentric social-religious sects that identify with the late Ethiopian emperor Haile Selassie. Hence, the socioreligious use pattern is found in places with large numbers of Rastafarians, including Jamaica, the Eastern Caribbean, Guyana, Trinidad and Tobago, and Grenada. Quite importantly, though, not only Rastafarians use ganja.

Cocaine abuse in the Caribbean results from a spillover from the illicit cocaine trade. Crack cocaine is readily available in many places. According to the U.N. International Drug Control Program (UNDCP), evidence of crack production in the Caribbean first came from Trinidad and Tobago. This problem is found mainly in the principal transit states: the Bahamas, Jamaica, Belize, the Dominican Republic, Guyana, Puerto Rico, and Trinidad and Tobago. Needless to say, cocaine addiction can lead to singularly devastating acts, as in Guyana where a thirty-year-old deranged crack addict murdered six people, including his own mother, at one swoop in a cutlass attack on December 9, 1994, at Buxton-Friendship, a village along the Atlantic Coast (Waddell 1994a, 1994b).

Trafficking and Money Laundering

Apart from trading their own ganja in the United States, Canada, and Europe, some Caribbean countries are important transshipment centers for South American cocaine, heroin, and ganja bound for Europe and North America. For more than two decades, the Bahamas, Belize, and Jamaica dominated this business, but recently Barbados, the Dominican Republic, Guyana, Haiti, Trinidad and Tobago, and Eastern Caribbean countries have featured more prominently.

For instance, in Barbados, authorities reported seizing 35 kilos of cocaine and 1.65 metric tons of marijuana and arresting 546 people during 1998 (INCSR 1999, 242). In Guyana, 1993 cocaine seizures were 1,000 percent higher than in 1992, amounting to 463 kilograms. The amount dropped in 1994 to 80 kilos, but this certainly does not mean that less trafficking occured; it indicates that less is being seized. On January 4, 1995, 5,000 pounds of marijuana valued at U.S.$2 million were discovered behind a false fiberglass wall of a container about to be shipped from Georgetown to Miami. In 1998 the largest ever drug bust was made when authorities successfully interdicted 3,154 kilos of cocaine in transit from Panama to Holland, where the cover cargo was a shipment of rice (INCSR 1994, 189, 215; Hassim 1995, 1). In Trinidad and Tobago, cocaine seizures during 1998 increased by more than 60 percent and narcotics-related arrests more than tripled (1,388 people) compared to 1997 (INCSR 1999, 236).

The geography of the Bahamian archipelago makes it an excellent candidate for drug transshipment, given its seven hundred islands and strategic location in the airline flight path between Colombia and south Florida. When the Bahamas first became a transshipment center, the drug involved was mainly marijuana, with a few consignments of hashish. Evidence dates drug trafficking as far back as 1968, when 250 to 300 pounds of marijuana were flown from Jamaica to Bimini. One of the earliest cocaine seizures was made in 1974; 247 pounds of pure cocaine, with a 1974 street value of U.S.$2 billion, at an airport in George Town, Exuma. That same year, the Bahamas police discovered off Grand Bahama a store of marijuana over six feet high and more than two miles long. In February 1998 Bahamian and U.S. law enforcement officials boarded a coastal freighter in Grand Bahama and seized 2,236 kilos of cocaine, and later that year seizures from airdrops with loads ranging from 300 kilos to 600 kilos occurred in March, May, September, and October. Overall for 1988, the seizures were 3.68 metric tons of cocaine and 2.68 metric tons of marijuana, for which 1,982 people were arrested (Government of Bahamas 1984, 7–8; INCSR 1999, 200).

The geography and topography of Belize also make that country ideal for drug smuggling. There are large jungle areas, sparse settlements, and about 140 isolated airstrips that facilitate stops on flights from South America to North America. Moreover, there is virtually no radar coverage beyond the thirty-mile radius of the international airport at Belize City. Recently, though, there has been an increasing use of maritime routes. Crack has also been featured more prominently. According to the 1994 International Narcotics Control Strategy Report, "for the first time [in 1993], there was evidence of Belizean export of crack cocaine to the United States." Aruba, which is just twenty miles from Venezuela and eighty miles from Colombia, is also becoming more implicated in trafficking. In 1998, authorities there seized 794 kilos of cocaine and 6 kilos of heroin, 95 percent and 100 percent more, respectively, than in 1997 (INCSR 1999, 194).

Several features of the Dominican Republic also make that country a prime trafficking candidate: proximity to Colombia, the Bahamas, Puerto Rico, and the southern United States; a long, often desolate, 193-mile-long border with Haiti; a coastline of nearly 1,000 miles; and poorly equipped police and military authorities. The scope of their problem is reflected in the fact that in 1993, the country's national antidrug directorate, supported by the navy, seized 1,073 kilograms of cocaine, 305 kilograms of marijuana, 1,444 grams of crack, and other drugs. Also confiscated were 183 vessels, 222 motorcycles, and 164 firearms. These were the results of 812 antidrug operations where 5,635 people were arrested. In 1994 the seizures were 2.8 metric tons of cocaine, a 160 percent increase over 1993, and 6.8 metric tons of marijuana. Arrests numbered 3,000. In 1999 it was estimated that approximately 1.5 metric tons of cocaine and approximately 2 metric tons of marijuana flow to the United States and Puerto Rico through the Dominican Republic each month. These figures are based on the number of known and estimated trafficking events and reports of trafficking success (see INCSR 1994, 184–85; INCSR 1995, 168–69; INCSR 1999, 211).

Jamaica has long been key to the drug trade, given its long coastline, proximity to the United States, its many ports, harbors, and beaches, and its closeness to the Yucatan and Windward Passages. Trafficking takes place by both air and sea. According to the 1995 International Narcotics Control Strategy Report, 179 kilos of cocaine, 47 kilos of hashish oil, and one kilo of heroin were seized, and 886 people were arrested for trafficking in 1994. The 1999 report stated that in 1998 cocaine seizures totaled 1,144 kilos, compared with 414 kilos in 1997; hash oil seizures totaled 144 kilos, down from 383 kilos in 1997; and hashish seizures totaled 41 kilos, down from 67 kilos in 1997 (INCSR 1999, 227).

Money laundering is another aspect of the narcotics phenomenon. The countries known to be involved are Aruba, the Bahamas, the Cayman Islands, and Montserrat. Indeed it is partly the money laundering "reputation" of the Caribbean that made Anguilla the choice for Operation Dinero, a major money laundering sting operation that began in January 1992. By the time the operation ended in December 1994, American and British authorities had seized nine tons of cocaine and U.S.$90 million worth of cash and assets, including expensive paintings, one of which was Pablo Picasso's *Head of a Beggar*. They also made 116 arrests and gathered a wealth of intelligence on worldwide drug operations (INCSR 1995, 483).

Apart from Aruba, where Aruban exempt corporations (AECs) and bank secrecy have facilitated massive money laundering (see Sterling 1994, 230–31), most of the money laundering allegations point to the Bahamas and the British dependencies. A 1989 study by Rodney Gallagher of Coopers and Lybrand, a major accounting firm, revealed some telling reasons for this development. According to the Gallagher Report, over 525 international financial companies have had offices in one of these territories, the Cayman

Islands. The Caymans accommodated forty-six of the world's fifty largest banks, including Dai Ichi Kangyo and Fugi, Japan's two largest banks; Bank America; Barclays of the United Kingdom; Swiss Bank Corporation; and Royal Bank of Canada. Banking sector assets in 1987 were U.S.$250 billion.

The Caymans and other dependencies provide many incentives and benefits for doing business there. The Caymans, for example, have no income, corporate, or withholding taxes. Hence there are no international double taxation treaties. Companies that operate mainly outside the Caymans can register there as nonresident companies or incorporate as exempt companies, with the ability to issue bearer shares to nonresidents, and thus avoid disclosure of owners. In addition, bank secrecy is guaranteed under the 1976 Preservation of Confidential Relations Act. The offshore financial industry itself is critical to the economic security of the Caymans, having grown to U.S.$360 billion during the past decade. It provides one-third of the jobs in the Caymans and about the same proportion of their GDP (INCSR 1991, 366–67; Lohr 1992, 27ff).

Anguilla, another dependency, was home to 2,400 registered companies in 1988, including 38 banks and 80 insurance companies. The inducements to doing business there are freedom to move capital without exchange controls, no domestic taxes, and minimum disclosure requirements. The British Virgin Islands (BVI) has a tax regime, although a light one. They had 13,000 companies registered in 1988. Although they now have only six major banks, money launderers reportedly use their services extensively. However, BVI and U.S. authorities have been able to obtain vital bank records and freeze drug-related money. In 1991, for example, over U.S.$3 million were transferred to the United States for forfeiture and sharing between the United States and the BVI (INCSR 1991, 367–68; INCSR 1992, 421–22). Thus an observation by two investigators into the BCI debacle about how the Cayman Islands have been caught in the money laundering matrix is an indictment that, unfortunately, has applied to elsewhere in the Caribbean: "Beneath the veneer of respectability carefully polished by the big banks with offices there, the islands thrive on three principal commodities: money laundering, money from drug sales and other criminal activities, and illegal capital flight. . . . The criminal element simply slid in comfortably behind the reputable corporations and used the same mechanisms for their own ends" (Beaty and Gwynne 1993, 113).

The above discussion clearly suggests that the Caribbean is not implicated merely in the trafficking of drugs, as many officials within the region would prefer to believe, and as some observers outside it think. Drugs are increasingly available in Caribbean countries by design and default, even when the countries themselves are not the intended destinations (and in many cases they are). In the former case drugs are used in lieu of cash for the payment for trafficking services, and in the latter instance failed trafficking operations often result in the availability of drugs intended for elsewhere. Even Cuba, with its tight political and security control, is confronting a drug problem, as indicated by its national prosecutor in a November 1995 interview with the official newspaper, *Gramma*: "Years ago, since this merchandise had no commercial value, everyone who found a packet of this type handed it over to the authorities. Now people have discovered how much that's worth and they don't always hand it over" (Lee 1996, 57). Fidel Castro himself acknowledged the existence of the problem during a speech on January 5, 1999, in Havana (see Johnson 1999) and on July 26, 1999, in Cienfuegos (see "Statement on Drug Trafficking" 1999).

Crime and Criminal Justice

The concern here goes beyond the perpetration of criminal acts to criminal justice in general, which affects social justice and has several local-global linkages. Crime itself can be viewed in several ways typologically. One study sees two basic categories of drug crimes: "enforcement" crimes and "business" crimes. The former involves crimes between traffickers and between traffickers and civilians and police, triggered by traffickers' efforts to avoid arrest and prosecution. The latter category encompasses crimes committed as part of business disputes and acquisitive crimes, such as robbery and extortion. Another typology posits three types of crime: "consensual" ones, such as drug possession, use, or trafficking; "expressive" ones, such as violence or assault; and "instrumental" or property crimes, such as theft, forgery, burglary, and robbery (Kleiman 1989, Anglin and Speckart 1988).

Irrespective of which typology is used, there is a wide range of drug-related criminal activity in the Caribbean. There is no firm evidence of regionwide causal linkages between drug activities, on the one hand, and fraud, homicide, theft, and assault on the other. However, three observations are apposite. First, these are precisely the crime categories likely to be associated with drugs. Second, in a few countries there is clear evidence of linkage. For instance, in Jamaica, where there were 561 reported cases of murder in 1991, the Planning Institute of Jamaica indicated that "there was a 75 percent increase in the incidents of murder linked directly or indirectly to drug trafficking" (Planning Institute of Jamaica 1992, 21.3–21.4). Third, the countries with high and progressive crime reports in the theft, homicide, and serious assault categories are the same ones featuring prominently over the last decade as centers of drug activity: the Bahamas, the Dominican Republic, Puerto Rico, Jamaica, Trinidad and Tobago, the U.S. Virgin Islands, Guyana, and St. Kitts–Nevis.

Drug-related crime is even more important for some of these very countries because it affects tourism, a national economic enterprise. The link between drugs and tourism needs substantive assessment, but there is evidence to suggest a negative effect of drug trafficking on tourism due to media reports that scare potential tourists away and the high incidence of drug-related crime in some places. Caribbean observers have known for some time what the *New York Times* reported in April 1994: that drug-related crime has transformed the "paradise" character of the U.S. Virgin Islands and other Caribbean vacation spots, driving fear into locals and tourists alike and depressing tourism (Rohter 1994). Indeed, Gordon "Butch" Stewart, one of the region's leading tourism entrepreneurs, has called crime "the evil of tourism" (Bohning 1995, BM 43).

Dudley Allen, a former Jamaican commissioner of corrections, once remarked, "It is no longer possible to think of crime as a simple or minor social problem. . . . Mounting crime and violence have been declared leading national problems, and the issue of law and order has assumed high priority in national planning and policymaking. Fear of crime is destroying . . . freedom of movement, freedom from harm, and freedom from fear itself" (Allen 1980, 29). Allen first made this statement in 1976, but it is still relevant over two decades later, now even more dramatically so. He also was speaking mainly in the Jamaican context, but the observation now has region-wide validity because, for a variety of reasons that cannot be explored here, crime has skyrocketed.

Part of the local-global nexus of drug-related crime is reflected in the fact that the crime is not all ad hoc, local crime; some of it is organized, extending beyond the region to North America, Europe, and elsewhere. The most notorious organized crime is perpetrated by groups called "posses" in Canada, the Caribbean, and the United States and "yardies" in Britain. They are organized criminal gangs composed primarily of Jamaicans or people of Jamaican descent, but increasingly involving African Americans, Guyanese, Panamanians, Trinidadians, Nigerians, and Afro-Dominicans from the Dominican Republic. Although the posses are known most for the trafficking of drugs and weapons, they also have been implicated in money laundering, fraud, kidnapping, robbery, burglary, prostitution, documents forgery, and murder (see Headley 1996, Gunst 1989, Small 1995, Kovaleski and Farah 1998, A1).

Another important aspect of the local-global nexus, to which insufficient attention is paid by scholars, pertains to deportees. Drug-related criminal activity within some Caribbean countries is complicated and aggravated by the activities of nationals who are convicted, sentenced, and later deported from elsewhere. In a July 1993 speech to the Jamaican parliament as part of the parliamentary budget debate, National Security Minister K. D. Knight, stated: "Nearly a thousand Jamaicans were deported from other countries last year, with over 700 coming from the United States. Most of them, nearly 600, were deported for drug-related offenses" (see Knight 1993, 11). That was just the tip of the iceberg. Between 1993 and 1997, over 6,000 Jamaican deportees were returned to the island from countries in Europe and the Americas. The number returned in 1993 was 923; in 1996 it was 1,158; and in 1997 it was 1,647, according to law enforcement sources in Jamaica (Annamunthodo 1998).

Most of the deportees come from the United States. However, the United States is not the only country that sends criminals back to their homelands. For example, of the 1,647 people returned to Jamaica in 1997, 1,213 were from the United States, 257 were from Canada, and 121 were from the United Kingdom. Of course, Jamaica is not the only Caribbean nation to be forced to accept nationals in the diaspora who have walked on the wrong side of the law. As a matter of fact, Jamaica is not the Caribbean country to which most deportees are returned. That dubious distinction falls to the Dominican Republic. U.S. immigration sources indicate that between 1993 and 1997, deportees to the Dominican Republic from the United States alone numbered 6,582 (while those sent to Jamaica from the United States during the same period numbered under 5,000) (Taylor and Aleinikoff 1998).

The population size of the Dominican Republic and Jamaica and the size of their diaspora make it understandable that they might have such huge numbers of their citizens returned from countries in Europe and the Americas. But the stark contrast between the numbers from those two nations and the numbers elsewhere is no consolation to policy makers or scholars in any of the countries involved. Some of the countries with "small" 1993-97 United States deportee numbers are: Aruba, 10; Bahamas, 265; Belize, 374; Dominica, 57; Guyana, 427; St. Lucia, 52; and Trinidad and Tobago, 1,036. Needless to say, these are not the only Caribbean countries with deportees from the United States or from elsewhere. For example, Suriname and French Guiana frequently return people to Guyana; the Cayman Islands do the same with Jamaicans (Best 1998, 28).

Government officials throughout the Caribbean have complained that deportees become involved in crime, both drug-related and nondrug-related. Jamaica's Economic and Social Security for 1995 noted, for instance, that deportees are heavily involved in crime, "particularly the importation and use of firearms, the drug trade, and money laundering" (Planning Institute of Jamaica 1996, 23.3). Moreover, at the special CARICOM "Drug Summit," a special meeting dedicated to the issue of drugs held on December 16, 1996, in Barbados, Caribbean leaders noted, at Item 5 of the Summit Communique, "The challenge facing the region from indiscriminate deportations leading to increased criminality" (CARICOM Secretariat 1996).

It was noted earlier that the Dominican Republic, Jamaica, and the other larger nations are not the only ones facing deportee problems. One important difference between the problem in the larger countries and that in the smaller ones is the size factor. Because of the very small size of the populations of eastern Caribbean countries, for example, and hence of their migrant populations, and the smaller scale on which their nationals become involved in drug crimes, they have far fewer deportees. Yet precisely because of their small size, the (re)introduction of criminal behavior into those societies by deportees has a dramatic and traumatic effect on them.

Not only is the problem taxing the resources of Eastern Caribbean and other countries, but some of the deportees are former U.S. servicemen, and they bring their military training and knowledge of weapons and military hardware to their criminal enterprise, creating both a greater sense of apprehension by law enforcement officials and a bigger practical headache for them. In one May 1997 case in Guyana, a bungled burglary and shooting incident at the home of the former chairman of the elections commission, Rudy Collins, involved the use of laser-guided weapons by the would-be robbers, all five of whom were killed in a shoot-out with police; several of the bandits had been deportees (Alstrom and Richards, May 5, 1997).

Response of the State

The deportee headache has both interstate foreign policy and intrastate domestic policy aspects. Caribbean nations have attempted and initiated actions at both the international and domestic levels. In the former they have attempted individually and collectively to stem the tide of returnees from places from which most nationals are sent, the United States and Canada. In the case of the United States, the matter was a high-priority item on the agenda of the summit between President Bill Clinton and the fifteen Caribbean leaders that was held in Barbados in May 1997.

Efforts by the Caribbean leaders to halt the practice were futile, but the summit agreed to streamline the management of the deportees. Section 9 of the Plan of Action, which came out of the May 1997 U.S.-Caribbean summit, outlines the intended actions:

> We recognize the right of each state to determine its policies on deportations subject to international law, and agree to:
>
> 9.3 provide adequate advance notice to designated authorities prior to a criminal's deportation;
> 9.4 provide appropriate information regarding the persons to be deported;
> 9.5 establish, prior to the deportation, that the deportee is a national of the receiving state;
> 9.6 hold consultations on other issues associated with deportation; and
> 9.7 work to improve arrangements by which the deportee has access to his or her assets located in the sending country.
>
> We note that the United States intends to offer technical assistance in establishing parole and monitoring systems. (Caribbean/United States Summit 1997)

Implementation of some of the terms of the U.S.-Caribbean agreement on deportee management, as well as on other issues, has begun. But while these measures are necessary, they are not sufficient. Other actions within Caribbean countries in a variety of areas are also important. One area relates to the passage of new legislation.

For example, in 1994 Jamaica passed the Criminal Justice (Administration Amendment) Act. It provides for deportees to be deemed restricted persons, and under Section 54 restricted persons are subject to the imposition of orders, for up to twelve months at a time, to restrict their residence, force their registration, and compel them to report to police authorities on a weekly basis. They are also required to inform the police about intended absences from the registered address when the absence is for more than a week, and about any planned change of address. Moreover, the new law provides for a central registry of restricted persons as well as for twelve-month prison terms for violation of monitoring provisions or for false reporting. The act also creates a five-member Restricted Persons Review Tribunal to hear appeals from persons placed under restriction, and to advise the government on the maintenance of the system. Guyana plans to emulate Jamaica's legislative lead in this respect, according to Dr. Roger Luncheon, cabinet secretary and head of the presidential Secretariat, at a June 1997 press conference in Georgetown.

This Jamaican legislation, however, has serious implications for constitutional freedoms, especially association and movement. The government has argued that its actions are constitutional given the "exception clauses" of the fundamental rights section of the constitution. For example, under Section 23 of the constitution, which guarantees freedoms of assembly and association, there is the provision that "Nothing contained in or done under the authority of any law shall be held to be inconsistent with or in contravention of this section to the extent that the law in question makes provision (a) which is reasonably required (i) in the interest of defense, public safety, public order, public morality, or public health, or (ii) for the purpose of protecting the rights and freedoms of other persons." Nevertheless, Glen Andrade, a former director of public prosecution for Jamaica, himself once speculated that the law's constitutionality would be challenged with the very first case brought under it because of the delicate constitutional issues involved (Andrade 1995). Some of these same issues worry lawyers and human rights activists in Guyana, as the authorities there plan to follow Jamaica's lead in this area.

Caribbean governments have found it necessary to extend the legislative reach beyond the issue of deportees, of course. New and revised antidrug legislation has also become necessary in most countries. For instance, Jamaica passed the Dangerous Drugs Act in 1987; the Narcotic Drugs and

Psychotropic Substances Act was approved in Guyana in 1988; Barbados adopted the Drug Abuse (Prevention and Control) Act in 1990; in 1991 Trinidad and Tobago's Dangerous Drug Act became law; Antigua-Barbuda passed the Proceeds of Crime Act in April 1993; and St. Lucia adopted a similar law four months later. Calls have been made for capital punishment for certain drug offenses, but generally the new laws impose stiff fines and terms of imprisonment and provide for asset forfeiture. The nature of some drug offenses often prompts judges to apply the law fully. In one instance in March 1992, the chief magistrate of Guyana (now a judge), Claudette La Bennett, refused bail to a nine-month pregnant woman accused of possessing six pounds of cocaine and weapons and ammunition. The woman, Sharon Morgan, appealed La Bennett's decision and was released on G$100,000 bail. While on bail she delivered her baby, but then failed to attend trial on three occasions. She was later convicted and sentenced to four years in prison in absentia (*Stabroek News* 1992a, 1992b).

The breadth of some of these laws and the potential for abuse because of the wide discretion and power that they give to law enforcement officials are cause for some concern. A former Jamaican attorney general had just this in mind in observing:

> In our effort to rid our societies of the scourge of drugs and with some international pressures we are being invited to reverse burdens of proof and adopt a retroactive confiscatory regime. All this is understandable. The perceived danger is real, the consequences of the mischief which we would excise disastrous. As we contemplate effective measures, the nagging question, though, for all of us remains: Are they just?
>
> I remember too that in Jamaica, the mongoose was imported from India to kill out the snakes. It did a very good job. The snakes were eliminated. The mongoose then turned its attention to the chickens. There is a lesson in this. Effective measures against vermin may be turned to effective use by the ill intentioned against decent and law abiding citizens. (Government of Jamaica, May 10, 1991, 7)

As a consequence of the increased crime, and serving to further aggravate the criminal justice situation, is the problem of prison overcrowding. Given the tough, often mandatory, imprisonment terms in some of the antidrugs legislation, successful drug arrests and prosecution create the need for more prison space, something that does not exist. Most Caribbean prisons are overcrowded, and in most cases the prisoners are there because of a variety of drug-related offenses. In the Dominican Republic, for instance, a 1996 survey done by the General Directorate of Prisons revealed that the people convicted of drug crimes constituted the single largest group of prisoners in the country, 30 percent of the 10,359 prisoners at the time of the study.

In Guyana, former prisons director Cecil Kilkenny once indicated that the Georgetown prison, which was built to house 350 prisoners, was forced to accommodate over 800 people in 1994, and had accommodated as many as 1,000 prisoners during early 1992. The Georgetown prison now has a higher official capacity—510—but significant overcrowding still exists there and in most of the other prisons in Guyana. As regards Jamaica, in December 1991 the total inmate population of adult correctional centers was 3,705, about 33 percent above the official capacity of 2,781 (*Economic and Social Survey* 1991, 21.7). The survey also notes that 72 percent of all female admissions for 1990 were for drug offenses. The justice minister himself acknowledged, "The overcrowding in our two maximum security correctional institutions, the General Penitentiary and the St. Catherine District Prison, is serious, and has triggered serious problems over the years. Each of these prisons contains about twice as many inmates as they were designed to hold" (Knight 1993, 78). In 1994 the overage was 611, in 1995 it was 508, and it was only slightly better in 1996.

A 1993 inquiry into the situation in Jamaica highlighted the appalling conditions of their prisons. The inquiry, led by Justice Lensley Wolfe, now Jamaica's chief justice, found that prisoners were required to eat with their hands for security reasons, a situation it deemed "inhuman and degrading treatment." Meals were found to be generally "revolting in appearance and taste." In some places, "the diet fed to the cell occupants should be consumed only by pigs." The Wolfe study concluded that prison indiscipline abounded, and that all sorts of malfeasance and abuse occurred in Jamaican prisons. A few reforms have been implemented since the presentation of the Wolfe report, but the situation is still unpalatable. No wonder, then, that several serious prison riots erupted in Jamaican prisons in 1997, some of them resulting in fatalities. (This is not to suggest, though, that overcrowding and the horrible conditions alone explained the riots.)

In the case of Trinidad and Tobago, most of the country's seven penal institutions house three and four times the number of people for which they were intended. The Port-of-Spain prison, for instance, built in 1812 to accommodate 250 inmates, had a 1993 daily average inmate population of 978, up from the 1992 figure of 916. That prison housed an average of 1,100 people during 1994, and a little less in 1995. The serious overcrowding presents several critical problems affecting provision of medical services, especially given the high incidence of prisoner addiction; maintenance of discipline, particularly given increased gang and other violence in some prisons; physical safety of prison officers; and provision of recreational facilities, among other things.

The deplorable conditions of prisons in Trinidad and Tobago were highlighted in July 1998 when a judge blocked the execution of a death row inmate on grounds that he had already been subjected to cruel and inhuman punishment during his imprisonment over the years his trial worked its way back and forth in the criminal justice system. Justice Peter Jamadar noted that the convict Darrin Thomas had been forced to live with insufficient light, was handcuffed during breaks, and given inadequate food, among other things. The reponse by Justice Jamadar to prison conditions itself raises larger questions of criminal justice fairness and equity in Trinidad, questions that certainly are applicable to other countries in the region (*Miami Herald*, July 23, 1998).

Yet, as was stressed in the first two sections of this essay, the drug challenge is not faced only by "Manley's country" and "Jagan's country." Further, crime and criminal justice are not only critical aspects confronting the managers of the state in the region. Thus it is useful to offer an appreciation even if only a brief one of the response of the state to the drug phenomenon beyond the areas of crime and criminal justice.

Responses beyond Crime and Criminal Justice

A range of counterdrug coping strategies is being adopted by states in the Caribbean. Countermeasures are multidimensional, multilevel—national, regional, and international—and multiactor. They need to be multidimensional because drug operations and their impact occur on many different dimensions; they need to be multilevel because drug operations and many of the problems they precipitate are both national and transnational. Moreover, they have to be multiactor for the above reason plus the fact that Caribbean governments lack the necessary financial and other resources to meet the threats and challenges facing their nations. Hence, antidrug efforts require the involvement not only of governments but also of corporate bodies, nongovernmental organization (NGOs), and regional and international agencies such as the Regional Security System (RSS), the Caribbean Community (CARICOM), the Organization of American States (OAS), the Inter American Drug Abuse Control Commission (CICAD), and the U.N. International Drug Control Program (UNDCP).

The kind and impact of efforts introduced and maintained depend on three main factors: perceptions of the nature and scope of the predicament, national capacity, and foreign support. National efforts are wide ranging in scope, if not sufficiently substantive in character. They include law enforcement, education, interdiction, demand reduction, rehabilitation, crop substitution, improved port management, better regulation of financial services, and legislation. Circumstances are such that measures cannot be undertaken only sequentially; education, rehabilitation, interdiction, and the other measures have to be applied at the same time. Indeed, in many places it was a failure to adopt simultaneous measures, based on misperception of the situation, that has contributed to its deterioration. Most countries have, therefore, adopted the inclusive approach, actively reaching out to NGOs, corporations, and international agencies for partnership in countermeasures. Generally, though, even the combined available resources of governments and NGOs are insufficient, making foreign state and nonstate assistance necessary.

In some cases foreign support becomes so central to programs that its withdrawal results in the program's collapse. A case in point is Jamaica's Operation Buccaneer. It began in 1974 with U.S. support and some ambitious aims: eradication of all marijuana cultivation; arrest of all persons, equipment, aircraft and marine vessels engaged in trafficking; and destruction of all illegal airstrips. The U.S. obligations were usually for salaries for twenty-five to thirty people to cut and burn marijuana fields; fuel for the helicopters, boats, and vessels used in operations; funds to purchase chemicals, equipment, and supplies to cut and spray fields; and the lease of helicopters for use by the Jamaican military. The United States also provided vessels for the Jamaica Defense Force (JDF) Coast Guard, and helped with intelligence gathering. Operation Buccaneer was interrupted for almost eleven years, largely because of U.S. antipathy toward the socialist posture of the Jamaican government under Manley. It was restarted in 1985 and continued as an annual exercise, interrupted in 1988 when Hurricane Gilbert hit Jamaica and destroyed most of the island's marijuana fields. Because of budget constraints, the United States stopped funding of Operation Buccaneer in 1993. However, residual funds from previous years enabled drastically reduced operations through 1996. The program has since folded.[2]

Foreign assistance to Caribbean states is not only bilateral, as in the case of Operation Buccaneer, but multilateral as well, coming from the European Union, the OAS, and the UNDCP, among other places. Most Caribbean countries have national drug councils that are supposed to set policy on countermeasures. They usually are composed of officials from various government agencies as well as NGOs and the private sector. The National Council on Drug Abuse (NCDA) of Jamaica, Programa para la prevención del uso indebido de drogas (PROPUID) of the Dominican Republic, the National Advisory Council on Drugs (NACD) of Guyana, the National Council for Drug Abuse Prevention (Na CoDAP) of the Netherlands Antilles, and the National Drug Council (NDC) of the Bahamas are a few examples of these bodies. Understandably, structures and operational efficiency vary from country to country (see Griffith 1997, 249–56; and http://www.cicad.oas.org). Among other things, the national councils are mandated to create national master plans to establish overall policies for fighting drugs.

Several countries have mounted demand reduction programs, and one—Jamaica—has pursued crop substitution. The latter project covers farms in the parishes of St. Ann, St. Catherine, St. Elizabeth, and Westmoreland. Substitute crops include yams, carrots, coffee, citrus, and papaya. The program also includes cottage industries for processing agricultural produce, and dressmaking, embroidery, and needlecraft. Like crop substitution initiatives in Latin America, efforts in Jamaica raise the issue of the comparative economic advantage, from the standpoint of the farmers, of cultivating marijuana as opposed to the alternative crops. Planners in Jamaica are pragmatic in this regard, noting, "While it is not realistic to expect this plan to generate income capacities as marijuana production, a sufficient level of income will be generated devoid of risk and negative social impact [that comes] with production of the illegal crop" (Jamaica, Ministry of Agriculture, 1994, 2)

At the regional and international levels, Caribbean countries participate in a variety of networks and organizations, including UNDCP, CICAD, the Caribbean Financial Action Task Force, and the OAS Money Laundering Expert Group. Caribbean countries are also part of several international counternarcotics regimes. Notable ones are the 1961 United Nations Single Convention on Narcotic Drugs; the 1971 Convention on Psychotropic Substances; and the 1988 Convention Against Illicit Traffic in Narcotic Drugs and Psychotropic Substances. Indeed, one Caribbean country—the Bahamas—has the distinction of being the first country to ratify the 1988 convention, on January 30, 1989. The convention includes provisions on drug trafficking, money laundering, organized crime, and arms trafficking. It requires states that are party to it (153 up to October 1999, according to the UNDCP) to strengthen laws concerning financial reporting, extradition, asset forfeiture, and other subjects. It also urges adherents to improve cooperation in intelligence, interdiction, eradication, and other areas.

In terms of bilateral agreements, most Caribbean states have Mutual Legal Assistance Treaties (MLATs) with the United States. MLATs provide for training, joint interdiction, asset sharing, extradition, intelligence sharing, and material and technical support. Some countries, such as the Bahamas and Jamaica, long have had several complementary agreements with the United States. Bilateral treaties exist with countries other than the United States, though. For instance, Belize has agreements with Mexico for intelligence sharing between the two and for Mexican assistance with demand reduction and rehabilitation. Bilateral agreements also exist between Suriname and Colombia, Suriname and Guyana, Cuba and Guyana, Venezuela and Guyana, Jamaica and Mexico, Suriname and the Netherlands Antilles, Trinidad and Tobago and Venezuela, Cuba and Panama, and other sets of countries.[3]

Conclusion

Clearly then, there is no easy way out of the Caribbean drug dilemma. The "war on drugs" fought in Jamaica, Guyana, and throughout the region will be a long one. Moreover, it has to be a "total war," conducted on several fronts simultaneously and by several nations collectively. Antidrug measures must be flexible, sustained, and results oriented. However, they should not be driven by political dictates for "quick fixes" as the issues involved are multifaceted. This is something both Manley and Jagan appreciated, although they wished otherwise. The jury is still out on whether the "war" can be "won." But no one should dispute that the "war" must be "fought." The alternative is too unpalatable even to contemplate. The drama of drugs presents the kind of travail to Caribbean (and other societies) such that, remembering the words of poet Martin Carter, unless all are involved, all may well be consumed.

Notes

1. Understandably, it is impossible to discuss here all the possible drug-related matters affecting Jamaica and Guyana, examination of which makes evident the two features of Manley and Jagan identified earlier. The issue of criminal justice stands out, though. It will, therefore, be the main subject of discussion.

2. See Griffith, 1997b: 199–200. A 1999 status update was provided by a restricted source at the U.S. Southern Command on December 20, 1999.

3. For more on the response of the state, see Griffith (1997b, 197–232); Government of Guyana (1997); Government of Jamaica (1997); Griffith (2000, chapters 10–13).

References

Allen, Dudley. 1980. "Urban Crime and Violence in Jamaica." In *Crime and Punishment in the Caribbean,* ed. Rosemary Brana-Shute and Gary Brana-Shute. Gainesville: University of Florida Press.

Alstrom, Albert, and Andrew Richards. 1997. "Cops Kill Five Men—Robbery Foiled." *Stabroek News Online,* May 5.

Anglin, M. Douglas, and George Speckart. 1988. "Narcotics Use and Crime: A Multisample, Multimethods Analysis," *Criminology* 26, no. 2: 197–233.

Beaty, Jonathan, and S. C. Gwynne. 1993. *The Outlaw Bank.* New York: Random House.

Best, Tony. 1998. "Deportation Policy Has Gone Astray." *New York Carib News,* June 9.

Bohning, Don. 1995. "For Resorts, Crime=Crisis." *Miami Herald,* April 10.

Brana-Shute, Rosemary, and Gary Brana-Shute, eds. 1980. *Crime and Punishment in the Caribbean.* Gainesville: University of Florida Press.

Caribbean-U.S. Summit. 1997. *Plan of Action.* Bridgetown, Barbados, May 10.

CARICOM Secretariat. 1996. *Communique of Fifth Special Meeting of the Conference of Heads of Government of the Caribbean Community.* St. Michael, Barbados, December 16.

Carter, Martin. 1997. *Selected Poems.* Georgetown: Red Thread Press.

Government of Jamaica, Ministry of Agriculture. 1994. *Alternative Systems for an Illegal Crop*, September.
Government of Jamaica, Ministry of Justice. 1991. *Crime and Justice in the Caribbean* (Keynote Address by the Hon. Carl Rattray, Q.C., Minister of Justice and Attorney General of Jamaica), May 10.
Government of Jamaica, Parliament. 1993. *Presentation of the Hon. H. D. Knight, Minister of National Security and Justice, Budget Sectoral Debate*, July 15.
Government of the Bahamas. 1999. *Report of the Commission of Inquiry into the Illegal Use of the Bahamas for the Transshipment of Dangerous Drugs Destined for the United States*. Nassau.
Griffith, Ivelaw. 1993–94. "From Cold War Geopolitics to Post–Cold War Geonarcotics." *International Journal* 48 (winter).
———. 1997a. "Caribbean Security: A Reality Check." *Caribbean Affairs* 7, no. 6.
———. 1997b. *Drugs and Security in the Caribbean: Sovereignty Under Seige*. University Park: Penn State University Press.
———. 2000. *The Political Economy of Drugs in the Caribbean*. London: Macmillan.
Gunst, Laurie. 1989. "Jamaica Drug Gangs: Johnny-too-Bad and the Sufferers." *The Nation*, November 13.
Hassim, Alim. 1995. "Marijuana Container Valued at U.S.$2M." *Stabroek News*, January 6.
Headley, Bernard. 1996. *The Jamaican Crime Scene: A Perspective*. Washington, D.C.: Howard University Press.
Henke, Holgar. 1998. "Drugs in the Caribbean: The 'Shiprider' Controversy and the Quest for Caribbean Sovereignty." *European Review of Latin American and Caribbean Studies* 64.
Kavoleski, Serge, and Douglas Farrah. 1998. "Organized Crime Carries Clout in the Islands." *Washington Post*, February 17.
Kleiman, Mark A. R. 1989. *Marijuana: Costs of Abuse, Costs of Control*. Westport, Conn.: Greenwood Press.
Lee, Rensselaer W. 1996. "Drugs: The Cuba Connection." *Current History*, (February): 55–58.
Lohr, Steve. 1992. "Where the Money Washes Up." *New York Times Magazine*, March 29.
McDonald, Scott B. 1988. *Dancing on a Volcano*. New York: Praeger.
Planning Institute of Jamaica. 1992. *Economic and Social Survey, 1991*. Kingston.
———. 1996. *Economic and Social Survey, 1995*. Kingston.
Rohter, Larry. 1994. "Slaying in St. Thomas Stains Image of an American Paradise." *New York Times*, April 19.
Rubin, Vera, and Lambros Comitas. 1976. *Ganja in Jamaica*. New York: Anchor Books.

Small, Geoff. 1995. *Ruthless: The Global Rise of the Yardies*. London: Little, Brown, and Co.

Stabroek News. 1992a. March 3, p. 14.

Stabroek News. 1992b. April 14, p. 16.

Sterling, Claire. 1994. *Thieves World*. New York: Simon and Schuster.

Taylor, Margaret H., and J. Alexander Alienikoff. 1998. *Deportation of Criminal Aliens: A Geopolitical Perspective*. Inter-American Dialogue Paper, June, available at http://www.iadialogue.org/taylor.html.

U.S. Department of State. 1994–99. *International Narcotics Control Strategy Report* (INCSR).

U.S. Senate Committee on the Judiciary. 1989 (November 6), and 1990 (March 27). "Statement by the Hon. Michael N. Manley, Prime Minister of Jamaica," *U.S. International Drug Policy-Multinational Strike Force—Drug Policy in the Andean Nations*, Joint Hearings before the Committee on the Judiciary and the Caucus on International Narcotics, 101st. Cong., 1st and 2nd Sessions.

U.S. Southern Command. 1999. "Operation Columbus-K9-99-0009/UEZ1F, October 15."

Waddell, Ronald. 1994a. "'Baby Arthur' was a Crack Addict." *Stabroek News*, December 11.

———. 1994b. "Deranged Man Murders Mother, Five Others." *Stabroek News*, December 10.

12

The Role of Emigration in the Caribbean Development Process

MONICA H. GORDON

Migration has always been a central force in Caribbean formation and transformation. The search for economic opportunities after emancipation began the reversal of the in-migration that had dominated the region for the previous four centuries. The freedom to move after emancipation triggered the migratory flow outward, which has continued to the present time. Although this emigration was propelled by economic conditions, the movement also involved more complex issues of human, political, and social underdevelopment.

The complex reasons for migration from the English-speaking Caribbean can be linked to social, economic, and political changes and development in the region. The approach in this essay includes the psychosocial motivations of individuals; the structural factors that make migration a sociopolitical mandate; and how some individuals have used their immigrant experience and/or benefited from periodic mass migration from the region. The focus is not on the immigrant experiences in host countries, but instead on the linkages and relations between immigrants and home countries. The perspective that shapes this analysis is the dependency relationship between the English-speaking Caribbean and the industrialized world of North America and Great Britain, and the extent to which the dependency has shaped economic and social development in the region. In this context, migration from the region helps to frame the sociopolitical context and leadership roles. Political leaders often find that they have constituencies outside their natural borders and that those constituents impact events in their home countries. Jamaica's Michael Manley and Guyana's Cheddi Jagan shared those experiences. This essay will explore the ways underdevelopment shapes the migration culture as a push factor and whether emigrants themselves can contribute effectively and efficiently to sustainable development in the region.

Personal Factors in Migration

Literary works on migration focus on the complexity of the psychosocial and cultural aspects of individual experience. The essence of this complexity is captured in Wilfred Cartey's 1991 title, *Whispers from the Caribbean: I Going Away, I Going Home*. Although the book is a critical review of Caribbean novelists, it serves adequately as a metaphor for the circulatory movement of emigrating and returning home. Cartey defined "I Going Away" as the shaping of the Caribbean personality and "I Going Home" as the evolution of the Caribbean presence. The going away provides the opportunity to rethink the self, shaped by the forces of colonialism and its corollaries. Presence or going home, Cartey argues, is a cultural or spiritual term that suggests being in one's own "spiritual interiority," a selfhood that emanates from the values, worldview, and mores of one's own people. Thus, according to Cartey, personality and presence are in a constant state of tension and interaction in a transformative process whereby the Caribbean personality fragments and reassembles into a Caribbean presence. Going away is "a breaking away from dysfunctional sociopolitical forces," and going home is going "to a possible new fusion of elements," a holistic society (Cartey 1991, xiii–xvi).

Emigration is a conscious and practical act, which involves the leaving from a specific place to some predetermined destination and often for some specific purpose. In going away, persons leave behind all the external constraints that contributed to the shaping of their personalities. At the destination, in the new environment, the fragmentation of personality begins as new forces intervene, replacing the old influences and establishing new standards. The going away provides new opportunities, new beginnings, new journeys into selfhood and, in that process, generates visions of the society of origins and the possibilities for its transformation. Cartey, a Trinidadian immigrant to the United States, understood this process of personality evolving into presence, as immigrants become conscious of the significance of others and the meaning of community. All professionals, including almost all those who would become political leaders, shared this experience.

Stuart Hall suggested that migration is a one-way trip because there is no "home" to go back to (Chambers 1994, 9). This statement is also metaphorical and comparable to Cartey's metaphor of "I going away," where, in the process of going, transformation takes place so that both person and place are altered. The Guyanese writer and critic Wilson Harris explained that experiences of movement and marginality do not merely refer to geographical locations but provide perspective on "cultural formations and emerging cultural capacities" (Chambers 1994, 27). The persons who go away are not psychologically and socially the same persons who return; neither is "home" exactly as they left it. The point is that the emigration experience has the potential to transform individuals just as the individuals, in turn, can use the experience for social transformation in their homelands. This has been the path of change and development in the modern Caribbean. Cheddi Jagan, who went to Howard University, explains his transformation:

> You see my education in the United States was not just formal going to university and all that. I was working my way through and did all kinds of odd jobs. . . . So I was able to see both sides, which normally students are not able to see. This helped my orientation toward politics. . . . Looking back, I would say that my youth on the sugar plantation, the oppression of it, not only physically but sociologically, and then my experience in the States, and seeing the debasement and how working black people lived there, these were the main things which influenced my whole outlook in life. Thus my role in going into politics. (Sealy 1991, 132)

Jagan included India's struggle for independence as part of his political education and social awareness, especially about colonialism. He was able to extrapolate the physical manifestations of social injustice in the United States to his own Guyanese experience and to the broader context of the struggle against colonialism. On the other hand, Michael Manley, in the words of Norman Girvan, was born to privilege but spent most of his life fighting against the entrenched structures of privilege in his native Jamaica and in the wider world (1998). Manley's political consciousness came from his

Fabian Socialist family combined with his exposure to socialist philosophy at the London School of Economics. Both men went back home and activated the political and social knowledge gained abroad.

Structural Factors in Migration

The complexity of migration is the combination of the individual psychosocial motivation with the socioeconomic one, often conceptualized as "the search for a better life." This search for a better life, according to Palmer, is a circular process whereby economic gains in the host country are shared through remittances to their home communities (1990, 5). In this way, those who depart contribute to the economic and social well-being of family members left behind since the remittances pay for consumption goods, land, education, or even business start-ups. The emigrants' contributions bring new resources into the communities and with the resources, the potential for changes, even if the emigrants themselves never return to their places of origin.

The Caribbean migration phenomenon as a movement of people to multiple destinations in search of a better life puts economic considerations at the core of the migration. This focus is reflected in the frequent use of the push-pull theory of migration to explain the movement. Lee identified four factors associated with migration: area of origin, area of destination, intervening obstacles, and personal factors (1966). Lee argued that for each factor there are pull, push, and neutral factors. The intervening obstacles and personal factors become the selective factors that mitigate the decision to stay or migrate. In the Caribbean, structural conditions of underdevelopment are push factors and perceived opportunities at the destination are pull factors. The desire to migrate can be activated only when obstacles have been removed. For example, individuals who wished to pursue higher education prior to the 1950s had to meet certain educational prerequisites and have the necessary financial resources. This migration was limited to those seeking social advancement or status maintenance and was usually temporary. On the other hand, migration of large numbers of individuals in search of economic rewards was dependent on the availability of work at the destination. This latter type does not exclude individuals who are also motivated by the opportunity for social improvement, and many immigrants have used migration to advance both economic as well as social goals.

More recent scholars claim that the push-pull theory of migration is inadequate to explain the nature of and pattern of contemporary migration. Following the general guidelines of the modern world systems theory advanced primarily by Wallerstein (1974), they conceptualize migration as part of the trend in late capitalism toward a global labor market. Accordingly, labor migration largely follows a south to north pattern, or periphery to center, where capital is accumulated. The south or periphery comprises those countries whose economies have been stagnated by colonialism and imperialism and who continue in a pattern of dependency on countries with capital accumulation, usually former colonial powers. The periphery is characterized as areas of "reserve labor" to be recruited when and where needed (Petras 1983, Sassen-Koob 1978, Watson 1976). Nikolinakos agreed in general with the pattern of the migration and the relation to capital accumulation but sees migration as a many-sided phenomenon to be viewed from different perspectives (1975). The many sides of this phenomenon include people moving between and within countries, individuals making decisions that affect the lives of entire families, and class differences that involve the proletarianization of masses of people.

One can therefore state that the Caribbean, with no capital accumulation, is dependent on migration to areas of capital accumulation. Individual decision making is done within the context of the privileges extended to potential immigrants who are selected based on the needs and provisions of the receiving countries. Current observers of recent immigrants' behaviors use the term "transnationalism" to "define the process by which immigrants forge and sustain multi-stranded social relations that link together their societies of origin and settlement." Basch et al. explain that they used the term transnationalism to emphasize that many immigrants today build social fields across geographic, cultural, and political borders (1994). Such immigrants, called transnationals, live equally in the home and host societies. This level of involvement is potentially a powerful source for immigrants' intervention for social change in the Caribbean.

The Significance and Background of Caribbean Migration

Caribbean migration is a demographic phenomenon that can be assessed statistically in terms of human characteristics such as age, sex, race/ethnicity, education, occupation, and the total number of persons leaving or entering a country in any particular year. These factors have implications for the sending and receiving societies in the context of contributions and deficits. Emigration of surplus labor is a gain for the sending country but the emigration of highly trained and skilled workers may represent a net loss. Caribbean migration is also about how emigrants maintain contact, involvement with their home countries, and how they contribute to and influence the development of their home countries. Caribbean migration is about emigrants who returned to their countries of origin and get actively involved in social development and transformation efforts in their countries.

All these are the aspects of Caribbean migration that have helped to define the social, economic, and political contours of Caribbean life (Pastor 1985, Palmer 1990). Migration goals may be conscious or subliminal, articulated or repressed, but there is the expectation that "going away" should effect some transformation in those who go away. Those who remain also share this belief. It is a cultural phenomenon. The expectations from those who emigrate are self-improvement and regular assistance to family (including extended kin). Individual transformation is measured by accomplishments, which may include education and professional attainment, accumulation of material goods, and/or ideas that can be translated into action on behalf of the wider community. The ideas and goods that emigrants acquired contributed significantly to the changes that began to take place in the Caribbean from the last decade of the nineteenth century. Those who returned to their home countries began to realize that the quest for a better life for themselves also required changes in the social and political infrastructure to substantiate their improved economic status. Many Caribbean immigrants, whether they return to reestablish residence, continue to live abroad, or become transnationals, have contributed to social infrastructural development in their home countries.

The Caribbean background of chattel slavery and indentureship imposed severe restrictions on personal freedom to move. Yet, according to historian Gordon Lewis,

> The essence of Caribbean life has always been movement.... It also explains the socioeconomic phenomenon of migration. Migration, as the vast restless circulatory movement of whole peoples ... has its roots, historically, in the immediate past. For the first century of European colonization, migration meant the influx of European.... After

that came the African influx, . . . Following that again, was the influx of Indian indentured labor.(1990, xii)

The reversal of this in-migration began when the enslaved people were free to move in search of work and other opportunities. This freedom to move intensified with the early search for work around the Caribbean and Central American region during the latter half of the nineteenth century and expanded to North America and Europe for much of the twentieth century. The economic needs that spurred the migration led David Lowenthal to the observation that West Indians learn early that success—psychological as well as economic and social—requires emigration (1972, 216). This theme has long been articulated among writers such as V. S. Naipaul, who claimed that people are just born in the West Indies; they want to go away. As George Lamming puts it, writers (including Naipaul), "simply wanted *to get out* of the place where they were born . . . in the hope that a change of climate might bring a change of luck" (1992, 41). The psychosocial needs as the basis of an individual's decision to migrate hinted at by writers is complemented by theoretical perspectives that look beyond the individual's needs to structural and other situational factors that influence migration.

Migration has been a major, if not the major, element in the social, political, and economic history of the Caribbean. From the mid-nineteenth century to about the first decade of the twentieth century, the migratory movements were largely around the Caribbean region, following the pathways of economic activities in the region (Gordon 1979, Bryce-Laporte 1976). The second wave coincided with the outbreak of World War I. Men were recruited for the British army while the open door migration policy of the United States allowed entry to Caribbean people. Those recruited for the war effort in Britain were largely repatriated after the war, but those who went to the United States had the option to remain. The United States' open door immigration policy was rescinded by the mid-1920s under the National Origins Quota Act. From then on, until World War II, migration from the region was severely restricted.

World War II opened a new phase in migration from the Caribbean that has continued to the present time. First there was the demand for labor in postwar Britain. This generated a massive outflow of job seekers from the Caribbean. Thompson cited a newspaper headline in 1948, "492 Jamaicans arrive to seek work. . . . Among them singers . . . pianists, boxers, and complete dance bands" and there "were law students, dockers, potential chemists and scientists, who had left their homeland because of the difficulties of getting employment there" (1990, 39). This cohort, Thompson observed, was welcomed and assisted in finding jobs. As migration from the Caribbean to Britain intensified, the welcome changed to fear of what the dramatist/folklorist Louise Bennett called "colonisation in reverse." Great Britain, the quintessential colonial power that never had to deal with the dark-skinned colonial subjects except as elite students or soldiers, had absorbed hundreds of thousands of working-class immigrants from the Caribbean and elsewhere. The migration was summarily curtailed by the passage of the 1962 Commonwealth Immigration Act. By 1984, the estimated Caribbean population in Britain was over a half million (James 1993). Increase in this population is most likely to have come from reproduction rather than migration.

The next destination for emigrants was Canada that opened its doors, tentatively, with a limited program for domestic workers starting in the early 1950s. A more comprehensive immigration policy, similar to the U.S. 1965 Immigration Act, instituted a selection system based on qualification and labor force needs (Richmond and Mendoza 1990). Canada's 1996 census reported 279,405 Caribbean (including Bermuda and, likely, non-Anglophone countries) immigrants residing there, excluding nonpermanent residents.

The United States has been a primary destination for most Caribbean emigrants since the passage of the 1965 Immigration Act. The various amendments and additions to this reformulated policy, which eliminated race-based selection, reopened the United States as a destination for Caribbean emigrants. Approximately a million immigrants from the Anglophone Caribbean arrived in the United States between 1960 and 1994. This figure does not include nonresident emigrants, pre-1960 emigrants, or children born in the United States to immigrants.

Although the United States and Canada currently remain in the category of receiving states for immigrants, the general consensus is that open and unrestricted migration is a thing of the past. The selective recruitment of individuals considered valuable additions to the existing labor force is not likely to bring large numbers from the Caribbean in the foreseeable future. Service and family categories have been the largest cohorts in the migration from the Caribbean to the United States, but the emphasis is now on education, training, and skills (Gordon 1997, 173–76).

The Emerging Modern Caribbean Immigrants' Contribution to Social Change

The period between the two world wars marked the beginning of significant and far-reaching changes in the economic, political, and social organization in the Caribbean. Those who returned home from sojourns abroad had the opportunity to get involved and become catalysts for change. Palmer sees migration as "not a set of linear flows but a collection of circular movements" (1990, 5). These circular movements link the emigrants to their countries of origin and maintain a pattern of exchange, primarily through remittances, that has significance for the patterns of development in those countries. This circular migration has been the pattern of migration that Caribbean people have followed since they gained the freedom to move.

Fraser (1990, 19–37) and Richardson (1985) researched the early migratory movement of British Caribbean people (laborers, teachers, tradespeople) as they moved around the Caribbean and Central American region as free laborers from 1860 into the twentieth century. They worked on sugar and banana plantations, they built railways and the Panama Canal, and even worked as coachmen in Port-au-Prince. The work available to the emigrants was largely in seasonal agriculture or in infrastructure development—the railway and the canal—from which the workers would be released once the particular phase of the work ended for which they were hired. Some returned home, others moved on to the next place, and some remained. Many also died.

Social transformation in the Caribbean is closely associated with the ideas and actions of people who had lived and some that continued to live abroad. Commenting on the impact on the societies of the emigrants who returned home, Lowenthal suggests:

> The effects on emigrants themselves are also manifold: often atypical from the start, experience abroad makes them yet more unlike those at home. But insights acquired overseas ultimately affect the homeland too. Many emigrants return only briefly or late in life, if ever. But others come home to play significant roles in Caribbean society. Their energy and self-awareness equip them at least to articulate if not to solve problems that defy traditional approaches. Virtually every major Caribbean leader, in fact, has spent several years abroad. (1972, 223)

Thomas-Hope made similar observation and opined that return migration is a compound and complex process that includes a series of returns often over an extended period of time. This return, she argued, involved not just numbers but "people with specific orientations, views, skills, ideas, and the ability to readjust, who must fit back into the existing structural framework of the Caribbean. To varying degrees these people accept the status quo or become agents of change." Emigrants were exposed to new ideas about democracy and social justice, and developed new definitions of themselves as human beings. They learned the efficacy of workers' unions, began to understand politics, experienced racism that their color-coded system muted, and began to understand the patterns of social organization in their societies. They acquired leadership and organizing skills that placed them into activist and/or leadership roles (1985, 157–8).

The role emigrants can play when they return to their homeland or from where they reside changes according to the social and political climate of the time. Migration gives Caribbean people from different territories the opportunity to meet and interact. Michael Manley mentioned his associating with the West Indian Student Union, an activist forum that, he claimed, prepared them "for the immediate struggle for freedom and the latter task of remaking colonial society" (1975, 19). In another country, the United States, another Caribbean leader-to-be, Cheddi Jagan, was exposed to world politics and also returned home to pursue the cause of social justice (Sealy 991, 127–42).

Jagan's and Manley's Experiences with Migration

Guyana under the leadership of Cheddi Jagan (especially from 1950 to 1968) and Jamaica under Michael Manley (especially from 1972 to 1980) experienced political turbulence as a result of their attempts to bring about changes in the social systems of their countries. As mentioned above, both men, in keeping with their times, studied abroad. The act of studying abroad is not a mandate for social action, but among Caribbean leaders those who did or who traveled for other purposes were more likely to enter the public arena with ideas for change. Emigration and immigrants played key roles in the national elections of Guyana (1968) and Jamaica (1970s). The events of those times are well known (see Thomas 1988, St. Pierre 1982) and this chapter is not oriented to discuss them, but it is important to note that returning and departing emigrants affected the governments of Cheddi Jagan and Michael Manley.

In the case of Jagan, it is believed that allowing overseas resident Guyanese to vote in the 1968 general election contributed to the defeat of Jagan's People's Progressive Party since the majority of those voters were Afro-Guyanese who voted for Burnham's People's National Congress Party. Michael Manley, on the other hand, experienced out-migration and capital flight during his first two terms as prime minister largely as a result of his move toward democratic socialism. Stephens and Stephens, in their analysis of emigration patterns from Jamaica during the period of 1967 to 1980, note the early departure to Canada of managers, administrators, proprietors, and officials (1986, 98–99). Professionals and technical personnel followed this exodus in 1977. Perceived economic hardships and highly publicized violence seem to have motivated the emigration of these individuals (1986, 195).

The high-profile sociopolitical movements were not the only transforming activity in the region, especially as these movements affected only a relatively small percentage of workers. The remittances the emigrants sent home to relatives, the investments in the purchase of land, the building of homes, savings, and other investments have made quiet but significant transformations in communities where government resources have not reached. The money earned while abroad has also made it possible for some emigrants to achieve limited upward mobility by investing their money in land and small businesses (Richardson 1985, Philpott 1968, Frucht 1968, Rubenstein 1983).

Contemporary Emigrants' Relations with the Home Countries

The transnational theoretical perspective helps explain patterns of contemporary emigration. Emigrants from the Caribbean move frequently between host and home countries or return to reestablish residence permanently. Families and communities benefit from those who migrate and maintain contact through a variety of exchanges. Governments and international organizations have acknowledged and calculated monetary transfers by emigrants to their places of origins, possibly because it is relatively easy to keep track of transfers involving currency exchange. Other goods—food and clothing (the infamous barrel), for example—probably totaling millions of dollars annually, are shipped to various Caribbean destinations. Caribbean emigrants' charitable organizations are increasingly providing needed services: medical and dental care and medicines, and technology transfers to individuals and organizations in the Caribbean. Whereas an organization like the Jamaica Progressive League was political in orientation, contemporary organizations are more socially conscious and make contributions to "needy cases": individuals, and social welfare and educational agencies.

Emigrants create a bridge between the host and home countries in very tangible ways. Through a variety of exchanges between emigrants and their sending countries (relatives, friends, business and exchange visits, goods and services), emigrants have managed to diminish the separateness that distance normally produces. This condition is, of course, mitigated by the technological opportunities of modern times. Emigrants' investment in their countries is tangibly demonstrated by remittances. In Guyana, remittances represented 25.5 percent of GNP in 1992 ($13 million). In the same year, Jamaicans remitted $248 million (7.2 percent of GNP) and in 1994, $479.8 million (Baker 1997, 192). Emigrants contribute in other ways. Caribbean countries have increased export goods to the expanded emigrant market. Agricultural products, art and entertainment, and travel industries benefit from the emigrant communities. In addition to material goods, emigrants have knowledge and skills in a variety of areas that can be used by governments and nongovernmental organizations (NGOs) in human development efforts.

Concerns for Future Development

Rubenstein raised concerns about the impact of remittances and other goods on development in the Eastern Caribbean (1983). He argued that remittances rarely contribute to rural economic development: "rather than ameliorating economic conditions remittance and the entire migratory system, of which they are a part, may be exacerbating West Indian rural stagnation." He does not deny that some people benefit significantly, but he argues that the system itself is not inherently capable of meaningful development.

This observation goes to the heart of the argument advanced by Pastor, who pointed out that although emigration is related to Caribbean economic development and political stability, "few nations have considered relating their policies on migration with their development strategies, let alone systematically doing so" (1985, 3). He further argued that neither the United States, which aims to contain emigration in the region, nor Caribbean regional leaders, who view development as a core objective, have attempted to make connections between emigration and their policy objectives. He notes that financial institutions and aid-granting institutions do not factor migration into their development activities, either.

It is possible that a major reason for not factoring migration into the development equation can be found in Girvan's observations on the development process (1991, 11–21). Girvan argued that development is a succession of stages that must connect economic growth and structural change with the broader social and political systems. He conceptualized development as a three-tiered phenomenon: (1) development as economic growth; (2) development as growth and structural change and transformation; and (3) development as a multifaceted process with economic, social, cultural, and political dimensions. The third concept of development is pertinent to the Caribbean because it incorporates the idea of sustainable development. Sustainable development requires a focus on human resource development, efficient management of natural and human resources, social and public policies that are knowledge based, and the commitment to social justice to successfully operationalize these principles.

Although more likely to result in a sustainable program, this multifaceted approach has never been well articulated, planned, or activated effectively. Henry and Johnson briefly assessed the socialist development philosophies of Burnham in Guyana and Manley in Jamaica during the 1970s and noted that their well-intended polices contributed to the loss of what those countries needed most: trained, skilled workers. Henry and Johnson located the "major impetus for emigration" in the structure and functioning of the Caribbean economies (1985, 274). They concluded, as did Anderson (1985), that emigration is a part of the system of structured dependency, and sustainable development remains an elusive goal.

Guyana and Jamaica are prime examples of nonsustained development. Each country enjoyed brief periods of rapid growth during the 1950s and 1960s only to fall into debt and be subject to direct interference from international economic regulatory bodies. Both Guyana (under Jagan and Burnham) and Jamaica (under Manley) attempted to reorganize their economies under state supervision to achieve social goals, possibly at the expense of profit. Manley reflected in the epilogue to his seminal work "The Politics of

Change" that the social justice orientation of his policies and programs were not grasped by a significant percentage of the Jamaican people, nor could they understand the difficulties of introducing change into an institutional structure born out of colonialism (1990). In advocating new approaches to development, Girvan suggested that equitable and sustainable human development requires a far wider range of actors than the traditional dichotomy between the state and private sector (1994). Given the fact that Guyana and Jamaica have been reduced to "poor" countries in relation to others in the region indicates the need for the collective efforts of NGOs, the international community, debt relief, and priority focus on human development.

Currently, emigrants represent important and viable resources for the holistic, integrative, and sustainable development needed in the Caribbean. These resources are not only money and goods but knowledge and skills. Emigrants can redirect their expertise and knowledge toward sustainability, since this is the social and economic concern of the time. Emigrants represent an international network that can connect the Caribbean meaningfully into the global economy. However, this use of emigrant resources needs conscious effort, planning, and organization to harness. In other words, it needs to be managed. One factor that will have to be considered is changing immigration laws internationally; physical "going away" from the Caribbean is likely to diminish in the coming decade when the United States changes its regulations.[1]

It seems unlikely that there will be great demand for waves of unskilled labor from the Caribbean when the labor-recruiting countries have been closing their doors (Gordon 1997, 174–76; New York City Dept. of Planning 1996, 1–3). The Caribbean immigrants are aging along with the rest of the world's population and are retiring from paid employment. At this stage in the life cycle, "going home" or "engaging" with home becomes a strong possibility. As mentioned earlier, home is not the same place they left as emigrants, yet many are now better able to make positive contributions to their countries if their reentry into the home societies can be managed effectively. It is possible that the experiences of living abroad has made emigrants more appreciative and willing to pursue the ideas of social justice, which Cheddi Jagan and Michael Manley advanced but were unsuccessful in incorporating into effective social and human development. Emigrants are a vital resource that can and should be incorporated into any development policy initiative in the Caribbean as part of the development strategies.

Notes

1. The United States has remained the primary destination for immigrants from the Caribbean for the last three decades, but there are indicators that the numbers will decline in the not too distant future. The Immigration Act of 1990 actually increased the number of immigrants allowed over the 1980 annual level, but this move should be accepted with caution. The three important changes incorporated in the 1990 act were: (1) increase in the number of visas allocated for family reunification, (2) the introduction of a "diversity pool" program, and (3) expansion of the number of occupational and skill-preference visas. The "diversity lottery" primarily benefits Europe and other countries from which migration in the previous decade had been low because they did not benefit from the family provision. Jamaica and other Caribbean sending countries with high annual migration are barred from participation in the diversity lottery. Furthermore, a minimum educational qualification of high school or its equivalent is required for this visa. The majority of immigrants from the Caribbean qualify under the family reunification act. The categories under this provision have been numerically reduced (unmarried children of U.S. citizens and their children and married children of U.S. citizens and their families).

References

Anderson, Patricia. 1985. "Migration and Development in Jamaica." In *Migration and Development in the Caribbean*, ed. R. A. Pastor. Boulder, Colo.: Westview Press.

Baker, Judy L. 1997. "Poverty Reduction and Human Development in the Caribbean." World Bank discussion paper 366.

Basch, Linda, N. Glick-Schiller, and C. Blanc-Szanton. 1994. *Nations Unbound: Transnational Projects, Postcolonial Predicaments, and Deterritorialized Nation-States*. Langhorne, Pa.: Gordon and Breach.

Bennett, Louise. 1966. "Colonisation in Reverse." In *Jamaica Labrish*. Kingston: Sangster Bookstore.

Bryce-Laporte, Roy. 1972. "Black Immigrants: The Experience of Invisibility and Inequality." *Journal of Black Studies* 3: 29–56.

Cartey, Wilfred. 1991. *Whispers from the Caribbean: I Going Away, I Going Home*. Los Angeles: Center for Afro-American Studies at UCLA.

Chambers, Iain. 1994. *Migrancy, Culture, Identity*. New York: Routledge.

Cooper, Dereck. 1985. "Migration from Jamaica in the 1970s: Political Protest or Economic Pull?" *International Migration Review* 29, no. 1: 728–45.

Girvan, Norman. 1991. "Notes on the Meaning and Significance of Migration." In *Gender in Caribbean Development,* ed. P. Mohammed and V. Shepherd. Mona: Institute of Social and Economic Research, University of West Indies.

———. 1994. "New Partnership for Global Development." *Caribbean Affairs* 7, no. 4: 134–42.

———. 1998. "Michael Manley: A Personal Perspective." Paper delivered at the Caribbean Perspectives on Labor and Politics Conference, Wayne State University, April. Http://members.aol.com/Beleiver/Manley.htm

Gordon, Monica H. 1992. "The Dynamics of Political Integration and Ethnic Identity among African-Caribbean Immigrants in New York City." Unpublished paper presented at Caribbean Studies Association Conference, Grenada.

———. 1997. "Caribbean Migrations in the 1990s: Some Policy Implications." In *Caribbean Public Policy,* ed. J. A. Braveboy-Wagner and D. Gayle. Boulder, Colo.: Westview Press.

Hall, Stuart, and Paul duGay, eds. 1996. *Questions of Cultural Identity.* Thousand Oaks, Calif.: Sage.

Hart, Richard. 1984. "Origins and Development of the People's National Party." Lecture given at the Vernon Arnett Party School, Kingston.

Henry, Ralph, and Kim Johnson. 1985. "Migration, Manpower, and Underdevelopment of the Commonwealth Caribbean." In *Migration and Development in the Caribbean,* ed. R. A. Pastor. Boulder, Colo.: Westview Press.

James, Winston. 1993. "Migration, Racism, and Identity Formation: The Caribbean Experience in Britain." In *Inside Babylon: The Caribbean Diaspora in Britain,* ed. Winston James and Clive Harris. New York: Verso.

Kasinitz, Philip. 1992. *Caribbean New York: Black Immigrants and the Politics of Race.* Ithaca: Cornell University Press.

Lamming, George. [1960] 1992. *The Pleasures of Exile.* Ann Arbor: University of Michigan Press.

Lee, Everett. 1966. "A Theory of Migration." *Demography* 3, no. 1: 47–57.

Lewis, Gordon K. 1990. Foreword to *In Search of a Better Life: Perspectives on Migration from the Caribbean,* ed. Ransford Palmer. New York: Praeger.

Lewis, W. Arthur. [1939] 1977. *Labor in the West Indies: The Birth of a Workers Movement.* Research Series No. 44. London: Fabian Society.

Lowenthal, David. 1972. *West Indian Societies.* New York: Oxford University Press.

Manley, Michael. 1975. *A Voice in the Workplace.* London: Andre Deutsch.

———. 1990. *The Politics of Change.* Rev. ed. Washington, D.C.: Howard University Press.

Mintz, Sidney. 1990. "Labor Needs and Ethnic Ripening in the Caribbean Region." In *Anales del Caribe,* Centro de Estudios del Caribe. Havana, Cuba: Casa de las Americas.

New York Dept. of City Planning. 1996. "The Newest New Yorkers, 1990–1994." Report. New York: New York Dept. of City Planning

Nikolinakos, Marios. 1975. "Notes toward a General Theory of Migration in Late Capitalism." *Race and Class* 17, no. 1: 5–17.

Palmer, Ransford, ed. 1990, "Caribbean Development and Migration Imperative." In *In Search of a Better Life: Perspectives on Migration from the Caribbean*. New York: Praeger.

Pastor, Robert A., ed. 1985. *Migration and Development in the Caribbean*. Boulder, Colo.: Westview Press.

Petras, Elizabeth McLean. 1983. "The Global Labor Market in the Modern World Economy." In *Global Trends in Migration: Theory and Research on International Population Movements*, ed. M. Kritz, C. Keely, and S. Tomasi. New York: Center for Migration Studies.

Reid, Ira. [1939] 1968. *The Negro Immigrant*. New York: AMS Press.

Richardson, Bonham. 1985. *Panama Money in Barbados, 1900–1920*. Knoxville: University of Tennessee Press.

Rubenstein, Hymie. 1983. "Migration and Underdevelopment: The Caribbean." *Cultural Survival Quarterly* 7, no. 4: 30–32.

Sassen-Koob, Saskia. 1978. "The International Circulation of Resources and Development: The Case of Migrant Labor." *Development and Change* 9: 509–45.

Sealy, Theodore. 1991. *Caribbean Leaders*. Kingston: Eagle Merchant Bank and Kingston Publishers, Ltd.

Stephens, Evelyn H., and John D. Stephens. 1986. *Democratic Socialism in Jamaica*. Princeton: Princeton University Press.

Sutton, Constance, and Susan Makiesky-Barrow. 1987. "Migration and West Indian Ethnic Consciousness." In *Caribbean Life in New York City: Sociocultural Dimensions*, ed. Constance Sutton. New York: Center for Migration Studies.

Thomas-Hope, Elizabeth. 1985. "Return Migration and Its Implications for Caribbean Development." In *Migration and Development in the Caribbean*, ed. R. A. Pastor. Boulder, Colo.: Westview Press.

Thompson, Mel. 1990. "Forty-and-One Years On: An Overview of Afro-Caribbean Migration to the United Kingdom." In *In Search of a Better Life*, ed. Ransford Palmer. New York: Praeger.

Wadinambiaratchi, George. 1989. "Management in the Development Process: The Missing Ingredient." *Caribbean Affairs* 2, no. 2: 125–44.

Selected Bibliography

ELLA DAVIS

Cheddi Jagan and Michael Manley were both astute in keeping their views in the public arena. They were prolific in their formal writings, whether in the form of major books or articles. They also gave many speeches over their lifetimes, some of which have been captured although many have been lost. Because they were such controversial figures, there is a growing literature on their political stances and the impact those have had on the Caribbean and beyond. What follows is a small sample of what is available on each man. The intent is to encourage readers to learn more about these two fascinating men of the Caribbean.

Cheddi Jagan

Books and Articles by Cheddi Jagan

British Guiana: A Challenge to Labor. London: Labour Publishing Society, 1954.
"Chile: The Beginnings of a New Era." *New World Review* 39, no. 1 (1971): 16–26.
Forbidden Freedom: The Story of British Guiana. London: Lawrence and Wishart, 1954.
Global Dilemma: Economic Growth, Sustainable Development, and the Debt Burden. Georgetown, Guyana: n.p., 1994.
"Guyana: A Reply to the Critics." *Monthly Review* 12, no. 4 (1977): 36–49.
"Guyana at the Crossroads." *Black Scholar* 5, no. 10 (1974): 43–47.
"Guyana at the Crossroads." *New World Review* 38, no. 2 (1970): 72–75.
Guyana Needs Cheddi: The Fight for Guyana's Freedom. Astoria, N.Y.: Association of Concerned Guyanese—USA, 1990.
A New Global Human Order. Milton, Ont.: Harpy, 1999.
PPP Struggles for TUC Freedom: Selected Materials on Guyana's Labour Movement. Georgetown, Guyana: People's Progressive Party, 1985.

"Strengthen the Party, Defend the Masses, Liberate Guyana: Text of the Central Committee." Report delivered by General Secretary Cheddi Jagan at the Twenty-first Congress of the People's Progressive Party, Mon Repos, July 30–August 2, 1982. Georgetown, Guyana: People's Progressive Party, 1982.

Unity and Action in the Youth Movement: Addresses. [n.p.: New Guyana Co. Ltd.], 1986.

"Urgent Need for a New Consensus on Social Reform." *Caribbean Affairs* 6, no. 2 (1993): 39–48.

The West on Trial: My Fight for Guyana's Freedom. London: Joseph, 1966. Reprint, Berlin: Seven Seas, 1972.

Talks, Speeches, and Letters

Cheddi Jagan: Selected Speeches, 1992–1994. London: Hansib, 1995.

Cheddi Jagan letters to Alan McLeod. 1971, 1972. Rare Books Room, University Library, Pennsylvania State University, University Park.

"Cheddi Jagan on Critical Support." Address to the Twenty-fifth Anniversary Conference of People's Progressive Party, August 3, 1975.

"Cheddi Jagan Speaks at Freedom Rally, Feb. 9, 1964." Georgetown: New Guiana Co. for People's Progressive Party, 1964.

"Cheddi Jagan Speaks to Workers on May Day, 1986." Georgetown, Guyana: New Guyana Co. for People's Progressive Party, 1986.

A Talk with Cheddi Jagan. Berkeley, Calif.: Pacifica Tape Library. Interview. Recorded for WBAI during a visit to New York in 1994.

Secondary Sources

Akhtar, Shameem. "British Guiana: A Study of Marxism and Racialism in the Caribbean." M.A. thesis. Southern Methodist University, 1962.

Ankum-Houwink, J. C. "Guyana, 1953–1966." *Speigel Historical* [Netherlands] 8, no. 12 (1973): 651–60.

Bathrick, David Delos. "Cheddi Jagan's Role As Nationalistic Leader in Guyana." M.A. thesis. Arizona State University, 1971.

"Bright Prospects for People's Power" Documents from the Fifth Caribbean Conference of Trade Unions, 1987. Georgetown, Guyana: Guyana Agricultural and General Workers' Union, 1987.

"Country Report: Guyana." *Courier* (March–April 1995): 30–51.

Datt, Norman. *Cheddi B. Jagan: The Legend.* Pickering, Ont.: N. Datt, 1997.

Dr. the Honourable Cheddi Jagan, Premier of British Guiana, Biographical Note. Georgetown: Government Printing and Stationery Office, 1961.

"Entrevista con Cheddi Jagan, líder socialista de Guyana" [Conducted by Margarita Haugaad]. *El Caribe Contemporaneo* no. 7 (1983): 115–24.
For a Revolutionary Democratic Alliance. Lacytown, Guyana: People's Progressive Party, 1985.
Garcia Muniz, Humberto. "Guyana: El Macrodesarrollo de las Fuerzas de Securidad." *Secuencia* [Mexico] 8 (1987): 145–68.
Hintzen, Percy C., and Ralph R. Premdas. "Race, Ideology, and Power in Guyana." *Journal of Commonwealth and Comparative Politics* [London] 21, no. 2 (1983): 175–94.
Huntley, Eric L. *The Life and Times of Cheddi Jagan.* London: Bogle-L'Ouverture Press, 1994.
Interview with Dr. Cheddi Jagan, Prime Minister of British Guiana. Sunday, October 15, 1961 (proceedings of *Meet the Press,* v. 5, no. 40). Washington D.C.: Merkle Press, 1961.
Jagan, Janet. *When Grandpa Cheddi Was a Boy and Other Stories.* Leeds, England: Peepal Tree Books, 1993.
Karran, Kampta. *National Unity and Racial Equality: Celebrating Dr. Cheddi Brahat Jagan, 1918–1997.* Guyana: Offerings Publications, 1997.
Kaufman, Victor. "Domestic Politics As a Catalyst for United States Intervention in the Caribbean: The Case of British Guiana." *Journal of Caribbean History* 3, no. 1–2 (1996): 107–31.
Lakhan, Chris V., ed. *Cheddi Jagan: Selected Contributions on his Life and Legacy.* Windsor, Ont.: Summit Press, 1997.
Premdas, Ralph R. "Guyana: Socialism and Destabilization in the Western Hemisphere." *Caribbean Quarterly* [Jamaica] 25, no. 3 (1979): 25–43.
———. "Guyana: Socialist Reconstruction or Political Opportunism." *Journal of Interamerican Studies and World Affairs* 20, no. 2 (1978): 133–64.
Sallahuddin. *Guyana: The Struggle for Liberation, 1945–1992.* Guyana National Printers, 1994.
Simms, Peter. *Trouble in Guyana: An Account of People, Personalities, and Politics As They Were in British Guiana.* London: Allen and Bacon, 1966.
Singh, Chaitram. "Changing the Basis of Civilian Control over the Military in Guyana." *Journal of Third World Studies* 14 (fall 1997): 113–31.
Spinner, Thomas J., Jr. "Nationalism, Socialism, and Culturalism: Pluralism in Guyana." *Queen's Quarterly* [Canada] 84, no. 4 (1997): 582–92.
Steps toward Caribbean Unity: The Views of Cheddi Jagan, James Mitchell, Julian Hunte, Oscar Allen, James Millette, and Vere Bird. Georgetown, Guyana: People's Progressive Party, 1989.
Yes to Marxism! Georgetown, Guyana: N.G.C.L. for People's Progressive Party, 1984, 1986.

Michael N. Manley

Books and Articles by Michael Manley

Drumblair: Memories of a Jamaican Childhood. Kingston: I. Randle Publishers, 1996.
"Grenada in the Context of History: Between Necolonialism and Independence." *Caribbean Review* 12, no. 4 (1983): 6–9, 45–47.
"The Integration Movement, the CBI and the Crisis of the Mini-State." *Caribbean Affairs* 1 (1988): 6–15.
Introduction. *Two Can Play.* By Trevor D. Rhone. Lexington, Ky.: KET Books, 1984.
Jamaica: Struggle in the Periphery. London: Third Word Media in association with Writers and Readers Publishing Cooperative Society, 1982.
"Overcoming Insularity in Jamaica." *Foreign Affairs* 49, no. 1 (1970): 100–110.
"Parallels of Equity: New Horizons in Economic Cooperation." *Round Table* [Great Britain] 260 (1975): 335–47.
The Politics of Change: A Jamaican Testament. Washington, D.C.: Howard University Press, 1975.
The Poverty of Nations: Reflections on Underdevelopment and the World Economy. London: Pluto Press, 1991.
"Southern Needs." *Foreign Policy* 80 (1990): 40–51.
"Third World Development and the International Economic System." *TransAfrica Forum* 3, no. 4 (1986): 83–93.
Up and Down Escalator: Development and the International Economy—a Jamaican Case Study. Washington, D.C.: Howard University Press, 1987.
We Are a Country without a Conscience: Quotations. [n.p.]: D. H. Consulting, 1988.
"The Year Ahead: Excerpts from Address by Prime Minister Hon. Michael Manley, on September 11, 1977." Kingston: Agency for Public Information, 1977.

Lectures, Interviews, and Speeches

Evening Exchange. Exclusive interview with Michael Manley. Videocassette. United States: WHMM-TV, 1990.
An Interview with Michael Manley. Videocassette. Taped at the Schomburg Center for Research in Black Culture, New York Public Library, New York City, 1986.
Lecture by Michael Manley given at Florida International University, March 7, 1986.
"Operation Construction: A text of a broadcast to the nation by Prime Minister, Hon. Michael Manley, on March 30, 1980." Kingston: Agency for Public Information, 1980.
"Our Movement Is Irreversible—because Our Cause Is Just." Speech by Prime Minister Michael Manley at the Sixth Summit of the Nonaligned Nations in Havana, Cuba, Sept. 4, 1979. Kingston: Agency for Public Information, 1979.

"The Policy of the People's National Party." Speech made by the Honourable Michael Manley, prime minister of Jamaica, at Denbigh, 1974.

The Search for Solutions: Selections from the Speeches and Writings of Michael Manley. Oshawa, Ont.: Maple House Publishing Company, 1976.

"Statement by Michael Manley at the Twenty-seventh Session of the United Nations, Oct. 2, 1972." Kingston: G. P., 1972.

Recordings and Videocassettes

Michael Manley says the advantage that raw-material- and food-producing countries currently enjoy is probably temporary. Recording. Broadcast on NET, February 10, 1976.

Michael Manley defines "Third World" and talks of his own emergence as a Third World leader. With Bill Moyers on *Bill Moyers' Journal.* Recording. Broadcast on PBS, May 4, 1975.

Michael Manley says Washington operates on a series of self-destructive myths about the nature of the "devil" communist conspiracy. Recording. Gift of Terry Link. Recorded at Calvin College (Grand Rapids, Michigan), fall 1981.

Michael Manley speech. Audiovisual. 1 Videocassette: sd., col.; 3/4 in. Baruch video; UMT 075-076, 1986.

Secondary Sources

Arawak, Christopher. *Jamaica's Michael Manley: Messiah, Muddler, or Marionette?: Has His Disastrous Experiment with "Democratic Socialism" Wrecked Jamaica's Economy Beyond Repair?* Miami: Sir Henry Morgan Press, 1980.

Ashley, Paul W. "Natural Resource Diplomacy: Non-Alignment versus Regional Cooperation." *Boletin de Estudios Latinoamericanos y del Caribe* 33 (1982): 139–54.

Bernal, Richard L. "The IMF and Class Struggle in Jamaica, 1977–1980." *Latin American Perspectives* 11, no. 3 (1984): 53–82.

———. "Restructuring Jamaica's Economic Relations with Socialist Countries, 1974–80." *Development and Change* [Netherlands] 17, no. 4 (1986): 607–34.

Boulton, Adam. "Jamaica's Bauxite Strategy: The Caribbean Flirts with the International System." *SAIS Review* 2 (1981): 81–91.

Brown, Devon. "A Comparison of the Political Style and Ideological Tendencies of Two Leaders—Michael Manley and Edward Seaga—Using Parliamentary Speeches." *Social and Economic Studies* 31, no. 3 (1982): 191–214.

Campbell, Horace. "Socialism and Pseudo-Socialism in the Caribbean: Cuba, Jamaica, and Guyana." *Taamuli* [Tanzania] 13 (1983): 39–55.

Danielson, Anders. "Surplus and Stagnation in Jamaica: Further Notes." *Social and Economic Studies* [Jamaica] 41, no. 1 (1992): 45–66.

Davies, Omar. "Economic Transformation in Jamaica: Some Policy Issues." *Studies in Comparative International Development* 19, no. 3 (1984): 40–59.

Edie, Carlene J. "Domestic Politics and External Relations in Jamaica under Michael Manley, 1972–1980." *Studies in Comparative International Development* 21, no. 1 (1986): 71–94.

———. "Socialism, the State, and Rural Development in Tanzania and Jamaica." *Journal of African Affairs* 14, no. 3 (1987): 141–51.

Gardels, Nathan P., ed. *At Century's End: Great Minds Reflect on Our Times.* La Jolla, Calif: ALTI Pub., 1995.

Girvan, Norman, and Richard Bernal. "The International Monetary Fund and the Foreclosing of Development Options: The Case of Jamaica." *Investigacion Economica* [Mexico] 40, no. 156 (1981): 159–76.

Graham, Pamela M. "Alternative Strategies for Development: An Analysis of the Bauxite and Agricultural Programs of the Manley Government in Jamaica." M.A. thesis. University of North Carolina at Chapel Hill, 1989.

Grosfoguel, Ramon. "Migration and Geopolitics in the Greater Antilles: From the Cold War to the Post–Cold War." *Review* [Fernand Braudel Center] 20, no. 1 (1977): 115–45.

Harsch, Ernest. *U.S. Intervention in Jamaica: How Washington Toppled the Manley Government.* New York: Pathfinder, 1981.

Hart, Richard. *Michael Manley: An Assessment and Tribute.* London: Caribbean Labour Solidarity, 1997.

Headley, Bernard D. "Behind a Manley Victory in Jamaica." *Monthly Review* 38, no. 9 (1987): 17–30.

Hoffman, Linda M. *Politics of the Manley Regime in Jamaica, 1972–80.* Ph.D. diss. University of Wisconsin at Madison, 1983.

Jackson, Lois A. "Canadian Bilateral Aid to Jamaica's Agricultural Sector from 1972–86." *Social and Economic Studies* [Jamaica] 41, no. 2 (1992): 83–101.

Kaufman, Michael. *Jamaica under Manley: Dilemmas of Socialism and Democracy.* London: Zed Books, 1985.

Keith, Nelson W., and Novella Z. Keith. *The Social Origins of Democratic Socialism in Jamaica.* Philadelphia: Temple University Press, 1992.

Kopkind, Andrew. "Jamaica: Socialism 'Soon Come.'" *Working Papers for a New Society* 5, no. 1 (1977): 44–52.

Lefkowitz, David I. "Socialist Experiments in the Third World: Michael Manley's Failure in Jamaica." Senior honors thesis. Brandeis University, 1981.

Levi, Darrell E. *Michael Manley: The Making of a Leader.* Athens: University of Georgia Press, 1990.

———. *Michael Manley: The Making of a Leader.* Kingston: Heinemann Publishers, 1989.

Lewin, Arthur. "The Fall of Michael Manley: A Case Study of the Failure of Reform Socialism." *Monthly Review* 33, no. 9 (1982): 49–60.
Lewis, Vaughan A. "The Small State Alone: Jamaican Foreign Policy, 1977–1980." *Journal of Interamerican Studies and World Affairs* 25, no. 2 (1983): 139–69.
Mandle, Jay R. "Caribbean Dependency and Its Alternatives." *Latin American Perspectives* 11, no. 3 (1984): 111–24.
Manley, Farewell: A Scrapbook. Kingston: Mowtown Limited, 1997.
Manley, Rachael. *The Slipstream: A Daughter Remembers.* Toronto: A. A. Knopf Canada, 2000.
Muñoz, Laura M. "El Nuevo Gobierno De Manley: ¿Transformaciones Con Equidad?" *Secuencia* [Mexico] 26 (1993): 119–29.
Nettleford, Rex. "Masters of the Game: Cricket As Social Metaphor, Michael Manley As Historian." *Caribbean Affairs* [Trinidad] 1, no. 3 (1988): 194–99.
———. "Michael Manley, Jamaica: Struggle in the Periphery." *Caribbean Quarterly* [Jamaica] 28, no. 3 (1982): 47–52.
O'Flaherty, J. Daniel. "Finding Jamaica's Way." *Foreign Policy* 31 (1978): 137–58.
Paul, Alix-Herard. "The Destabilization Program of the IMF in Jamaica." *Inter-American Economic Affairs* 37, no. 2 (1983): 45–61.
Payne, Anthony. "The 'New' Manley and the New Political Economy of Jamaica." *Third World Quarterly* [Great Britain] 13, no. 3 (1992): 463–74.
Profile: The Hon. Michael Norman Manley, Prime Minister of Jamaica. Kingston: Jamaica Information Service, 1989.
Ramsay, Ken. *The Dream Lives On.* Port Antonia, Jamaica: K. Ramsay, 1997.
Reaching for the Future: A Timely Trilogy. Black Rock, St. Michael, Barbados: West Indian Commission Secretariat, 1991.
Sealy, Theodore. *Sealy's Caribbean Leaders.* Kingston: Eagle Merchant Bank of Jamaica in association with Kingston Publishers, 1991.
Simms, Glenda Patricia. *Political Messianism: The Case of Michael Manley.* Edmonton: University of Alberta, 1985.
Stephens, Evelyne Huber, and John D. Stephens. "Democratic Socialism in Dependent Capitalisms: An Analysis of the Manley Government in Jamaica." *Politics and Society* 12, no. 3 (1983): 373–411.
———. "The Transition to Mass Parties and Ideological Politics: The Jamaican Experience since 1972." *Comparative Political Studies* 19, no. 4 (1987): 443–83.
Stephenson, Oliver. "'Who the Cap Fit . . .': Whither Goest Jamaica?" *Freedomways* 16, no. 4 (1976): 245–50.
Steppin', Steppin': A Film. Washington, D.C.: Institute for Policy Studies. Videocassette. Bono Film and Video Services, 1995.
Stone, Carl. "Jamaica in Crisis: From Socialist to Capitalist Management." *International Journal* [Canada] 4, no. 2 (1985): 282–311.

———. "The Jamaican General Election of 1989." *Electoral Studies* [Great Britian] 8, no. 2 (1989): 175–81.

———. "Jamaica's 1980 Elections: What Manley Did Do; What Seaga Need Do." *Caribbean Review* 10, no. 2 (1981): 40–43.

———. "The 1976 Parliamentary Election in Jamaica." *Journal of Commonwealth and Comparative Politics* 15, no. 3 (1977): 250–65.

———. "Political Change in Jamaica: Life's Better but the Polls Are for Manley not Seaga." *Caribbean Affairs* [Trinidad] 1, no. 2 (1988): 31–46.

A Tribute to Michael Manley. Largo, Md.: International Development Options, 1998.

Waters, Anita. "Half the Story: The Uses of History in Jamaican Political Discourse." *Caribbean Quarterly* [Jamaica] 45, no. 1 (1999): 62–77.

Woolcock, Jean C. "Framing the Demise of Manley's Government: The Case of the *Jamaica Daily Gleaner.*" M.A. thesis. San Jose State University, 1997.

Contributors

BRINDLEY BENN, a former Guyana high commissioner to Canada and a cabinet minister in the Jagan PPP government in the 1960s, is now retired and working on his memoirs in Georgetown, Guyana.

ANTHONY BOGUES is professor and chair of Africana Studies at Brown University and a visiting scholar at Dartmouth College. He is the author of *Caliban's Freedom: The Early Political Thought of C. L. R. James* (1997) and *Black Heretics and Prophets: Radical Political Intellectuals* (2003), and the associate editor of the Caribbean journal *Small Axe*.

A. LYNNE BOLLES is professor of women's studies and affiliate faculty in anthropology, Afro-American studies, American studies, and comparative literature at the University of Maryland, College Park. Her research focuses on the African diaspora, particularly the Caribbean. She is the author of *We Paid Our Dues* (1996) and *Sister Jamaica* (1996). Bolles was president of the Caribbean Studies Association (1997–98) and chair of the Association of Feminist Anthropology (2001–3).

ELLA DAVIS is a lecturer in the department of Africana Studies, Wayne State University.

NORMAN GIRVAN is director of the Association of Caribbean States. He is the former director of the Consortium of Graduate Schools of Social Sciences, University of the West Indies/University of Guyana. He is the author and coauthor of over ten books and monographs, and is editor or coeditor of several books on the political economy of Caribbean development. Besides his academic appointments, he has worked as director of planning in the government of Jamaica.

MONICA H. GORDON is human services faculty mentor at Walden University and adjunct associate professor of sociology at the City University of New York. Her scholarly areas of specialization include race and ethnic relations, Caribbean and gender studies, and Third World development. She has an ongoing interest, reflected in her publications, in international migration and the integration and experiences of immigrants.

IVELAW L. GRIFFITH is professor of political science and dean of the Honors College at Florida International University. A specialist in Caribbean and inter-American security and narcotics issues, he has published several books, among them *Drugs and Security in the Caribbean: Sovereignty under Siege* (1997) and *The Political Economy of Drugs in the Caribbean* (2000). He is a past president of the Caribbean Studies Association (1999–2000).

JOAN MARS is assistant professor in the department of sociology, University of Michigan, Flint. She was a former attorney-at-law in Guyana and is the author of *Deadly Force, Colonialism, and the Rule of Law: Police Violence in Guyana* (2002).

PERRY MARS is professor and chair of the department of Africana Studies, Wayne State University, Detroit. He was formerly a professor of political science in the Institute of Development Studies, University of Guyana. He is the author of *Ideology and Change: The Transformation of the Caribbean Left* (1998).

KRISTINE B. MIRANNE is managing director of the Skillman Center for Children at Wayne State University. Her research focuses on a gendered perspective of the changing welfare state, children's poverty, and youth violence. She recently coedited *Gendering the City* with Alma H. Young, and edited the special issue on welfare reform reauthorization in the *Journal of Family and Economic Issues*.

MAURICE ST. PIERRE is professor of sociology and chair of the department of sociology and anthropology at Morgan State University in Baltimore, Maryland. Among his recent publications are *Anatomy of Resistance: Anti-Colonialism in Guyana, 1823–1966* (1999) and the coauthored *Giving Voice to the Poor: Poverty Alleviation in West Bengal and Bangladesh* (2002).

CLIVE THOMAS is director of development studies at the University of Guyana. He is the author of several books, among them *Dependence and Transformation* (1974) and *The Rise of the Authoritarian State in the Periphery* (1998).

HILBOURNE WATSON is professor of international relations at Bucknell University, Lewisburg, Pennsylvania. He has published extensively on issues in international political economy with special emphasis on the Caribbean. He recently published "Globalization as Capitalism in the Age of Electronics: Issues of Popular Power, Culture, Revolution, and Globalization from Below," *Latin American Perspectives* 29, no. 6 (November 2002).

ALMA H. YOUNG was the Coleman A. Young professor of urban affairs and the dean of the College of Urban, Labor, and Metropolitan Affairs at Wayne State University. She was a former president of the Caribbean Studies Association (1986–87) and chair of the governing board of the Urban Affairs Association (2000–2001). Her most recent publications included *Gendering the City* (coedited with Kristine B. Miranne).

Index

Abeng, 61n. 10
Accabre Ideological College, 14
Adams, Grantley, 13, 100, 101
AFL-CIO, 99–100, 102, 106, 107, 113, 117, 153–54
Afro-Guyanese: and capitalism, 105–6; and ethno-politics, 149, 150, 152, 156; and policing, 71, 73, 78, 79, 80–81, 82
Allen, Dudley, 211
Alliance for Progress, 107
American Institute for Free Labor Development (AIFLD), 107, 112–14, 117, 153–54
Anderson, Beverly, 167
Anderson, Patricia, 169–70, 237
Anglo-American Caribbean Commission, 96
Anguilla, 208, 209
Antigua-Barbuda, 133, 134, 216
Antoine, Rose-Marie Bell, 138
Antrobus, Peggy, 187
Arnett, Vernon, 44, 46
Artisans Union, 41

Bahamas, 134, 205, 206, 207, 208–9, 211, 220, 221
Bandung, 109
Barbados, 133, 134, 176, 177, 185, 193, 202–3, 206, 216
Barbados Industrial Trade Union, 6, 44, 46
Barriteau, Eudine, 184, 185
Basch, Linda, 229
Bauxite industry, xiv, 13, 33, 40, 48, 49, 58, 59, 105
Belize, 203, 204, 206, 207, 221

Benn, Brindley H., xxxii, 152
Benn, Denis, 33
Bennett, Louise, 232
Berlin, Isaiah, 45
Bernard, Aggie, 167
Bishop, Maurice, 94, 154
Black Friday, 77
Black Power Movement, 50
Blacks. *See* Afro-Guyanese
Blanc-Szanton, C., 229
Blanshard, Paul, 103–4
Bogues, Anthony, xiii
Bookers Company, 105, 106
Bosch, Juan, 102
Brazil, 102
British Labour Party, 47
British Virgin Islands, 209
British West Indies, 90, 95–98, 100. *See also* Caribbean; individual countries
Buchanan, Hugh, 41
Burnham, Linden Forbes Sampson, 12; and antigovernment riots, 76; British support for, xviii, 30; corruption of, xi; death of, 160; election of, 32; ethnopolitics of, 152; and international relations, 160; and Jagan, xvi, 156, 160; and migration, 235; and People's National Congress, 75, 106; and People's Progressive Party, xi; and political policing, 81; and race, 32; and racial conflict, 150; on religion in education, 28–29; and socialism, 237
Bustamante, Lady Gladys, 173
Bustamante, Sir Alexander, 3, 13, 41, 103–4, 173

Bustamante Industrial Trade Union, 41, 109, 147, 173
Butler, Smedley, 96

CADORIT (Caribbean Area Division of the Organizacion Regional Interamericana De Trabajadores), 102, 106, 107, 114
Canada, 191, 206, 211, 212, 232, 235
Capitalism, 147, 153; cold war project of, 89, 91, 94, 113–14, 117–18; commodification of labor under, 90; and democracy, 93, 104, 153; global, xxii–xxvi, 105; in Guyana, 105; instability in, 94; and Inter-American Treaty of Reciprocal Assistance, 91; and Jagan, xxiii, xxiv, xxv, 116; and Jamaica Labor Party, 109; and Manley, xxiii, xxiv, xxv, 56–57, 58, 120; and middle class, 115; and migration, 119, 229; negative aspects of, 121; and People's National Party, 109; and Resolution 1080, 93, 114–15; and trade unions, 90, 113; and United States, 93–94
Caribbean, xxiv; arrested modernization of, xxiii; and capitalist cold war project, 91; civil society in, xxiv; and Cold War, 130; and colonialism, 43; crime in, 210, 212; drugs in, 203–10, 212, 213, 215–16, 219, 220–21; economy of, xix, xxii–xxvi, 236–38; emigration from, 225–39; foreign destabilization of, 153–55; and global economy, xxii–xxvi; and globalization, 129–31; history of, ix, xxii; international influences in, 161–62; labor in, xxiv–xxv; labor law in, 138–39; and labor vs. capital, 147; low-intensity warfare in, 113; plantation system of, xxii; political policing in, 65–66; polyarchic political system in, 150, 153, 161, 162; poverty in, 10; prisons in, 216; United States interference in, xvii–xviii; women in, 185. *See also* British West Indies; individual countries
Caribbean Basin Initiative, 130
Caribbean Bauxite Mine and Metal Workers Union, 49
Caribbean Community, xiv; and cold war project, 90; and drug problem, 219; economy of, 129, 133–34, 140–41; individualism in, 118; and International Confederation of Free Trade Unions in, 114
Caribbean Community Harmonization Project, 138
Caribbean Congress of Labor (CCL), 107, 112, 113
Caribbean Labor Congress (CLC), 106, 107
Caribbean People's Development Agency, 194
CARICOM. *See* Caribbean Community
Carter, Jimmy, 160
Carter, Martin, 21, 33, 201, 222
Cartey, Wilfred, *Whispers from the Caribbean,* 226, 227
Castro, Fidel, 210
Catholicism, 53
Cayman Islands, 208–9
Central Intelligence Agency, xix, 99, 102, 106, 108, 109, 154
Chase, Ashton, x, xxi, 11, 12, 21, 22
Chile, xviii
China, 153
Chinese, 150
Civil Service Association, 76, 77
Civil society, xxiv
Class: and Jagan, xxvii, 32, 144, 148, 156, 161; and Jamaican women, 170; and Manley, 42–43, 48, 56, 148; and race/ethnicity, 144, 145, 161, 163; subordinate, 145, 146; and women, 169, 170, 171, 172
Clientalism, 149
Cognitive praxis theory, 19–20
Cold War: and Caribbean, 130;

destabilization during, 153; and economy, 130; effect on working class project, 143; end of, 91, 133, 160; and Great Britain, xvii; and Jagan, 34, 160; and Jamaican communism, 41; and labor movement, xxii; and Manley, 42; significance of, xvii–xviii, xix; and United States, xvii
Cold war project, 89–121; defined, 89–91, 93
Colombia, 155, 207
Colonialism: in Caribbean, 43; in Guyana, 64, 66; and Jagan, xvi, 11, 13, 14, 21, 26–27, 30, 33–34, 35; in Jamaica, 43–44; labor in, 149–50; and labor law, 138; and Manley, 42–43; and migration, 229; People's National Party, 41; role of police in, 64, 68–69, 70; and women, 168
Commonwealth Caribbean countries, 90
Communism: and American organized labor, 98; destabilization of, 153; failure of, 155; and Great Britain, 103, 106; and Guyana, 74, 105, 106; and Jagan, 28, 30, 31, 34, 35; and Jamaica, 41, 61n. 12, 97, 102; and labor movement, xxii; and Manley, 41–42, 109; and People's National Party, 97, 109; and People's Progressive Party, xi; in Political Affairs Committee, 21–22; and United States, 92, 96, 97–98, 102; Western opposition to, xvii. *See also* Marxism; Socialism
Communist Party of Jamaica, 109
Coombs, Allan George, 41
Crime, xxx, 136, 210–13, 216. *See also* Drugs
Critchlow, H. N., xxi
Cuba, xvii; and drug problem, 210; and Jagan, 107, 147; and Jamaica, xvi, 112, 154; and Manley, xiv, xvi, 6, 109, 147; and People's National Party, 109; and Resolution 1080, 93; and United States, 30, 92, 96, 107

D'Aguiar, Peter, 76, 77, 107
Deere, Carmen Diana, 186
Demba strike, 25
Democracy: and capitalism, 93, 104, 153; and cold war project, 89, 104; in Guyana, xii; and Jagan, xii, xv, xvi, xx, xxvi, 26–27, 31, 34; and labor, 127, 140, 163; and Manley, xiii, xv, xvi, xx, xxvi, 43, 44, 48, 52–54, 57; and middle class, 93; and migration, 234; People's Progressive Party policy on, xi; polyarchic, 150, 153; representative, 93; trade union, 115; and working class, 93, 104, 163; in workplace, 48, 52–54, 57
Democratic socialism: and Jagan, 31, 35; in Jamaica, 116; and Jamaica Labor Party, 109; and Manley, xiii, xiv, 41–42, 43, 54, 57, 103, 109, 110, 116, 119–20, 147; and migration, 235; and People's National Party, 56, 102–3, 109. *See also* Socialism
Development Alternatives for Women in a New Era, 194, 196
Domination, matrix of, 169, 170, 171
Dominican Republic, xviii, 102, 155, 205, 206, 207–8, 211, 212, 217, 220
Drugs, xxix–xxx, xxxiv, 200–222
Duncan, D. K., 50, 62n. 15, 152

East Indians: in colonial division of labor, 150; ethno-politics of, 152, 156; Indo-Guyanese, 105–6, 120; and Jagan, 32, 33; and People's Progressive Party, 149; and political policing, 71, 72, 73, 78, 79, 81, 82
Economy: of Barbados, 133, 134; of Caribbean, xix, xxii–xxvi; of Caribbean Community, 129, 133–34; and Cold War, 130; and cold war project, 92; decentralization of, 139; deconcentration of, 139; destabilization of, 154; developed, 130; developing, 131, 133; development of, 237; effect

Economy: of Barbados *(continued)* of crime on, 211; global, xxii–xxvi, 185–88; globalization of, xx; of Guyana, 104–5, 128, 132, 133–37, 154, 237; integration of, 140–41; international, 15–16, 159, 161; and Jagan, xix, 14, 15–16, 31, 34–35, 105, 161; of Jamaica, 6, 7, 8, 50, 110, 133–37, 154, 237–38; labor in, 126–41; and Manley, xiii, xiv, xvi, xix, 3, 5, 6, 7–8, 42, 43, 49, 54–55, 57, 58, 131, 159, 161, 237–38; market, 58; migration in, 225, 228, 229, 230, 231, 235–37; and New International Economic Order, xvi, xvii, 6, 49, 131, 159; and People's National Party, 110; and People's Progressive Party, xi, 14, 105; preferences dependent, 129; privatization of, 159; remittance in, 228, 233, 235, 236; socially managed, 8; sovereign, xix; structural adjustment of, xix, 128, 132, 135, 154, 159, 184–85, 186, 188; of United States, 130; and women, 169, 183–97; and working class, 143–44, 159

Education, xxviii, 28–29, 136–37, 169, 190, 228, 232, 234

Edwards, Joseph, 61n. 8

Enmore estate riots, xv, 25–26, 36n. 6, 147

Equality: and Jagan, xx; in Jamaica, 42–43, 50; and Manley, xx, 42–43, 55, 56, 57, 59, 60; and neoliberalism, 117; for women, 166, 170, 173, 184

Ethnicity. *See* Race/ethnicity

Ethno-politics, and working class, 143–63. *See also* Race/ethnicity

Family, 169, 170, 185, 187

Federal Bureau of Investigation, 97

Federation of Independent Trades Unions of Guyana, 160

Feminism, 169, 193

Fordism, 100

Fraser, 233

Free riders, 19

French Guiana, 205

Garvey, Marcus, 3, 41, 97

Gay, Jane Phillips, 177

Gender, 168–72, 184–85, 186. *See also* Women

Georgetown Declaration, 15–16

Girvan, Norman, 227, 237, 238

Girvan, Thom, 6

GIWU. *See* Guiana Industrial Workers' Union (GIWU)

Glasspole, Florize, 174

Glasspole, Halcyone Idelia, 173–74

Glick-Schiller, N., 229

Globalization, xx; and Caribbean Community, 129–30; cold war, 90, 91; competition from, 133; corporate control of, 8; of economy, xx; effect on ethno-politics, 144; and labor market, 130; and labor policies, 128; and Manley, 7–8; and Resolution 1080, 93; and trade unions, 139; and United States, 8; and women, xxviii–xxix

Goldberg Commission, 45

Gonzalves, Ralph, 147, 149, 151

Goulart, João, 102

Great Britain: and Burnham, xviii, 30; and Caribbean, xvii; and Cold War, xvii; and cold war project, 101; as colonial power, 34; and communism, 103, 106; crime in, 211–12; deportations from, 212; destabilization by, xvii, xxvi, 153; electoral system change by, 31, 108; and Guyana, 104–5, 106, 107; and Jagan, xviii–xix, 14, 26–27, 30, 34, 35, 64, 107, 108; and labor movement, xxii; and migration, 225, 231–32; and People's National Party, 103; and People's Progressive Party, xi, 14–15, 29, 30, 64, 74; and political policing, 66–67, 69, 80; and poverty in Caribbean Community, 10; and race, 32; and sugar industry, 104–5; and

INDEX 259

United States, 31, 34, 108; and Waddington Constitution, xviii, 27, 29, 30, 74, 75; and women, 168, 173
Green, Enid, 175
Grenada, xviii, 94, 154, 193, 206
Grenfruit Women's Cooperative, 193
Group of 77, 109
Guatemala, xviii, 92
Guiana Industrial Workers' Union (GIWU), 29, 106
Gunst, Laurie, 109
Guyana: AFL-CIO in, 99–100, 106, 107; capitalism in, 105; Central Intelligence Agency in, 106, 108; Cold War interference with, xvii–xix; and cold war project, 102, 104–8; colonialism in, 64, 66; communism in, 74, 105, 106; crime in, xxx, 136, 211; democracy in, xii; deportations to, 215; destabilization of, 94; development in, 237; drugs in, xxxiv, 201, 203, 204–5, 206, 216, 220; economy of, 104–5, 128, 132, 133–37, 154, 237; ethno-politics in, 149, 152, 156, 157–58; and Great Britain, 104–5, 106, 107; human rights in, 128; independence of, xi; international influences on, 161–62; and International Monetary Fund, 159; labor law in, 138; and Labor Relations Bill, 77, 105, 106, 154, 158; Mackenzie/Wismar incident in, 79, 80; and migration, 134, 234–35; and Police Act of 1957, 71; police role in, 64–84; and political policing, 66; polyarchic political system in, 161; poverty in, 134–35, 238; prisons in, 217; proportional representation in, 108; public sector layoffs in, 132; public services in, 135; race/ethnicity in, 71, 78–82, 105–6, 107, 108, 127, 136, 149, 150, 151, 154; remittance to, 236; social fabric of, 136; and socialism, 109; structural adjustment of, 128, 132, 135, 154; sugar industry in, 104–5;
suspension of constitution of, xviii, 29, 30, 74, 75, 106; trade unions in, xv, 25–26, 101, 108, 136, 137, 147–48, 160; trade with, 135; unemployment in, 132, 134, 136; and United States, xvi–xvii, 90–91, 92, 93, 94, 106, 107; urbanization of, 134; violence in, 136; and Waddington Constitution, xviii, 27, 67; women in, 137, 175, 177; workers of, 102, 105–8, 127, 132, 134, 136–37, 155. *See also* Jagan, Cheddi
Guyana Agricultural Workers Union, xv, 25, 78, 147
Guyana Industrial Workers Union, 105, 177

Haiti, 155, 206, 207
Hall, Stuart, 46, 227
Harris, Wilson, 227
Hart, Richard, xxi, 101, 151
Hector, Tim, xiv–xv
Henry, Ralph, 237
Hill, Ken, xxi, 151
Holloway, John, 115
Home, Lord, 31
Hoover, J. Edgar, 97
Hoyte, Desmond, xi, xii
Hubbard, H. J. M., 11, 12, 21
Hubbard, Jocelyn, x

ICFTU. *See* International Confederation of Free Trade Unions (ICFTU)
Ideology, 89, 92, 93, 149, 187
Inter-American Defense System, 100
Inter-American Treaty of Reciprocal Assistance, 91–92, 93, 94, 96, 100, 105, 106, 107, 109, 112
International Bauxite Association, 49
International Confederation of Free Trade Unions (ICFTU), 99, 101, 106, 113
International Labor Organization, 138
International Monetary Fund, 134, 139, 154, 188; and International

International Monetary Fund *(continued)* Confederation of Free Trade Unions, 114; and Jagan, 159, 160; and Jamaica Labor Party, 159; and Manley, xiv, xix, xx, 7, 159; and New Global Human Order, 16; protests against, xxv; and trade unions, 139, 162. *See also* Economy
International Trade Secretariats (ITS), 107
Ishmael, Richard, 107
Issacs, Allan, 46

Jagan, Cheddi: and Accabre Ideological College, 14; and AFL-CIO interference, 102; on agriculture, 13; and American Institute for Free Labor Development, 154; background of, 20; and bauxite industry, 13, 33; and Benn, xxxii; and Burnham, xvi, 156, 160; and capitalism, 116; and Central Intelligence Agency, 108; and Chase, 11, 21; and class, xxvii, 32, 143–44, 148, 156, 161; and Cold War, 34, 160; and cold war project, 116; and colonialism, xvi, 11, 13, 14, 21, 26–27, 30, 33–34, 35; and communism, 28, 30, 31, 34, 35; on crime, xxx; critical discourse of, 27–28; and Cuba, 107, 147; and Demba strike, 25; and democracy, xii, xv, xvi, xx, xxvi, 26–27, 31, 34; and democratic socialism, 31, 35; and destabilization, 94; and drugs, 201, 221; and East Indians, 32, 33; and economy, xix, 14, 15–16, 31, 34–35, 105; education of, 10–11; as educator, 11, 21–23; and Enmore estate riots, xv, 25–26, 147; and equality, xx; and ethno-politics, 120, 144, 152, 157–58, 160, 161, 163; and Federation of Independent Trade Unions of Guyana, 160; foreign interference with, 154, 155, 158, 160; and Georgetown Declaration, 15–16; and global capitalism, xxiii, xxiv, xxv; and Great Britain, xviii–xix, 14, 26–27, 29, 30, 34, 35, 64, 107, 108; and Guyana Agricultural and Workers Union, xv, 25, 147; and Hubbard, 11, 21; imprisonment of, 29–30; and independence, 30, 32, 33, 35; and Indo-Guyanese, 105–6, 120; and Inter-American Treaty of Reciprocal Assistance, 105; and international economy, 15–16, 161; and International Monetary Fund, 159, 160; and international relations, 147, 159–60; knowledge production by, 29–30, 35; and Labor Relations Bill, 105, 106, 154, 158; leftist politics of, 145; legislative experience of, 11–12, 23–24; life of, ix, x, xi, xii; limited power of, 160–61; and Man Power Citizens Association, 25; and Marxism, 34, 35, 147; and middle class, xxvii, 144, 156, 161; and migration, 227, 234–35; as movement intellectual, 20–23, 31, 33; on nationalization, 31; National Press Club speech, 30–31; and neoliberalism, 116, 119–20; and New Global Human Order, 15–16; and New International Economic Order, xvii, 131; and 1964 Guyanese race riots, 78, 79; and People's Progressive Party, x–xi, 12, 14, 26; and Police Act of 1957, 71; policy mistakes of, 34, 148; and Political Affairs Committee, 11, 21, 22; political meetings of, 22–23; and political policing, 66, 67–68, 71, 74, 75, 76, 78, 80, 84; and political space, 21, 24, 35; and polyarchic politics, 150; and protest, 36; and race, 32–33, 35, 78, 79, 120, 148, 150, 155, 156–57, 160; Race Relations Commission of, 160; reputation of, xvi; and Rice Producers Association, 11; and Sawmill and Forest Workers Union, xv, 25, 147; and socialism, xiv, 14, 28, 29–30, 31, 35, 76,

116, 119–20; on social reform, 31; and Soviet Union, 107, 147; and status quo, 156; and sugar industry, 22–23, 24, 25, 33; time in London, xiv; and trade unions, xv, 11, 13, 25–26, 35, 101, 131, 143–44, 147, 160, 162; and United Nations, 14; and United States, xi, xiv, xvi–xvii, xviii, 13, 14, 27, 30–31, 34, 35, 107, 108, 227; and University of Ghana, 14; violence during rule of, 136; welfare policies of, xi; and West Indies Federation, 13; and women, 183–84, 194, 196–97; and workers, xxv, xxvii, 13, 25–26, 29, 126, 127, 128, 136, 138, 141; and workers movement, xvi, xxii, 148; and working class, xv, xix, xx–xxi, xxvi, xxvii, 11, 20, 32, 143–44, 147; and Working People's Alliance, 120. *See also* Guyana; People's Progressive Party

Jagan, Janet Rosenberg, x, xii, 11, 12, 21, 28, 32

Jamadar, Peter, 218

Jamaica: agriculture in, 220; Central Intelligence Agency in, 109; clientalism in, 149; and Cold War, 41; and cold war project, 101–4, 109, 112; colonialism in, 43–44; and communism, 41, 61n. 12, 97, 102; Creole nationalism in, xiii, 43–44; crime in, xxx, 136, 211–12, 213, 216; and Cuba, xvi, 112, 154; democratic socialism in, 116; deportations to, 212, 213, 215; destabilization of, 94, 109–11; development in, 237–38; drugs in, 201, 202–3, 205, 206, 208, 211–12, 215–16, 219–20, 221; economy of, 6, 7, 8, 50, 110, 133–37, 154, 237–38; equality in, 42–43, 50; Essential Services Law, 49, 52; ethno-politics in, 152, 158; foreign destabilization of, 154; health care in, 188; human rights in, 128; and Inter-American Treaty of Reciprocal Assistance, 109, 112; international influences on, 161–62; Joint Trade Union and Research and Development Center, 60n. 4; labor law in, 50–52; labor market in, 136–37; Labor Relations and Industrial Disputes Act, 52, 112, 158; low-intensity warfare in, 110–11; master and servants law of, 51; and migration, 134, 234–35, 239n. 1; nationalism in, 3; National Minimum Wage Act, 51; and neoliberalism, 116; plantation system in, 43, 44, 50; political unionism in, 46–47; polyarchic political system in, 161; poverty in, 134–35, 238; prisons in, 216, 217; public services in, 135; race in, 42–43, 127, 149, 150–51, 152, 158; reforms in, 6; remittance to, 236; slavery laws of, 50–51; social collectivism in, 112; social fabric of, 136; structural adjustment of, 128, 132, 135, 154; Termination of Employment Act, 51; trade unions in, 40–41, 46–47, 49, 50, 101, 136, 137, 147–48; trade with, 135; unemployment in, 134, 136; and United States, xviii, xix, 41, 90–91, 93, 94, 95, 96–97, 102–3, 109, 112, 219–20; upper class in, 149; urbanization of, 134; violence in, 136; women in, 61n. 11, 137, 166, 167, 170, 185, 193; workers movement in, 48, 50, 54, 60n. 4, 155; working class in, 101–4. *See also* Manley, Michael

Jamaica Broadcasting Corporation, 47–48, 61n. 9

Jamaica Defense Force, 110

Jamaica Democratic Party, 104

Jamaica Labor Party: and capitalism, 109; and cold war project, 103, 104; and democratic socialism, 109; destabilization through, 154; ethno-politics of, 149, 156; formation of, 41; and International Monetary Fund, 159; and neoliberalism, 116; and racial conflict, 151; and sugar industry, 53; and United States, xix, 98

Jamaica Union of the Teachers, 40
Jefferson, Thomas, 95
Jeffries, Sir Charles, 70
Johnson, Charles, 154
Johnson, Kim, 237

Kaufman, Michael, 94
Kennedy, Edward, xvii, 160
Kennedy, John F., xvi
Kenyatta, Jomo, 13
Kilkenny, Cecil, 217
Knight, K. D., 212
Knowledge, production of, 19–20, 26, 28, 29–30, 35
Kurzman, Dan, 99
Kwayana, Eusi, 32, 33

La Bennett, Claudette, 216
Labor market, 130, 132, 134, 136–37. *See also* Workers
Lachmansingh, J. P., 25, 26
Lamming, George, 231
Laski, Harold, xiv, 4, 42, 57
Latin America, 91, 204, 220
Lee, Everett, 228
Lennox-Boyd, Alan, 27
Lens, Sidney, 99, 102
Lewis, Gordon, 230–31
Liberation theology, 53
Lowenthal, David, 231, 233
Luckhoo, Lionel A., 27–28, 29, 105

Mackenzie/Wismar incident, 79, 80
Manifest Destiny, 95
Manley, Edna, xiii, 3, 42
Manley, Michael: and Abeng, 61n. 10; and Arnett, 44; background of, 42; banking policy of, 51; and Bustamante Industrial Trade Union, 44; and bauxite industry, xiv, 40, 48, 49, 58, 59; and Black Power Movement, 50; and capitalism, xxiii, xxiv, xxv, 56–57, 58, 120; and Caribbean Bauxite Mine and Metal Workers Union, 49; and Caribbean Community, xiv; charisma of, 62n. 14; civil disobedience of, 48; and class, 42–43, 48, 56, 148; and Cold War, 42; and cold war project, 101, 116; and collective bargaining, 58–59; and colonialism, 42–43; and communism, 41–42, 109; contradictory policies of, 148; on crime, xxx; and Cuba, xiv, xvi, 6, 109, 147; and democracy, xiii, xv, xvi, xx, xxvi, 43, 44, 48, 52–54, 57; and democratic socialism, xiii, xiv, 41–42, 43, 54, 57, 103, 109, 110, 116, 119–20, 147; destabilization of, 94; and drugs, 200–201, 221; and economy, xiii, xiv, xvi, xix, 3, 5, 6, 7–8, 42, 43, 49, 54–55, 57, 58, 131, 159, 161, 237–38; education of, 4; election campaign of, 50; on employee share-owning, 54, 58; and equality, xx, 42–43, 55, 56, 57, 59, 60; and Essential Services Law, 52; and ethno-politics, 144, 158, 161, 163; foreign interference with, 154, 155; and Girvan, 6; and globalization, 7–8; and Goldberg Commission, 45; housing policy of, 51; and International Bauxite Association, 49; and International Monetary Fund, xiv, xix, xx, 7, 159; and labor market, 136; and Labor Relations and Industrial Disputes Act, 52, 158; and Laski, xiv, 4, 42, 57; legislative work of, 49, 50–52, 59; life of, xiii–xiv; limited power of, 160–61; on low-intensity conflict, 95; and Marxism, xvi, 41, 54; on master and servants law, 51; and middle class, 48, 144, 156, 161; and migration, 234–35; and National Housing Trust, 51; and nationalism, xiv; and National Minimum Wage Act, 51; and National Worker's Union, xiii, xv, 4, 40, 44, 45, 147; on natural human rights, 48; as negotiator, 4–6, 59; and neoliberalism, 119–20; and New International Economic Order, xvi, 6, 49, 131, 159; organizational skills of,

45; parents of, xiii, 3, 42; and People's National Party, xv, 6, 44, 49, 58; and plantation system, 43, 44; political communication of, 44–45, 55–56, 59; political consciousness of, 227–28; and politicized labor, xxv, 47, 162; and polyarchic politics, 150; on poverty, xiv; as prime minister, 50; on public ownership, 57; and race, 42–43, 50, 60, 148, 150, 151–52, 155, 156–57; radicalism of, 50, 145; and Rastafarian movement, xvi; and Seaga, 156–57; and Shearer, 6, 45–46; and socialism, xiii, xiv, 41–42, 43, 54, 57, 58, 62n. 15, 103, 109, 110, 116, 119–20, 147, 219, 237; and Socialist International, xiv; and social justice, 238; and social programs, xiv; and social reform, 6; and status quo, 156; and sugar industry, 44–47, 48, 50, 53; and Sugar Workers Cooperative Movement, 53; and sympathy strikes, 48; and Termination of Employment Act, 51; and trade unions, 6, 40–60, 101, 131, 143–44, 147, 162; and United States, xiv, xviii, xix, 6, 7, 58, 103, 109, 219; and University and Allied Workers Union, 40; and Westminster electoral process, 147; and women, 166–67, 178, 183–84, 194, 196–97; and workers, xxii, xxv, xxvii, 4–5, 6, 40–60, 126, 127, 128, 136, 138, 141, 148; and Workers Bank, 51; and working class, xiii, xv, xix, xx–xxi, xxvi, xxvii, 43, 47, 147; and workplace democracy, 48, 52–54, 57; youth of, 3–4. *See also* People's National Party

Manley, Norman, xiii, 3, 13, 42, 151

Man Power Citizens Association, 25, 29, 105, 106, 107, 108

Mars, Perry, 32, 94

Marshall Plan, 99

Marxism, xxii, 34, 35, 41, 54, 147, 153. *See also* Communism; Socialism

McDonald, Alexandria, 175

Merriweather, Sandra, 176

Middle class: and capitalism, 115; and democracy, 93; ethno-politics of, 152, 158; global interests of, 116; as individualist, 118; and Jagan, xxvii, 144, 156, 161; and Jamaica Broadcasting Corporation strike, 48; and Manley, 48, 144, 156, 161; and neoliberalism, 117; and People's National Party, 110; political leadership of, 144, 148; privilege of, 169; and trade unions, 144, 148; women of, 170, 171; and working class, xxvi, xxvii, 144, 146, 148

Migration, 225–39; and capitalism, 119; and Guyana, 134, 234–35; and Jamaica, 134, 234–35, 239n. 1; and People's Progressive Party, 29; by women, 191–92

Military, 202, 213. *See also* Policing, political

Mohammed, Patricia, 169

Morgan, Sharon, 216

MPCA. *See* Man Power Citizens Association

Munroe, Trevor, 41, 97–98

Naipaul, V. S., 231

National Negro Congress, 97

National Worker's Union, xiii, xv, 4, 40, 41, 44, 45, 46, 101, 109, 147

Neoliberalism, 112–15, 116–17, 119–20, 153

Netherlands Antilles, 220

New Global Human Order, 15–16

New International Economic Order, xvi, xvii, 6, 49, 109, 131, 159

Nicaragua, 94

Nikolinakos, Marios, 229

Nixon, Richard, 100

Nixon Doctrine, 112

Nkrumah, Kwame, 13

North Atlantic Treaty Organization, 100

NWU. *See* National Worker's Union

Organization of American States Resolution 1080, 92–93, 102, 114–15, 120
ORIT (Organizacion Regional Interamericana De Trabajadores), 107

Palmer, Ransford, 228, 233
Pastor, Robert A., 236–37
Patterson, P. J., xiii
People's National Congress: and Afro-Guyanese, 78, 149; in antigovernment riots, 76; and Burnham, 75, 106; and cold war project, 108; ethno-politics of, 149, 152, 156, 157, 158; formation of, xi, xviii, 30; and International Monetary Fund, 159; and migration, 235; and neoliberalism, 116; and 1964 race riots, 78, 79; and People's Progressive Party, 15; and political policing, 78, 81; and race, 75, 78, 79, 150, 151; and socialism, 109
People's National Party: aims of, 41; and capitalism, 109; and cold war project, 101; and colonialism, 41; and communism, 97, 109; and Cuba, 109; and democratic socialism, 56, 102–3, 109; destabilization of, 109–11; and economy, 110; ethno-politics of, 149, 156, 158; formation of, xiii; and Great Britain, 103; and international capital, 148; leftist politics of, 145; and Manley, xv, 6, 44, 49, 58; and middle class, 110; and neoliberalism, 116; and racial conflict, 151–52; and Rastafarians, 149; and status quo, 156; and sugar industry, 53; and Sugar Workers Cooperative Movement, 53; and trade unions, 101; and United States, 97, 98; and West Indian solidarity, 147; and women, 167; and working class, 147. *See also* Manley, Michael
People's Progressive Party: and Burnham, xi; and Central Intelligence Agency, 108; and cold war project, 106; and communism, xi; and democracy, xi; demonstrations against, 76–78; and East Indians, 149; and economy, xi, 14, 105; ethno-politics of, 149, 152, 156, 157, 158, 160; formation of, x–xi, 12–13, 26; and Great Britain, xi, 14–15, 29, 30, 64, 74; and Guiana Industrial Workers' Union, 29; immigration policy of, 29; independence aims of, 26, 27, 28; and international capital, 148; and Jagan, 14, 26; knowledge production by, 26, 28; labor relations bill of, 29, 77, 78; leftist politics of, 145; and migration, 235; and 1964 race riots, 78, 79; and People's National Congress, 15; policies of, xi; and political policing, 67–68, 74, 75, 78, 80, 81, 84; and race, 33, 75, 78, 79, 149, 150, 151, 152, 156, 157, 158, 160; and religion in education, 29; socialism of, 76; split in, 108; and status quo, 156; subversion of, 14–15; and Sugar Producers' Association, 29; suppression of, 75; and trade unions, xv; and United States, 74; and working class, 15, 105. *See also* Jagan, Cheddi
People's Progressive Party/Civic, 116, 160
Peters, Maggie, 173
Phillips-Gay, Jane, xxi, 26, 177
Plantation system, xxii, 43, 44, 50
PNP. *See* People's National Party
Policing, political, 64–84
Political Affairs Committee, 11, 21–23
Politics: destabilization in, 154; exclusivist strategies of, 151–52; and labor, xxiii–xxiv, xxv, xxvii–xxviii; and migration, 225–26, 230, 231; and police, 64–84; polyarchic, 161; and trade unions, 46–47, 127; women in, 173, 175, 176–77, 184
Portuguese, 150
Poverty: in Caribbean Community, 10; in Guyana, 134–35, 238; in Jamaica, 134–35, 238; Manley on, xiv; recent

growth in, xxv; of women, 183, 187, 188, 191, 195
PPP. *See* People's Progressive Party
Progressive Youth Organization, 152
Project of Non-Alignment, 109
Public Services International (PSI), 107, 108
Puerto Rico, 205, 206, 211

Race/ethnicity: and Burnham, 32, 150; and class, 144, 145, 161, 163; exclusivist strategies of, 151–52; and Great Britain, 32; in Guyana, 71, 78–82, 105–6, 107, 108, 127, 136, 149, 150, 151, 154; and Jagan, 32–33, 35, 78, 79, 120, 148, 150, 155, 156–57, 160; in Jamaica, 42–43, 127, 149, 150–51, 152, 158; in labor movement, 127–28, 132; and Manley, 42–43, 50, 60, 148, 150, 151–52, 155, 156–57; and migration, 232; and Norman Manley, 151; and People's National Congress, 75, 78, 79, 150, 151; and People's Progressive Party, 33, 75, 78, 79, 149, 150, 151, 152, 156, 157, 158, 160; and political policing, 71, 72–74, 78–82; and violence, 71; and women, 169, 170, 171, 172; and working class project, 143–63
Rastafarians, 149, 205–6
Regional Organization of Workers, 102
Resolution 1080. *See* Organization of American States Resolution 1080
Resource mobilization theory, 19
Rice Producers Association, 11
Richardson, Bonham, 233
Richardson, Sir Arthur, 103
Rio Treaty. *See* Inter-American Treaty of Reciprocal Assistance
Robinson, William I., 150, 153
Romualdi, Serafino, 106
Roosevelt, Franklin D., 89, 94, 105, 117
Roosevelt, Theodore, 95
Rubenstein, Hymie, 236
Rusk, Dean, 31

Sanday, Peggy Reeves, 170
Sawmill and Forest Workers Union, xv, 25, 147
Schlesinger, Arthur, Jr., xvi, 160
Seaga, Edward, xix, 7, 151, 152, 156–57, 159
Shearer, Hugh, 6, 45–46
Slavery, 168–69, 170, 188–89, 230–31
Small, Hugh, 46–47
Smyth, Carmichael, 70
Socialism: and Burnham, 237; disintegration of, 133; failure of, 155; in Guyana, 109; and Jagan, xiv, 14, 28, 29–30, 31, 35, 76, 116, 119–20; in Jamaica, 116; and Jamaica Labor Party, 109; and Manley, xiii, xiv, 41–42, 43, 54, 57, 58, 62n. 15, 103, 109, 110, 116, 119–20, 147, 219, 237; and migration, 235; and neoliberalism, 116–17; and People's National Congress, 109; and People's National Party, 56, 102–3, 109; and People's Progressive Party, 76; and United States, 98; and working class, 145. *See also* Communism; Marxism
Socialist International, xiv
Social movements, 18–19, 36n. 3
Social services, 131–32, 187, 195
Social welfare, 183, 188
Society: civil, 132; and gender, 168–72; and migration, 226, 230, 231, 233–34; and structural adjustment, 132; weakness in, 136; women in, 184
South Africa, 6
Soviet Union, 107, 147, 153, 155
St. Kitts-Nevis, 133, 205
St. Lucia, 216
St. Vincent, 203
State: and cold war project, 91; commodification of labor under, 90; restructuring of, 132; sovereignty of, 92, 140; and women, 184–85, 187–88, 195
Stephens, Evelyn H., 94, 104, 235

Stephens, John D., 94, 104, 235
Sterling, Kenneth, 41
Stewart, Gordon "Butch," 211
Stone, Carl, 49, 149
Strachey, John, 11
Sugar industry: and Great Britain, 104–5; and Jagan, 22–23, 24, 25, 33; and Manley, 44–47, 48, 50, 53; and People's National Party, 53; and political policing, 78
Sugar Producers' Association, 26, 29
Sugar Workers Cooperative Council, 53, 61n. 12
Sunshine, Catherine, 112
Suriname, 205

Taft-Hartley Act, 98, 99
Tate and Lyle, 53
Third World, 94, 95
Thomas, C. Y., 127, 134–35
Thomas, Darrin, 218
Thomas-Hope, Elizabeth, 234
Thompson, Mel, 231–32
Tilly, Charles, 95, 104
Trade, international, 90, 129, 135, 187, 192
Trade Union Congress, 41, 44, 76, 101, 108, 153, 154
Trade Union Council, 77
Trade unions: assets of, 140; under capitalism, 90, 113; and cold war project, 101; conflict in, 136; and democracy, 115; economic policy of, 140; ethno-politics of, 149; and globalization, 139; in Guyana, xv, 25–26, 101, 108, 136, 137, 147–48, 160; independence of, xxviii, 162–63; and International Monetary Fund, 139, 162; and Jagan, xv, 11, 13, 25–26, 35, 101, 131, 143–44, 147, 160, 162; in Jamaica, 40–41, 46–47, 49, 50, 101, 136, 137, 147–48; and Manley, 6, 40–60, 101, 131, 143–44, 147, 162; member involvement in, 139; middle class leadership of, 144; and migration, 234; militancy of, 160; and People's National Party, 101; and People's Progressive Party, xv; and politics, xxvii–xxviii, 46–47, 127; as proactive, 139; rivalry between, 127; and structural adjustment, 154; and unemployment, 140; and United States, 98, 117; view of, 127; and women, 166, 167, 168, 171, 172–78; and working class, 145, 162; and World Bank, 139
Transnational corporations, 130–31
Transnationalism, 229, 230, 235
Trinidad and Tobago, 136, 152, 155, 170; and cold war project, 101–2; crime in, 211; drugs in, 203, 205, 206–7, 216; Industrial Stabilization Act, 158; prisons in, 217–18
Truman Doctrine, 99, 105
TUC. *See* Trade Union Congress

Unemployment. *See* Workers
United Force party, xi, xviii, 15, 32, 76, 107, 108, 156
United Nations, 14
United States: and bauxite industry, 105; and British West Indies, 95–98; and Caribbean, xvii–xviii; and Cold War, xvii; cold war project of, 89–121; and communism, 41, 92, 96, 97–98, 102; crime in, 211–12; and Cuba, 30, 92, 96, 107; deportations from, 212, 214; destabilization by, xvii–xviii, xxvi, 153; and drug problem, 202–4, 206, 207, 209, 219–20, 221; economy of, 130; global capitalist designs of, 93–94; and globalization, 8; and Great Britain, 31, 34; and Grenada, 94; and Guatemala, 92; and Guyana, xvi–xvii, 90–91, 92, 93, 94, 106, 107; as hegemonic state, 89–90; and international trade, 90; and Jagan, xi, xiv, xvi–xvii, xviii, 13, 14, 27, 30–31, 34, 35, 107, 108, 227; and

Jamaica, xviii, xix, 41, 90–91, 93, 94, 95, 96–97, 102–3, 109, 112, 219–20; and Jamaica Labor Party, xix, 98; and labor movement, xxii, 41; low-intensity warfare by, 93–95; and Manley, xiv, xviii, xix, 6, 7, 58, 103, 109, 219; and migration, 191, 225, 231, 237, 239n. 1; and National Worker's Union, 41; and New International Economic Order, xvi; and Nicaragua, 94; organized labor in, 98–101, 102, 106, 107, 113, 117, 153–54; and People's National Party, 97, 98; and People's Progressive Party, 74; security of, 91–92; and socialism, 98; and trade union movement, 117; and women, 173, 191; and working class, 117
United States Virgin Islands, 211
United Steel Workers of America, 41
University and Allied Workers Union, 109
University of Ghana, 14
University of the West Indies, 193
USAID, 112–13

Venezuela, 155

Wallerstein, Immanuel, 229
West Indians, 72, 147
West Indies Federation, 13, 33
Westmaas, Rory, 33
Westminster electoral process, 147, 150
Williams, Eric, 13, 152, 158
Wolfe, Lensley, 217
Women: in Barbados, 176, 177, 185, 193; in Caribbean, 185; and class, 169, 170, 171, 172; and colonialism, 168; discrimination against, 137; and economy, 169, 183–97; education of, 190; equality for, 166, 170, 173, 184; and family, 185; and globalization, xxviii–xxix; and Great Britain, 168, 173; in Grenada, 193; in Guyana, 137, 175; and higglering, 190; and ideology, 184, 187; and Jagan, 183–84, 194, 196–97; in Jamaica, 61n. 11, 137, 170, 185, 193; and Manley, 166–67, 177, 183–84, 194, 196–97; and matrix of domination, 169, 170, 171; of middle class, 170, 171; migration by, 191–92; networks of, 190–91, 193, 195; organizations of, 192–94, 195–96; and People's National Party, 167; in politics, 173, 175, 176–77, 184; poverty of, 183, 187, 188, 191, 195; power of, 167, 169, 170, 171–72, 184, 187; and race, 169, 170, 171, 172; role of, xxviii; and slavery, 168–69, 170, 188–89; social services for, 187, 195; and social welfare, 183; in society, 184; and state, 184–85, 187–88, 195; subordination of, 187; survival of, xxxiv, 183–97; and trade unions, 166, 167, 168, 171, 172–78; unemployment among, 134, 185; and United States, 173; wages of, xxix, 187, 193, 195; as workers, xxviii–xxix, 167, 168–69, 170, 171, 173, 184, 185, 186–92, 193, 195, 196
Women and Development Unit, 193–94, 196
Women's Construction Collective, 193
Workers: activism of, 154–55; under capitalism, 90, 147; under colonialism, 149–50; in democracy, 127, 140; and economy, 126–41; and globalization, 128, 130; and government, 186; in Guyana, 102, 105–8, 127, 132, 134, 136–37, 155; and International Confederation of Free Trade Unions, 113–14; and international policy, 132–33; and Jagan, xxv, xxvii, 13, 25–26, 29, 126, 127, 136, 138, 141; law concerning, 50–52, 127, 138–39; and Manley, xxii, xxv, xxvii, 4–5, 6, 40–60, 126, 127, 128, 136, 138, 141, 148; and migration, 230–32, 233, 238; and politics, xx–xxi, xxiii–xxiv, xxv, xxvii–xxviii; and race, 149–50; skin color of, 150; social partnerships with,

Workers (*continued*) 139; unemployed, 130, 132, 134, 136, 140, 185; unionization of, 137, 192; urban, 146; women as, 168–69, 170, 173, 184, 185, 186–92, 193, 195, 196

Workers Bank, 51

Workers Liberation League, 109

Workers Liberation Union, 46

Workers movement: accomplishments of, 126; and civil society, xxiv; and Cold War, xxii; and cold war project, 118, 120–21; and communism, xxii; democracy in, 163; destabilization of, 153; in economy, 128; ethno-politics in, 152–53; failures of, 127; and Great Britain, xxii; in Guyana, 102; and International Monetary Fund, xx; and Jagan, xvi, xxii, 148; in Jamaica, 48, 50, 54, 60n. 4, 155; political leadership from, 126; political unionism in, 127; race in, 127–28, 132; and United States, xxii; and women, xxviii–xxix, 167, 171, 173

Workers Party of Jamaica, 61n. 7, 109

Working class: and cold war project, 118; definition of, 146; and democracy, 93, 104, 163; and economy, 143–44, 159; in Guyana, 107–8; and Inter-American Treaty of Reciprocal Assistance, 91; international solidarity of, 145; and Jagan, xv, xix, xx–xxi, xxvi, xxvii, 11, 20, 32, 143–44, 147; in Jamaica, 101–4; and Manley, xiii, xv, xix, xx–xxi, xxvi, xxvii, 43, 47, 147; and middle class, xxvi, xxvii, 144, 146, 148; and People's National Party, 147; and People's Progressive Party, 15, 105; and Resolution 1080, 115, 120; and socialism, 145; solidarity of, 145, 151; and trade unions, 145, 162; and United States, 117

Working class project, xx–xxvi, 143–63

Working People's Alliance (WPA), 120, 157, 158

World Bank, xix; and International Confederation of Free Trade Unions, 114; and New Global Human Order, 16; protests against, xxv; structural adjustment by, 154, 188; and trade unions, 139. *See also* Economy

World Federation of Trade Unions, 99, 101, 106

World systems theory, 229

World Trade Organization, xxv, 130

Young Socialist League, 46

www.ingramcontent.com/pod-product-compliance
Lightning Source LLC
Chambersburg PA
CBHW071813230426
43670CB00013B/2444